the journal of strange phenomena

WEIRD YEAR 1996

EDITED BY
JOE McNALLY AND JAMES WALLIS

Published by
John Brown
Publishing Ltd.

STRANGE DAYS

The world is a bizarre place, and getting weirder. From stories of ghosts and alien abductions to new animals, life on Mars, bizarre deaths, weird sex, inept crimes, statues drinking milk, aphrodisiac chewing gum and the electric death worm – not to mention this year's new star of the paranormal, the Goatsucker – it's impossible to resist the lure of the strange and the unknown.

A collection of the most outlandish, funny, strange and inexplicable stories reported by *Fortean Times* magazine this year, gathered into more than fifty different sections, **Weird Year 1996** also contains over forty pages of new material by some of the world's leading experts on strange phenomena, and an array of the year's most startling and extraordinary pictures. Everyone's life needs a little more strangeness, and this is the place to find the very best of it.

forteantimes

WEIRD YEAR 1996

Edited by JOE McNALLY and JAMES WALLIS

General editor: MIKE DASH
Design: KEITH JACKSON
Cover design: ETIENNE GILFILLAN   Picture research: DAFFYDD BYNON
Contributors: BOB RICKARD, PAUL SIEVEKING, STEVE MOORE,
WILLIAM P BARRETT, MARTIN CANNON, BILL ELLIS, HUNT EMERSON, TED
HARRISON, DAVE LANGFORD, JENNY RANDLES, KARL SHUKER, IAN SIMMONS

First published in Great Britain in November 1996
by JOHN BROWN PUBLISHING, The Boathouse, Crabtree Lane, London SW6 6LU
Tel 0171 470 2400   Fax 0171 381 3930

© Fortean Times/John Brown Publishing 1996

How to find copies of Fortean Times

FORTEAN TIMES is on sale monthly in most large newsagents. You can also order copies to
be reserved for you in outlets which do not presently stock the magazine.

To order a sample copy or for details of subscriptions

 01454 202515

In the United States

 1-516 627 3836

British Library Cataloguing in Publication Data available
ISBN 1 870870 832

Printed in Great Britain by Stephens & George, Merthyr Tydfil

CONTENTS

the animal world

the human world

the natural world

the paranormal world

strange planet

Miracles

Some of the earliest Fortean phenomena on record are miracles - indeed it has been argued that these strange happenings, recurring in different cultures over the millennia, have been the driving forces behind the foundation of organised religion. From photographs of the gods to statues that move, drink, weep, sweat and menstruate, and from the liquefying blood of St Januarius to relics of the crucifixion, miracles and religious relics continue to inspire the faithful and challenge the agnostic.

HOLY LAUNDRY

THE SEAMLESS Robe or Holy Tunic, believed to have been worn by Jesus on his way to Calvary, was put on display in a sealed glass case in the cathedral in Trier, Germany's oldest city, for four weeks from 19 April. Four million tourists and pilgrims were expected to go to see it.

The garment does not look much like a robe, and certainly not one from Christ's time and wardrobe. It is more like a relatively modern liturgical garment. At some point, silk and taffeta adornments were added to the original fabric and the whole thing was dipped in a preservative rubber solution, rendering it impervious to carbon dating. The end result is a rigid material like canvas or felt with the smell of burning tyres. Textile historians say it is impossible to verify its authenticity.

According to legend, the relic was presented to Trier in the fourth century by the Empress Helena, a fanatical relic collector who also unearthed the True Cross and the Crown of Thorns on a visit to Jerusalem in 372. The earliest historical record dates to 1196 and the shirt became an object of veneration in the late Middle Ages. It has been displayed three times this century. In 1933 Nazi soldiers provided the guard of honour; and in 1959 the war-damaged building nearly collapsed under the weight of more than a million visitors. *Observer, 21 April; Guardian, 24 April; Independent, 30 April 1996.*

DAYLIGHT ROBERY: Pilgrims flock to see the Seamless Robe allegedly worn by Christ

Five remarkable religious relics

1. St Telio's skulls

This Welsh saint was so popular that after his death several churches claimed to house his relics – including three separate skulls, all famed for their ability to cure whooping cough. Down the centuries, all the supposed relics went missing, but in February 1994 a 'genuine' skull was installed at Llandaff cathedral. It had turned up in Hong Kong.

2. The holy handkerchief

Although the Turin Shroud has now been labelled a fake, two other images of Christ still exist in Italy. They are the Veronicas – relics which claim to be cloths on which Jesus wiped his face on his way to the crucifixion. One is in a Genoa convent, the other in the Pope's study at Rome. Neither has ever been photographed.

3. The incorrupt corpse

The apparently perfectly-preserved body of St Bernadette Soubirous is kept on display in the convent of Saint-Gildard in Nevers, France. St Bernadette is famed for her visions of the Virgin Mary, who instructed her to build what became the shrine at Lourdes. She died in 1879 and was exhumed in 1909. Many miracles have been attributed to her.

4. The holy lance

The lance which pierced Christ's side on the cross was successfully scryed by an itinerant holy man while the soldiers of the first crusade were besieged in Antioch at the end of the eleventh century. The miraculous recovery of the relic so inspired the troops that they sallied forth, defeated the Moslem forces in their path, and retook Jerusalem.

5. Christ's foreskin

There are several alleged relics of the sacred prepuce, originally severed when Christ was circumcised in the Temple, each of which causes the church considerable embarrassment. In the past the Vatican has threatened those who 'write or speak' of the prepuce with excommunication. Matters came to a head in 1983 when the holy foreskin of Calcata, near Rome, was stolen from the wardrobe of the parish priest.

TOWERING AMBITION

Villagers from Vilafranca del Penedes in Spain failing once again to build a human tower last July. It was the 105th successive year that they have over-reached themselves. *International Herald Tribune, 24 July 1995.*

POPPERFOTO/REUTER

Strange 1996

The cream of weirdness from around the globe

Goatsucker

The hottest topic of 1996 was Puerto Rico's mystery mammal mangler. While Goatsucker continued to gnaw its way through the island's food chain, no one could agree whether the creature was a strange bat, a CIA genetic experiment gone wrong, a UFO 'pet' loose on earth – or just a figment of the imagination. Then Goatsucker appeared on the American mainland...
See page 52

Area 51

In the year the US government barred ufologists from Freedom Ridge, the last piece of high ground overlooking the top-secret test facility where the US Air Force is rumoured to be flying saucers, Area 51 starred in the film *Independence Day* – and became a tourist attraction. The citizens of Rachel, Nevada (pop. 50) lobbied to have Route 375 renamed 'The Extraterrestrial Highway' and turned themselves into the centre of the UFO universe by welcoming researchers from around the globe to the newly-renamed 'Little A-Le-Inn' motel.
http://www.ufomind.com/area51/desert_rat/

Snail mail

A letter requesting a peanut-butter recipe arrived at Gordon Harrington's home in Michigan. It was addressed to his grandmother and had been caught in some postal limbo for 82 years. *The People, 18 Jul 1992.*

Life from Mars

A meteorite fragment from Mars, recovered from Antarctica, became the most celebrated lump of rock on the planet when scientists announced they had detected the fossilised by-products of life in it. 'Allan Hills 84001' is thought to have been catapulted into space when a meteor hit the then-warm and wet Martian surface about four billion years ago. Did life arrive on Earth from Mars?
See page 112

ALH84001,0

Crashed alien captured

Wild rumours of a possible UFO crash and the capture of at least one cowering alien brought ufologists hot-foot to the town of Varginha in Minas Gerais state. The facts may be even more difficult to disentangle from fiction than usual, but this is one story that looks set to run and run. **See page 8**

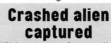

Mystery mineral

A supposedly new mineral, made up of fibrous crystals and a vivid blue in colour, was identified in March after being spotted by a holidaying geologist on a Moroccan souvenir stall. The Natural History Museum confirmed it was unknown, but later identified it as aerinite – very rare, but not new. *D. Telegraph, Times, Guardian, D. Mail, 19 Mar; Guardian, 26 Sept 1996.*

Green kitten

Pia Bischoff of Dybvad, Denmark, found a copper-coloured kitten in a hayloft. The mysterious moggie had green fur and claws, and the outlandish tint did not wash out. Copenhagen State Hospital was carrying out tests in the hope of finding out where the colour came from. *Politiken, 22 Nov 1995.*

Let's conger

A 76lb, nine-foot conger eel was fished from the sea off Schotland, Holland, in February. It was believed to be the largest eel ever taken from the North Sea. *De Telegraaf, 22 Feb 1996.*

Dirty linen

An ancient shirt – said to be the garment Christ was wearing when he was crucified – went on display in Trier cathedral in April. Any idea of subjecting the fabric to Turin Shroud-style carbon dating was frustrated by a nineteenth-century cleric who attempted to preserve the relic by coating it in rubber. **See page 4**

Motorboatosaurus

In April, *Fortean Times* published an exclusive story on possible film evidence for dinosaur survival in the Congo. Experts were divided on what the short video sequence, shot from a plane passing over steamy Lake Tele, actually showed. Some saw a monster – others two natives in a motorised canoe. **See page 19**

Pig-faced killer

The deaths of about 17 children in Uttar Pradesh in the central region of the state triggered a bizarre wave of rumours in the north Indian state. Some villagers claim the killer is a flying pig-faced monster that drives a white van, others that it has eyes and feet that glow, and can jump 25 metres in a single bound. The deaths have also been attributed to kidnappers, traders in human organs, and spies from Pakistan. **See page 116**

Fish out of water

Neil Wilson, a recluse from Toolondo, Victoria, was found dead in a field, encased in the home-made rubber fish suit he wore to swim in nearby Toolondo Lake. The tight-fitting suit had been fashioned from the remains of a water bed Wilson salvaged from a skip. **See page 104**

strange days

UFOs

Interest in Unidentified Flying Objects has probably never run higher. Since the release last year of Ray Santilli's film purporting to show an autopsy on an alien body recovered from the site of the 1947 Roswell 'crash', ufology has garnered more media attention than any other area of Fortean study. Whether UFOs are misidentifications of the planet Venus, psychic phenomena of some sort, or literal visitors from another world remains to be seen; what is true is that people continued to see inexplicable things in the sky and on the ground in 1996.

HURT ALIEN: An artist's impression of the creature

BRAZIL GOES NUTS OVER ALIENS

THE BIG UFO story of 1996 was undoubtedly a reported saucer crash in Varginha, Brazil. While reports still seem muddled, many ufological sources believe that live aliens were recovered from a crash site by the Brazilian government, and that there has been a bungled cover-up. There are conflicting accounts, but details have emerged of what could prove to be a case rivalling the legendary Roswell in its complexity and scale.

According to a press release issued by the Brazilian ufologist and writer A.J. Gevaerd, the story began on 20 January, when three young girls saw a strange animal in a field near their home in the Central Brazilian town of Varginha. From a few metres away they saw a creature squatting behind an old garage, apparently in pain.

Its hairless body was around five feet (1.5m) tall and dark brown, as though it had oil on its skin. It had two large, red eyes without pupils, a small nose and mouth, and a large, brown head with what appeared to be three horns. It also had an unusual smell, which the sisters' mother said was still evident when she visited the site. The girls fled when it moved. An elderly couple later claimed to have seen a submarine-like grey object skimming silently over the ground earlier that day.

The girls were interviewed by Dr Ubiraja Franco Rodrigues and Vitorio Pacaccini, two veteran ufologists who live locally, who were convinced that the girls had encountered an extraterrestrial. The ufologists located several more Varginha residents who had seen strange beings, along with others who had noted unusual numbers of military in the area. An anonymous military informant told them the fire department had been called out early that morning to capture a strange animal. The military had taken the captured animal to the nearby Escola Sargentos de Armas military base. The commander, Lt Col Olimpio Wanderley Santos, then declared it a "secret operation".

However, other military sources seemed willing enough to talk to the ufologists, and they soon had several reports of the capture of a second creature, possibly that seen by the girls, later that night. The creature was said to have died two days later after being treated at two different hospitals in the town. Its corpse, they were told, had been removed by 'S2' military intelligence officers, and anyone who had seen the creature was warned not to talk to the press or UFO researchers.

Next, the investigators heard, the creatures were both taken to a military facility in Campinas, São Paulo. The dead creature was taken to the city's university, where it was autopsied by Dr Badan Palhares, a distinguished pathologist who had performed the autopsy of Josef Mengele.

Since January many of the witnesses have changed their statements; the number of ETs seen has varied, and claims have surfaced that five of the creatures were chased from a park in Varginha. More witnesses have been found whose evidence corroborates that of others, including four military guards who claim to have been part of the convoy which transported the aliens to Campinas base. According to the mother of one of the girls who made the first sighting, a Man-In-Black style stranger offered her a "large" sum of money if she could convince her daughter to deny the story.

Official denial has been strenuous. The Brazilian military has implausibly denied that it would be interested in a crashed UFO. Dr Palhares has denied the rumours linking him to the putative autopsy, while the first hospital to which the aliens were said to have been taken say that the commotion which fuelled the stories of an injured alien were in fact down to the arrival of the body of a young man who had died in police custody.

AUFORA News, 30 May, 2 & 9 June 1996; UFO Roundup 23 June 1996; International UFO Magazine July 1996; ISCNIFlash 16 Jun 1996; translation from ISTO magazine (Brazil) by Regina Guimaraes; 'Human Mutilation in the Americas' by Scott Corrales in Paranoia, Spring 1996; Report by Matt Moffett in Wall Street Journal, 28 Jun 1996.

CRASH SITE?: The city of Varginha

BRITISH AIRWAYS JET BUZZED BY A UFO

THE MOST IMPORTANT British UFO story of the year came from two British Airways pilots who had a very close encounter with a triangular UFO approaching Manchester airport. Although the incident took place in January 1995, details were not released by the Civil Aviation Authority until this year.

At 6.48pm on 9 January, flight 5061, a Boeing 737 with 60 passengers on board, was 8-9 nautical miles (15-17km) south-east of the airport, at 4,000ft (1,200m) – just above cloud level. Captain Roger Wills saw the craft approach at high speed and pass silently down the starboard side of the plane in the opposite direction. He tracked it for about two seconds through the windows, and thought it had a number of small white lights. First Officer Mark Stuart apparently ducked, although he remembers seeing a dark stripe down its side.

Questioned separately, the officers agreed about the shape, size and colour of the UFO, but disagreed on its lighting. The captain put the object's size between that of a light aircraft and a small jet, although he emphasised that this was total speculation. Nothing was seen on radar, but the flight officers were certain that the object was solid and not a balloon or military stealth aircraft.

The official report into the incident, compiled by the Independent Joint Airmiss Working Group, was released in February 1996, concluding that while "[to] speculate about extra-terrestrial activity... is not within the group's remit," the incident "remains unsolved".

It has transpired that the British Airways pilots were not the only ones to see the unidentified craft. Mark Lloyd of Gatley was driving home when he saw the UFO. (Both Mr Lloyd and the press report implicitly assume that it was the same one).

"It looked like a massive space ship the size of Wembley Stadium, flying at about 4000ft," he said. "It was shaped like a Christmas tree." Mr Lloyd, who says he has a photographic memory, reconstructed what he saw with help from a local graphics student. *Civil Aviation Authority Airmiss Report No. 2/95; Times, 2 Feb; D. Mail, 3 Feb; Asian Age (New Delhi), 4 Feb; Stockport Express Advertiser, 26 June 1996.*

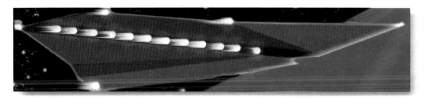

IDENTITY CRISIS: The picture above is an artist's impression of the unidentified craft based on the descriptions given by the two British Airways pilots. Below, graphics student Harold Withers' reconstruction of the object seen by Mark Lloyd. Did all three men witness the same thing?

China saucers

IN JANUARY, news reached us of a sighting in China the previous summer. People in three different areas of Guangsi province claimed to have seen UFOs at the same time, according to the semi-official China News Service.

On the night of 26 July 1995, dozens of workers saw a UFO three metres (10ft) in diameter, rising 1,500 to 2,000 meters from the ground just northwest of a mining area in Guangsi's Huanjiang county.

"The shape of the object was just like the sun perched on top of a crescent moon," the report said. "As it ascended, the size of the object grew gradually smaller while its glow faded. After approximately seven minutes, it disappeared completely."

At around the same time, a government official in Tian'e county witnessed a "strange star" in the sky. He reported that it was about the same size as the moon. "Its glow was similar to the moon, but it did not shine towards the ground," the man said. The "strange star" then rose into the air and vanished after about two minutes. *South China Morning Post, 9 Aug 1995.*

ALIEN PEACE

THE ROSWELL 'saucer crash' doesn't seem to have played out all its possibilities yet. Richard Hoagland of the Mars Mission/Enterprise Mission was reported to be of the opinion that the participants in the 1995 Bosnian peace talks at Wright-Patterson Air Force Base, Dayton, Ohio, were shown the bodies of aliens widely rumoured to be stored there, and allegedly recovered from the Roswell crash site.

Bufo Calvin, whose e-mail newsletter brought this to our attention, wonders if the reason might have been to show the hostile parties that the minor territorial squabble in the Balkans pales into insignificance beside some bigger problem facing the entire planet.

He reports that Hoagland has some idea what the problem might be: "We're being prepared for an interplanetary war." *Bufo's Weird World (e-mail: bufo.calvin@awaiter.com) 24 Nov 1994. For another story involving Richard Hoagland, see p97.)*

Simulacra

One of the most baffling of nature's tricks is the simulacrum, the naturally-occurring feature which manages to bear an uncanny resemblance to something - or even someone - else. Some are so familiar we barely think of them as simulacra - the Man in the Moon, for example. Our faithful readers keep us well stocked with these strange trees, rocks and puddles. A selection of some of our favourites is below.

GOAT'S HEAD

THIS EERIE wooden goat's head was photographed by Paul Weller (probably not the famous one) in the car park of Duloe Village Hall, Cornwall.

HUMANOID

This picture of a humanoid figure sprouting from a tree trunk was taken by Glen Turner of Barrow-in-Furness, Cumbria. When he took the original photograph, he was looking at the formation the other way up; it was only when it returned from the developer's that he noticed the haunting figure.

ROCK FACE

A photograph which lends a whole new meaning to the phrase "rock face"! This was taken at Alum Bay on the Isle of Wight by Jack Davis of Tenby; he only noticed the face once the film had been developed. "The rock," he writes, "was considered a dangerous extension of a layer of harder sandstone protruding out of the soft, coloured sand that Alum Bay is famous for."

JESUS

For some reason, religious imagery seems to be a regular feature of simulacra. Perhaps it's because many of us have become so accustomed to the iconography of religion; perhaps not. This photograph was taken by a drainage engineer working for Melbourne Water in 1988 after flooding of the Yarra river. It was sent to *FT* by the editor of the corporation's staff magazine, Greg Axford; he only noticed the Jesus simulacrum when the picture was turned sideways.

fortean times

Religious
round-up

by Ted Harrison

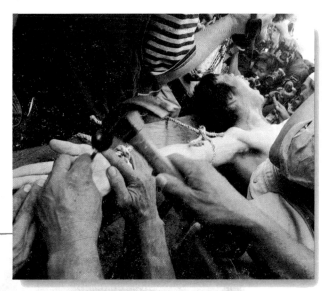

DEVOTION OR MASOCHISM? Shinichiro Kaneko is nailed to a cross

FT'S RESIDENT RELIGIOUS EXPERT casts an eye over some of the odder spiritual stories to appear in the magazine over the last year.

GOLD TOP: The faithful feed spoonfuls of milk to a statue of Ganesh, the elephant-god

IN JULY 1995, Father Christopher Jenkins, 63, a Benedictine monk and the acting parish priest at St Francis Xavier's Roman Catholic church in Hereford, had a remarkable recovery from a stroke. No one had expected him to live but he came out of his coma and began walking, talking and eating again – thanks, it is claimed, to the miracle curative powers of a severed hand. His recovery began shortly after a fellow priest had taken the mummified hand of St John Kemble and placed it on Father Jenkins' head as he lay in hospital.

St John Kemble was one of forty martyrs executed for treason in 1678 and canonised by the Pope nearly three centuries later. The story goes that St John Kemble's left hand, hacked off by the executioner, had been saved and had gained a reputation for its healing powers.

In August came reports from America that an unusually high incidence of fatal accidents on a 200-mile highway from Utah to New Mexico was being blamed on the road's number – Route 666, '666' being the dreaded number of the beast from the Book of Revelation. Christians and Navajo Indians were reportedly lobbying to get the number changed to something less apocalyptic.

September saw a frenzy of activity in the Hindu world, with claims that statues of the god Ganesh were drinking milk. On Thursday 21st, Delhi and much of northern India ran out of milk as rumours spread and the faithful converged on temples to offer their gifts to the gods.

Within hours the rumours had gone worldwide. In Southall – west of London – a local supermarket reported sales of 25,000 pints in one morning as 10,000 Hindus gathered at the Vishwa temple to feed the god by the spoonful. Apparently the milk vanished from sight as it was supped by the statues, without the stone from which they were made appearing damp or saturated.

Within days, however, the rumours died away with devout Hindus explaining that it was a short-term phenomenon designed by the gods to reassure the faithful of their continuing presence. When a Hindu statue is consecrated, it is believed

MISLEADING APPEARANCES: Three peasant children kneel before a vision of the Virgin Mary at Fatima, Portugal, in 1917. Moises Espirito Santo claims the area was named after the eldest daughter of Mohammed by an Islamic sect ten centuries earlier.

that the spirit of the god inhabits the material from which it is made.

On November 7th Julian Webb, a farmer from Western Australia, heard a voice coming from a pile of rocks on his farm. "Let I, the Lord, show you the way," the voice said. Two nights later Julian and his son returned to the same spot and found a granite slab on which there was an image of the face of Christ. One report said that a bright moonbeam led them to the 'holy tablet'. A month later, when it was put on public view, more than 1,000 pilgrims and tourists came to see the face. As the year ended opinion among the 1,400 townsfolk of nearby Beverley, W.A., was divided; some saw the face as a miracle, others as a hoax to attract tourists. There were rumours that a wealthy American was planning to buy the relic and up to half the town.

The sceptics claimed to have been vindicated when a silk-screen printer stumbled on a stock reproduction image of Christ bearing a striking resemblance to the 'Miracle Rock' while she scrolled through a computer art software package in search of a suitable graphic for T-shirts.

In November, officials at the Catholic shrine at Fatima in central Portugal were trying to stem an expected flood of Iranian pilgrims who believe that the spot was named after the eldest daughter of Mohammed, Fatima Zhara, or even that the vision by three peasant children in 1917 was of Fatima rather than the Virgin Mary. This idea was promoted by a docu-

MILKING IT: Milk shortages were reported as the faithful fed the statues

mentary broadcast several times on Iranian television.

The first Iranians were supposed to arrive in November, but a stiff protest by the Vatican to the authorities in Tehran, coupled with delays in getting visas, postponed their arrival. The Muslim community leader in Portugal, Sheikh Munir, a Sunni (most Iranians are Shi'ites) described the reports from Iran as 'perfectly ridiculous'.

The Iranian interest was originally triggered by a Jewish Portuguese sociologist, Moises Espirito Santo, whose study, which was circulated widely in Iran, maintained that Fatima had been named by Berber followers of a puritanical Islamic sect in the 9th and 10th centuries. The significance of the area was "much later perverted by the Roman Catholic hierarchy," he said. Sheikh Munir had not protested about the claims, he said, because this would have "turned Mr Espirito Santo into a Salman Rushdie".

Rumours that an apparition of Jesus had appeared high on a wall on Christmas Day and healed a paralysed Christian girl drew hundreds of Christians and Muslims to a three-storey apartment building in the Iranian capital, Tehran.

On 27 December, about 50 people gathered in front of the building in Avanessian Street, situated in an area of East Tehran inhabited mostly by Armenians. They pointed to a mark on the outside wall of the building and insisted that they could see a portrait of Jesus. Someone had spray-painted 'Death to rumour-mongers' just below the mark on the wall. Some of the crowd had other versions of the miracle. One old woman in a black chador said it had happened earlier and it was a Muslim man suffering from cancer who had been healed. She hoped that the miracle could help her husband, who also had cancer.

In February Mrs Ruksana Patel of Bolton became convinced that Allah would provide a special message for her to demonstrate how He was involved in the whole natural world. Her faith was rewarded when she bought an aubergine from a local mobile shop and, on cutting it open, discovered the seeds spelled out the phrase 'Ya-Allah' ('Allah exists') in Arabic.

Before long the allegedly divine vegetable was attracting about 50 pilgrims a day. Mrs Patel planned to leave the aubergine on display at her local mosque for a few weeks, after which it would be shared out among the faithful and eaten raw.

Finally, every Good Friday the village of San Fernando in the Philippines holds a re-enactment of Christ's crucifixion. Local Catholics allow themselves to be nailed to crosses for a brief period of painful but devout penance. This year, Shinichiro Kaneko from Japan asked to join the ceremony, in the hope that his suffering would persuade God to heal his critically ill younger brother. San Fernando's church readily agreed.

But Mr Kaneko was not a believer and had no sick relatives needing divine assistance. He was a pornographic actor specialising in sado-masochistic roles, and his crucifixion is to be released on video. When a Japanese magazine exposed the sham, Filipino Christians were understandably outraged.

However, a spokesman for V&R Planning, the video production company, could not see what was so disrespectful about filming religious rites. Foreigners often join in Shinto rites, he maintained, and no one complains because the locals do not take their own religion seriously.

PORN AGAIN: Filipilo Christians are scandalised by Shinichiro Kaneko's deception, shortly to be released on video.

The *curse* of
SUPERMAN

CHRISTOPHER REEVE: Wrote prescient poster

When actress Margot Kidder, who played Lois Lane in four *Superman* movies from 1978 to 1987, went missing for three days and was finally found on 23 April 1996, wandering "dirty, frightened and paranoid" in Glendale, California, her unexplained circumstances became part of a chain of misfortunes affecting principal actors from *Superman* movies, dating back to 1959.

MARGOT KIDDER: Car accidents and confusion

The best-known victim of the "curse of Superman" is actor Christopher Reeve, who broke his neck and damaged his spinal cord in a fall from a horse on 27 May 1995. In his last TV film, *Above Suspicion*, which was first broadcast in the same week as his accident, he played the part of a policeman paralysed from a spinal injury. He had also recently agreed to appear in a poster promoting safe riding. "In films I play an invincible hero," ran its wording, written by Reeve himself, "but in real life, I wouldn't think of riding without a helmet." A helmet and padded safety vest did not prevent the injury that paralysed the actor from the neck down.

Reeve's accident is strangely similar to Kidder's first brush with the "curse". In 1990 she suffered neck injuries in a car accident while filming a pilot for a new *Nancy Drew* TV series, and was confined to a wheelchair for a while. In 1991 the cost of her medical care forced her to file for bankruptcy. (Reeve's treatment works out at $400,000 a year, and his insurance will only cover him for three years.) Her career languished, accompanied by rumours of painkiller addiction.

On 20 April this year she was due to fly from Los Angeles International Airport to Phoenix, Arizona. Although she was seen at the airport she never boarded the flight, and three days later she was found wandering in a suburban back-yard 25 miles north-east of the airport. She was scratched, bruised and dirty, had cut off her hair in an attempt to alter her appearance, and claimed that she had been attacked and was being followed. Police said they did not believe she had been the victim of any crime. As of 25 April she was undergoing psychiatric tests.

Richard Pryor, who starred as a computer genius in *Superman III*, developed multiple sclerosis in the late 1980s. Like Reeve, he is now confined to a wheelchair.

RICHARD PRYOR: Multiple sclerosis

In a curious "lexilink", the first victim of the curse of Superman was George Reeves, star of the 1951 film *Superman and the Mole Men* and 104 subsequent episodes of the *Superman* TV series between 1951 and 1957. In 1959 his body was found, shot through the head. The police said it was suicide – Reeves had been depressed after failing to find other work due to typecasting – but rumours of foul play have persisted. *Hollywood Kryptonite* by Sam Kashner and Nancy Schoenberg (St Martin's Press), published this year, goes over the details of the mystery once again.

Jack Larson, who played Superman's pal Jimmy Olsen in the series, quit acting completely after Reeves' death. "I no longer wanted to come up against the same closed acting doors that I felt had driven George to his death," he said.

Given the enormous number of people involved in the *Superman* films over the years, four or five cases of medical misfortune may be nothing more than a statistical blip. All the same, the fact that it is the only series of films to have its own "curse", and that so much has happened to prove the frailties of actors who have been associated with the invulnerable superhero, gives the idea of a "curse of Superman" an interesting irony.
(Boston Herald, 25-26 April 1996; Guardian 22 August 1996; http://www.geocities.com/Hollywood/2459)

WHO'S NEXT? Will Dean Cain and Teri Hatcher find any future misfortunes blamed on the curse?

Cryptozoology

Cryptozoology, the study of unknown or mythical animals, is one of the most famous schools of Fortean investigation. Its subjects range from traditional favourites, such as the Loch Ness Monster and Bigfoot, to more recent phenomena such as alien big cats (ABCs) and the very fashionable Goatsucker. Here's a few of the best stories that came our way this year.

BIGFOOT UPDATE

LAST SUMMER odd screams were heard up in the Blue Mountains round Walla Walla in south-east Washington. Cattle began behaving oddly, as if disturbed by something. On 4 August, resident Wes Sumerlin drove up into the mountains with Paul Freeman, a veteran Bigfoot hunter, and Bill Laughery, a former game warden. As they entered an area where they had seen Bigfoot tracks before, Wes Sumerlin got "a whiff of something, like somebody skinning muskrats."

They reached a clearing where they found small trees twisted and broken, so fresh they were still dripping sap. There were large clumps of long hair, some black, some dark brown, caught on the broken trees.

Sumerlin and Laughery caught sight of a 7ft (2.1m) ape-like creature and heard the screams of two others. The creature was observed through binoculars at a distance of 90ft (26m), eating yellow wood violets. The trackers also found droppings, 2-5in (5-13cm) long, full of half-eaten carpenter ants, and fallen trees that had been pulled apart for the ants inside.

The hair clumps have been given to Frank Pourier, chairman of the anthropology department at Ohio State University, who is using a DNA test developed for the FBI to analyse hair strands without roots. If the hair turns out to come from an unknown primate, Pourier will compare it with a single hair reputed to be from a Chinese "wildman", given to him by Chinese peasants during a 1989 expedition. The latter does not match any known primate's hair, according to an analysis done at Shanghai University. *[AP] 6 Nov; Columbus (OH) Dispatch 3+6 Nov 1995; National Enquirer, 16 Jan; Guardian, 23 Jan; Charlotte (NC) Observer, 28 Jan; Los Ange-les Times, 4 Feb; Denver Post, 9 Mar 1996.*

DAVID COLMAN was driving down a country lane in West Lothian, Scotland, with his wife and three children when he saw what appeared to be a distinctly humanoid figure running down a forest path at what seemed like 70mph. This encounter with the "Quickfoot" happened in the Bathgate Hills, in an area known as Knock Forest. When the mysterious and fleet-of-foot creature realised that it was being observed, it turned on Colman and his family and snarled. "It was about six feet tall with a humanoid face," he said, "and seemed angry that we had disturbed it. My wife said, 'Did you see what I saw?'"

The date of this event is not given, but Mr Colman admitted to his interviewer: "It has taken me a long time to speak about this." *The People, 12 Nov 1995.*

CHERNOBYL

SCIENTISTS STUDYING wildlife in contaminated wastes around the Chernobyl nuclear power plant in the Ukraine discovered voles thriving on radioactive pollution. Ron Chesser of the University of Georgia and his colleagues examined the voles' genetic make-up and found it was mutating at an incredible rate. Since genetic diversity is what ensures the survival of a species, the supervoles were theoretically becoming more resilient.

The scientists examined a gene called Cytochrome B, found in the cell's mitochondria. Normally this gene changes at a rate of one mutation in every million letters of DNA code per generation, but in the supervoles the gene was producing a new mutation for every 10,000 letters of code.

One female vole, who had built her nest beneath a monument praising the Soviet workers who built the power station, produced five offspring, of which three had newly mutated versions of the Cytochrome B gene. Voles of the same species living 30km (19 miles) away, outside the contaminated "Zone of Alienation" had normal rates of mutation. "We're seeing more diversity in the mitochondrial DNA between two individual Chernobyl voles than we see between two different species, such as mice and rats,' said Chesser. *Los Angeles Times, 2 July 1995, 26 Feb 1996; Austin (TX) American Statesman, 26 Nov 1995; [R] 29 Feb 1996.*

MUTANT COW

A TWO-HEADED calf was born on the race track in the Russian city of Perm in the Ural mountains. It had two mouths and three eyes. The heads were joined at the top, with the third eye in the middle. Pollution from an adjacent oil plant was blamed. *Scotland on Sunday, 4 Feb 1996.*

BLACK PANTHER

A BLACK PANTHER sighting on Maui, Hawaii, the second in three months, led to a fruitless police search. Permission was being sought from landowners to set traps. *USA Today, 1 March 1995.*

DEVIL-FISH HUNTERS SQUIDS IN

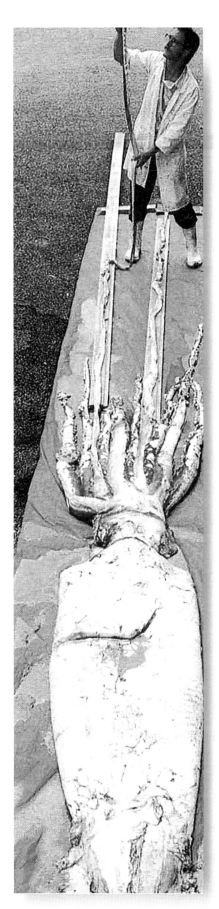

SINCE DECEMBER last year, biologists and fishermen around New Zealand have caught four giant squid (*Architeuthis dux*), including a 20ft (6m) male, one of the largest ever found, caught at only 1000ft (304m), less than one-third of the usual depth for the species. Males are smaller than females and for some reason extremely rare.

A $5 million expedition to observe the giant squid in its habitat for the first time will start diving near the Chatham Rise in the South Atlantic between November 1996 and February 1997. It will be led by Dr Clyde F. E. Roper of the National Museum of Natural History at the Smithsonian Institute, who plans to plumb the depths in a tiny submersible and film the leviathans.

The larger of the two female specimens shown here, 26ft (8m) long and weighing nearly a ton, was trawled up from 1400ft (426m) near the Chatham Islands, 600 miles (960km) east of New Zealand, on 31 December last year. It was one of only 20 of this size known to have been caught in the past decade. Its tentacles stretch 13ft (4m) and its head is nearly 6ft (1.8m) across, with eyes 10in (25cm) across. Scientists kept it in the ship's cold storage until the vessel reached Wellington in late January.

New Zealand has long claimed the squid record for one caught off Lyall Bay, Cook Strait, in 1887, which was said to measure 51ft (15.5m); but the Guinness Book of Records maintains that the biggest Atlantic giant was one netted in 1888 in Thimble Bay, Newfoundland. It had a 20ft (6m) body while one of its tentacles was 35ft (10.7m) long. However, it is believed that an adult squid can grow to a length of 70ft (21m).

Architeuthis dux is the world's most mysterious mollusc, with the largest brain of all soft-bodied sea-creatures. It has 10 tentacles studded with suckers which surround its beak-like jaws; well-developed eyes (the largest in the animal kingdom); tiny pigment sacs enabling it to camouflage itself quickly; and a water-jet propulsion system which lets it swim at up to 25mph (40kph).

What we know about them has been gleaned from remains found in whales' stomachs and from about 100 beached carcasses dating back to

1639 – although the very existence of *Architeuthis* was in doubt until the 1870s. A giant octopus 25ft (7.5m) long was found dead last September on the Matalascanas beach neat Doñana National Park in Spain's Heulva province. Its tentacles were 21ft (6.3m) long, its head 4ft (1.2m) and its weight estimated at several hundred kilos. The state of decomposition suggested it had been dead for at least a month.

"In many cultures," wrote David Heppell, keeper of mollusca at the National Museums of Scotland, "the larger octopus and the squid are regarded as the embodiment of evil and the term 'devil-fish' has often been applied to them. Elaborate rituals were devised to keep them at bay.

"Is it coincidence that Satan, the evil one, shares with the squid the same forked tail, occasional wings, the colours black and red, and is associated with the whiff of sulphur? In trying to make sense of a decomposing corpse with a forked tail, did our forebears start a train of horrific speculation that led to the Devil himself? Was Satan nothing more than a giant squid?" *Independent, 30 Jul 1990, 2 Feb 1996; El Pais (Spain), 13 Sept 1995; [AP] D.Mail, 1 Feb; NY Times, 13 Feb 1996.*

WHAT A WHOPPER: (Left) Marine scientist Steve O'Shea exmaines the New Zealand giantess. **(Above)** Lu Chung measures up a female giant squid caught off Australia's King Island.

JAH LION ROARS

SOUTH AFRICAN animal specialist Hym Ebedes has discovered 11 lions at a forgotten zoo in Addis Ababa, Ethiopia, bearing a striking resemblance to biblical lions thought to have died out in Africa decades ago. They have long, wide, black manes which reach under their bellies. The male cats, descendants of lions kept at the royal palace by Emperor Haile Selassie have the physical features of the North African Barbary lion or South Africa's Cape lion.

Barbary lions, from Morocco's Atlas Mountains, were imported by the Romans for use in gladiatorial contests. The last one was shot in the Atlas region in the 1920s. Cape lions, which resemble their North African cousins, were thought to have become extinct in the 1850s.

The two subspecies probably developed similar features because cool winters and the lack of dense bush allowed their manes to grow longer.

The history of the Ethiopian pride, which includes three males, four lionesses and four cubs, is unclear. They were probably taken from the royal collection in 1974 after the emperor was overthrown. *Times, 13 July 1996.*

TUSKER DO

A FEMALE elephant sprouting black tusks has been found in Thailand's northern Phayao province. It is extremely rare for female elephants to develop tusks, and even then they are almost invariably white. Veterinarians said the 3in (7.6cm) tusks sported by Noi, an elephant belonging to Kamnu Boadaeng, were authentically black and might grow a bit longer. Kamnu had Noi pulling timber from the forests, but he stopped working her three years ago when she developed the tusks.

In former days, domesticated or captured elephants with any distinctive characteristics had to be given to the king, as they were considered a symbol of his power and charisma. Kamnu said he would follow tradition and bestow the elephant on King Bhumibol Adulyaadej in honour of his 50 years on the throne. *[AFP] 25 July 1996.*

MANE LION: Does he look extinct to you?

PIGFACE BOUNCES IN

CREATURES THAT walk like dogs, have faces like pigs, eyes like bulbs and springs on their feet were sighted driving a white van through the central and eastern parts of Utter Pradesh, in northern India, in search of small children to eat, according to a report in *The Pioneer* newspaper on 25 June this year.

"This manai [man] walks both like a man and an animal. His eyes and shoes have bulbs, his shoes have springs and he jumps 80ft (25m) at one go," a man from Patti village was quoted as saying. "There are many like him. They come in groups in a white Maruti van, which can fly over any obstacle in the road."

Villagers say that at least 20 children have already fallen prey to the seemingly unstoppable beasts. Manju, an 8-year-old girl who says that she saw one of the creatures, described a man with the face of a pig who walked on all fours. A village woman said that the man first walked on four legs, but subsequently took flight.
[UPI] 26 June 1996.

JAPANESE CAPTURE AFRICAN DINOSAUR ON FILM – MAYBE

JURASSIC PARK it isn't, but a fifteen-second clip of videotape captured by a Japanese film crew may show a present-day dinosaur swimming in Lake Tele, in central Africa.

The film, shot from a light aircraft at a height of about 200 feet, was snatched as the crew, from the Japanese TV show 'The Presenter', was trying to take some panoramic footage for a documentary they were making about the lake, which has been reputed to be the home of *mokele mbembe* or *n'yamali*, a 30ft (9m) dinosaur.

Like much Fortean evidence, the film is maddeningly unclear. Shot on Beta SP video, it shows something large and apparently animate forging across the surface of the lake a few hundred metres from land, leaving a broad wake as it goes. The camera zooms in on the subject, wobbles, loses it, pans about and finally relocates it as it curves towards the shore. The camera refocuses just as the plane flies out of range. It banks around to circle the lake, but by now the object is gone, leaving only a disintegrating wake.

On analysis, the film seems to show a flattish shape with two tall, thin protuberances rising from it. A neck and a hump seems like one possibility; two men in a canoe is another, although the crew were adamant that there were no powered canoes on the lake that day. The object also submerged which, according to leading cryptozoologist Karl Shuker, suggests that it is an animal. "If you were willing the subject to be a dinosaur you could see it as that, but it could be one of the big freshwater turtles that live in the lake."

Lake Tele, a weed-clogged body of water about 3 miles (5km) across but little more than 20ft (6m) deep at most, has been linked to dinosaur sightings since 1980, and there are native rock-drawings of four-legged, long-necked animals which pre-date that. Many travellers in the area have observed large three-clawed footprints, some described as up to 3ft (90cm) across, although plaster casts of the prints usually measure less than half that size.

In the last twenty years several expeditions have set out specifically to look for *mokele mbembe*. In 1980/81 James Powell, a Texan herpetologist, and Roy Mackal of the

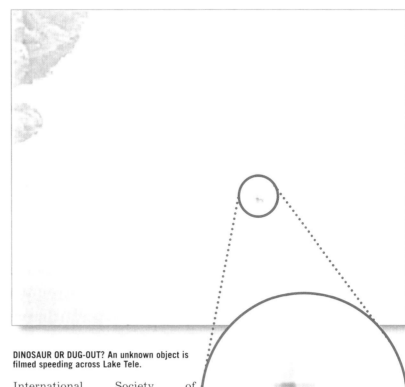

DINOSAUR OR DUG-OUT? An unknown object is filmed speeding across Lake Tele.

International Society of Cryptozoologists, collected several dramatic eye-witness reports. One, from a Congolese hunter named Nicolas Mondongo, described the beast as about 30ft (9m) long, with a 6ft (2m) head and neck the thickness of a man's thigh and crowned with a frill like a rooster, four sturdy legs and a tail longer than its neck. There was also a tantalising report of a mokole mbembe which had been trapped and eaten by a local village.

In 1983 an expedition led by Marcellin Agnagna, a zoologist from Brazzaville zoo, claimed a sighting of the animal, about 300 yards (275m) out in the lake. He described it as having a slim reddish head tipped with crocodile-like oval eyes and a slender muzzle, which it held about three feet (90cm) out of the water and turned from side to side as if looking for him. It also had a long black hump. Agnagna said he thought the animal was a reptile, but not a crocodile, python or freshwater turtle. Disappointingly, although several expeditions took photographs or films of their sightings, none are clear enough to offer any form of decent evidence.

Stories and sightings of *mokele mbembe* continue to intrigue cryptozoologists. The Japanese film cannot be regarded as any kind of proof of the creature's existence, but it may convince others that there is something worth investigating in the Congo.

WHAT A DRAGON

A WHITE KOMODO DRAGON has been sighted on the Indonesian island of Flores, according to Governor Herman Musakabe. Komodo dragons, the world's largest monitor lizards, are usually dark brown, like the one in Minnesota zoo, USA, which got a gourmet treat in September 1995 when a pink flamingo flew in from a nearby enclosure. Zoo workers found pink feathers and one leg. *Hong Kong Standard, 10 Jan 1996; USA Today, 13 Sept 1995.*

fortean times

Fringe Madness

Fortean Culture 1996

by Ian Simmons

WANKY FRANKIE: His masturbatory image upset the citizens of Normal

THE CULTURAL SCENE threw up a particularly vintage array of strangeness in '96, with, as usual, the world of art leading the way. An art exhibition in Normal, Illinois, turned out to be anything but normal. The exhibition, on the theme of Frankenstein, was originally going to feature work of children from local schools as well as professional artists, but the children were banned from attending and their art withdrawn when some of the professionals got a bit carried away. Some pictures showed naked bits of male anatomy, which is perhaps not surprising, but the one featuring the monster masturbating frantically would have given pause to anyone familiar with Mary Shelley's work.

Children had a more successful time with more notably priapic icon. In aid of a £1.5 million appeal for heart and lung research several hundred of them wearing red and blue T-shirts and carrying balloons recreated the image of the Cerne Abbas giant on the lawn of Kenwood House in London. Three hundred of them then changed position to give the giant a heart while the whole thing was photographed from the air. While he gained a heart the giant's most prominent feature, his penis, was missing. A spokeswoman said, "It might have offended the children, or if not them, their teachers."

Another phallic image at the art/medicine interface definitely did cause offence. An impotence clinic used a picture of New Zealand's 1928 Olympic athlete Stan Lay holding a 'limp' javelin. Unbeknownst to them, the appropriately named Lay was still very much alive, the country's oldest living male Olympian, and the use of his image in such a context without permission "outraged" his family.

Probably the most far-out art tale of 1996 was related in the *Phoenix New Times* in August. The article related the discovery of a 'lost Picasso' by David Barnes of East Texas which led to apparently vast revelations. 22 years ago, when the grandparents of Barnes's partner, Debbie, were living in a retirement community, they were given a picture their neighbours found in a skip. This was entitled 'Don Quixote and Sancho Panza' and bore the signature 'Picasso'.

Her grandparents hung it on their wall for a while then, tiring of it, put it away in a cupboard and forgot about it until they gave it to Dave and Debbie along with a load of other stuff when they moved to a new apartment. The Barneses kept it kicking around for a while, almost throwing it out several times and nearly losing it when a truck carrying all their belongings crashed during another move, but they never thought much of it until a couple of years ago when Debbie says an art student friend of hers looked closely at it and realised it was in fact a genuine Picasso, a revelation to her. They claim this was confirmed by the Picasso Museum in Barcelona, who offered them ten million for it, but they refused, because by now they'd figured out more about the picture.

David Barnes had spent hours staring at it and said, "I saw demons coming out of it. And the more I studied it, the more Picasso started talking to me. There's stuff in this

CERNE ABBAS EUNUCH: Open-heart prudery

PICASSO: Manipulated by dark forces?

painting that is going to come out in the End Times, when Christ comes again. I could give you numbers down to the year when Christ is going to return." He also claims it reveals him to be a direct descendant of Jesus, who will return in a spaceship, and that all this is being covered up by the government. Apparently it shows that Picasso was being manipulated by dark forces, but hid the face of Christ in the image as a signal of his eventual triumph. There's also a map of Europe showing where he and Matisse hid caches of priceless art from the Nazis, a secret suppressed by "forces in the underground art world".

In addition, the picture is painted over an original work by Goya and tells of everyone, including government officials, who were in Picasso's satanic circle. The art world, however, disagrees. Picasso expert Samuel Heath, whom the Barneses claim authenticated the miraculous image, sighs deeply when the couple are mentioned and said their picture was, in fact, a mass-produced lithograph distributed by a magazine in the 1950s and was worth, at most, $250. He remarked: "That's the wonderful thing about working in a museum: you get queries that are out of the blue. This was about as far out of the blue as I've seen."

In February Wenda Gu, artist in residence at a Nottingham gallery, appealed for volunteers to have their hair cut so that she could make bricks from the clippings and build a wall with them. The following month, pasta was the 'in' material. In the Cumbrian village of Silloth, Marjorie Harrison completed a 10-month labour of love, building a replica Celtic cross out of the stuff. Marjorie, organist at Christ Church in the village decided that what the church really needed was its own ancient monument and set about creating it herself. Rejecting stone as too costly, she settled on pasta as the ideal material, creating the detail with dried peas and lentils and colouring it with car spray paint. However, food art had darker consequences in Poland, where Urban Mittens attempted to build the world's largest ever pyramid of soup tins. Just as Mittens was adding his final touches after three years spent making a 63ft pyramid, the whole thing collapsed and crushed him to death.

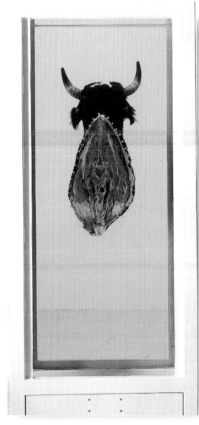

COW-ART: Sculpture or BSE-infected foodstuff?

Elsewhere, the vogue in art seemed to be "Think big". Oliver Bierhoff was seized by artistic inspiration and had a 62ft-high wooden chair built in the centre of the Italian city of Udine. Bierhoff is the German striker for the Udinese football club. In May Tom McClean, the first man to row across the Atlantic single-handed, created Moby, a 65ft long whale-shaped boat powered by diesel in which he intended to cross the Atlantic again; and Maidstone, Kent was up in arms about sheep. A giant floral sheep 18ft high, created by a local garden centre and weighing four tons, took its place in the town centre in June, but many locals condemned it as a waste of cash.

Also in trouble with the Philistines was Damien Hirst. Trying to import his sculpture 'Some Comfort Gained from the Acceptance of Inherent Lives in Everything' – two cows sawn into 12 segments and mounted in formaldehyde – into the United States, he fell foul of US

PHARAOH'S PINT: The new old beer

Customs. They impounded it because of their ban on British Beef as a result of the BSE scare, but eventually decided it was exempt being art rather than food. At least he did better than Constantin Brancusi who once had a bronze impounded because he would not pay US Customs duty on it as a machine part – Customs did not recognise anything non-figurative as sculpture.

BSE was also a problem for the Portuguese: their BSE variety of white wine was causing a stir among British visitors. Top London grocer Fortnum & Mason, however found yet another way to enjoy wine – they sell a CD of the sound of 14 different wines fermenting, recorded by Austrian winemaker Willi Opitz. It retails for £9.95. Beer also made the news with a new brew based on an ancient Egyptian recipe and called 'Tutankhamen's Ale' going on sale. Developed by Cambridge historians, it was brewed by Scottish and Newcastle. Whitbread, though, went for the aphrodisiac market – coming up with Myrrhy Christmas Ale, containing myrrh, a noted ingredient of love potions. Another aphrodisiac aroused the attentions of the Chinese bomb squad in Kunming. Examining a suspicious suitcase, they found it contained 1,500 dried dog penises, usually sold to improve people's sex lives.

In the US, it was dried pigs' dicks that caused all the flap. Oink-Oink Inc. of Iowa was required by the US Dept of Agriculture to start dyeing its best-selling dog treat, pork tenderloin, bright green so that it could not be used for human consumption. The company decided to kill the product, made from dried hog penises, rather than dye it, because they felt dogs would stop eating it if it were green.

Also unfit for human consumption was chef Geraldo Renaldez's prize-winning chilli con carne. He won more than 200 cookery competitions with his secret recipe, but when his ingredients were analysed, one of them was found to be cow manure.

In China, the Ministry of Internal Trading has stopped restaurants adding opium-poppy shells to their meals. Diners became addicted to them and kept returning to the restaurants to eat. Elsewhere in China, packaging was causing grief. In two apparently separate incidents snacks containing obscene novelties brought torrents of complaint. In Guangdong Province police arrested six staff at the Guangdong Wanda Food Production Factory after their snack foods were found to contain free gifts of plastic men and women having sex; and in Xuzhou the local ice-cream factory was subjected to a night raid when the sticks of their ice lollies turned out to be plastic naked women. The police seized 10,000 lewd sticks and 8,000 popsicles, and closed down the factory.

On the subject of concealed rude bits, the Disney corporation took a lot of stick in 1996 for allegedly having obscene subliminal images in its cartoons. While Disney allowed a Rio samba school to dress up as its characters for a carnival on the condition that none of the dancers had bare breasts, avid prudes were finding just that in a Disney production. Freezing the video of *The Brave Little Toaster* frame by frame revealed a bare-breasted woman wearing only star-shaped 'pasties' among photographs briefly held up by a character. The woman who made the discovery, Kathy Phelan of St Thomas, Ontario, said, "I think it's pretty sick, I don't think it's something I want my kids seeing."

Animators have long indulged in subliminal jokes, placing racy single-frame images in their work, knowing that it was invisible to anyone viewing the film at normal speed. Even video freeze-framing was hard to do accurately and tended to be blurred, but with laser discs it is possible to do accurate frame-by-frame analyses. That seems to be behind these revelations, starting in 1995 with the claim that a scene in Disney's *Who Framed Roger Rabbit?* includes a frame revealing Jessica Rabbit has no underwear.

It wasn't just the freeze framers that were giving Disney problems this year either, phone callers were too. Two numbers mentioned in Disney films turned out to have less than savoury connections in real life. In a Disney pig movie, *Gordy*, a lonely porker sets up a hot line to find his fellow swine, with the number 1-800-555-SOOEY, but when two Kentucky brothers called it for real, they got a sexually explicit recording urging them to give their credit card number for access to even harder material. Similarly, two kids who rang a number from the Disney movie *The Santa Clause*. On calling 1-800-SPANK ME they were told: "Welcome to hot, panting lesbians, sweaty man-to-man action and wild orgies". Their mother, Yvonne Brackman, planned to sue. But lest you should think it's just Disney who were getting subliminal stick, Coca-Cola got it too. They had to withdraw a poster from all over Australasia when it was found to contain a tumescent penis and an open mouth hidden in the artwork.

This just skims the surface of 1996's contribution to Fortean culture. Elsewhere Pepsi got sued for refusing to give a Harrier jump-jet as a competition prize; the log cabin where bluesman Muddy Waters was born went on tour; the big new thing in porn films was fully clothed women smoking sensuously; and the French Olympic Synchronised Swimming team was banned from performing a routine based on the Holocaust. Out on the fringes, life continues to get stranger.

REFERENCES

Frankenstein *S. Times 5 May 1996;* Giant *Times 22 June 1996;* Javelin *Guardian 2 Aug 1996;* Hair *Sun 24 Feb 1996;* Pasta *S. Post 3 Mar 1996.* Soup *Big Issue 22-28 Jul 1996;* Picasso *Phoenix New Times 8 Aug 1996;* Chair *Independent 28 Oct 1995;* Whale *Times 13 May 1996;* Sheep *Kent Messenger 28 June 1996;* Hirst *Int. Herald Tribune 2 May 1996;* BSE *S. Mail 12 May 1996;* CD *Times 12 June 1996;* Tut beer *Sussex Eve. Argus 6 Feb 1996;* Myrrh *D. Record 23.Nov 1995;* Dog Dicks *People 12 Nov 1995;* Pig Dicks *Idaho Statesman 4 Apr 1996;* Chilli *S. Mail 9 Jun 1996;* Opium *Sussex Eve. Argus 19 Jan 1996;* Guangdong *Victoria (BC) Times-Colonist 4 May 1996;* Popsicles *Victoria (BC) Times-Colonist 22 June 1996;* Rio *Irish Times 11 Jun 1996;* Disney *Victoria (BC) Times-Colonist 12 Nov 1995;* Pig *Economist 9 Sept 1995;* Pig *Victoria (BC) Times-Colonist 17 Nov 1995;* Santa *D. Mirror 2 May 1996;* Coke *Guardian 17 Jan 1996;* Harrier *Guardian 27 Jul 1996;* Cabin *Int. Herald Tribune 20 Mar 1996;* Smokers *D. Telegraph 2 Feb 1996.*

HARRIED: Pepsi never expected anyone to get the 7 million tokens to win a jump-jet. They were wrong.

CAT SCRATCH FEVER

CATS will be cats, but this moggy has ideas above its station. Leaping two yards into the air to attack a sea eagle at the Okayama nature reserve in Japan, the kamikaze kitty narrowly missed getting its claws into the seven-foot wing-span bird of prey. Perhaps it's just as well, as the eagle, with its razor sharp talons and flesh-ripping beak, would probably have given the foolish feline a harsh lesson in the difference between the hunter and hunted. *Mail on Sunday, 17 March 1996.*

FRANK SPOONER

Strange Deaths

We all have an appointment with the Reaper waiting at the end of our lives. Now and again, he lets his 'grim' identity slip, and despatches some poor unfortunate in a weird, wonderful or just plain stupid way. Here are some of our favourite strange deaths reported in Fortean Times in the last year.

RICHARD VERSALLE'S was the year's first strange death. He died when he fell ten feet (3m) from a ladder on the stage of the Metropolitan Opera House in New York on 5 January during the opening scene of Janacek's opera *The Makropulos Case*, about the secret of eternal life. It was thought that he had suffered a heart attack. Versalle, who was alone on stage at the time, was portraying a clerk named Vitek and was climbing a ladder to return papers to a filing cabinet. Somewhat ironically, the last line he sang was, translated from the Czech, "Too bad you can only live so long," a reference to a protracted lawsuit that was finally about to be settled. Versalle fell to the stage, landing on his back with his arms outstretched. The curtain was swiftly lowered and he was rushed to hospital, but was dead on arrival. *AP 6 Jan; NY Post, 6 Jan 1996.*

LISA POTTER, 21, went for a walk at night with her mother, Mrs Ann Everitt of Witham, Essex. When they came to the Moots Lane level crossing, where Lisa's father had been killed eleven years earlier, Mrs Everitt refused to continue. Lisa went and stood on the track and called, "Come on mum, it's all right." At that moment a train appeared and Lisa was run over and killed.
D. Telegraph, 10 Aug 1995.

AN EGYPTIAN searching for the treasures of the pharaohs was found in July sitting cross-legged on top of a mountain, his corpse pecked by crows.

Police in Southern Egypt were searching the area near Saqolta mountain in Sohag province for four of his relatives who accompanied him of the treasure hunt. *Reuter, 6 July 1995.*

YIANNIS KARAYANNOPOULOS, 87, a farmer in Oropedio, near Grevena in northern Greece, believed that his cat had been stolen by his neighbour, Thomas Koletsos, so he shot him dead as he left for work on 10 May. Mr Koletsos's wife, Chrysanthi, heard the shot, rushed out and was shot dead in turn. Karayannopoulos then turned the gun on himself. The cat returned later in the day. *AP, 12 May 1995.*

RALPH BREGOS waited two years for a heart transplant. When news arrived at his Kentucky home that a donor was available, Ralph, 40, got so excited that he had a massive heart attack and died. *D. Record, 9 Feb 1996.*

AN ISRAELI SOLDIER on leave from combat duty was sucked into a giant dough-mixer and kneaded to death at Jerusalem's Mystic Pizza. A co-worker at the pizzeria said that Moshe Dor-On, 21, had reached into the bottom of the mixer to pull up dough from the bottom when he was sucked in. *Reuter, 3 Aug 1995.*

VITTORIO VERONI was killed on the Via Cartoccio level crossing in Reggio Emilia, northern Italy, when his Renault 21 was hit by a train and carried along the line. His daughter Cristina, had been killed four years earlier at

the same crossing, by the same train, driven by the same driver. The crossing, over the Guastella-Reggio line – unmanned and without any protective bar, the legal norm for Italy's local railways – was near a bend in a flat landscape where the morning sun could be particularly blinding. Signor Veroni, 57, a builder from nearby Novarella, drove back and forth to work several times a day over the crossing. Suggestions that he decided to take his life at the place where his daughter died were repudiated by his family and the train driver, Domenico Serafino. Investigators said his death was accidental. They believed that he was either blinded by the sun or hindered from turning to look before crossing because of a plaster cast he was wearing around his chest following a workplace accident. *La Repubblica (Italy), 9 Nov; D. Telegraph, 10 Nov 1995.*

AN APHRODISIAC called 'Rock Hard', thought to have been imported from Hong Kong, killed four New York men over two years when they swallowed it instead of rubbing it on their genitals. The American Food and Drug Administration blamed the deaths on poor labelling. The product was said to contain dried toad secretions and a steroid. Oral ingestion caused an irregular heartbeat and vomiting. *AP, 25 Nov 1995.*

PEOPLE coming to see the film *Deadly Virus* in a Berlin cinema stepped over a dead usher's body in the darkened entrance, thinking he was a wax dummy advertising the movie. Some of the cinema-goers even kicked him. *D. Star, 27 Apr 1995.*

24

ANDREA RUGA, 47, had the same name, birthplace and date of birth as a Mafia godfather accused of terrorism and various kidnaps. Italy's police computers couldn't tell them apart and the "impeccably honest" ironmonger from Monasterace in southern Italy constantly had his house raided. At roadblocks his wife and children sat weeping as he was hustled off to have his papers checked. At hotels he suffered countless indignations as staff called the police. He was finally found dead in a lay-by near Naples after taking poison. Minutes before, he had phoned three senators, three magistrates, a newspaper editor and the local police chief to say that he couldn't stand the aggravation any more. *D. Mail, 25 Oct 1995.*

KATHY TAGUE DIGIROLAMO, 29, from Hatfield, Pennsylvania, suffered from bronchial asthma and an allergy to shellfish. As she dined in a restaurant one night, she developed breathing trouble after a waiter walked past her table with a steaming platter of shrimp. Her asthma inhaler was ineffective, her breathing worsened and, despite medical attention, her pulse rate plunged and her heart stopped. Such deaths merely from smelling certain foods are the result of a system-wide breakdown called anaphylactic shock, and are exceedingly rare. *Omaha World Herald, 4 Dec 1994.*

SEVERAL FRENCH World War I veterans died of joy after hearing that they were to receive the Legion of Honour to mark the anniversary of the end of the war, according to the Veterans' Affairs Minister. He said he knew of at least two who died filling in the form to receive it. *Reuter, 11 Nov 1995.*

AN ARSONIST boiled to death in Manila, Philippines, when he hid in a drum of water to protect himself from a fire he started. Renato Salazar, an employee of a haulage firm, entered the company's kitchen, opened two gas tanks and then hid inside the water-filled drum before tossing a lighted match at the tanks. The fire destroyed the building. *[AFP], Canberra Times, 7 Jan 1996.*

A MAN accidentally killed his two-year-old daughter at Bauma, near Zurich, by building a snowman on top of her. Dozens of neighbours joined the search for the girl, identified only as Priscilla, when she was discovered missing from the playground in front of the family's home. One person noticed something strange about the snowman and uncovered the frozen child curled up underneath. *AP, 4 Jan 1996.*

RACHEL DRAKE, a head teacher from Southampton, died instantly when a 500lb (225kg) deer was catapulted onto the roof of her car. Drake, 50, suffered massive head injuries after the stag ran into the road, was struck by an oncoming vehicle and landed on the roof of her car. *Huddersfield Daily Examiner, 10 Jan 1996.*

TWO WITCH-DOCTORS in Zimbabwe who claimed they could cure AIDS died from the disease after having sex with patients they believed they had cured. *AFP, 9 Dec 1995.*

IN JUNE last year a German woman of 75, identified only as 'Ema N', was declared dead from a heart attack and spent two days in a mortuary in Saxony-Anhalt. Two nurses saw the sheet-draped body move. The woman was re-admitted to intensive care, but died the next day from hypothermia. *Manchester Eve. News, 22 June; Sun, Today, 23 June 1995.*

A 75-YEAR-OLD MAN, walking his dachshund, in Berlin was attacked by a 43-year-old man who bit him on the neck, shouting, "I am Dracula!" Passers-by overpowered the attacker and handed him over to the police. He said he had been drinking. The unnamed victim went home and died an hour later from a heart attack. *Abend Zeitung, 6 Apr 1995.*

A FIJIAN FISHERMAN bled to death in March when a surface-skimming swordfish leapt at his night lamp and stabbed him in the face. Meli Kalakulu, 18, of Gau Island, was night-fishing near Suva in the South Pacific. *Wolverhampton Express & Star, 15 Mar; D. Express, 16 Mar 1996.*

GUNNAR LARSEN, 42, was carving his name on a giant oak in a high wind when a branch broke off, fell and crushed him to death in a public park in Herning, Denmark. *Sunday Express, 31 Dec 1995.*

PARAPSYCHOLOGY

BY JOE McNALLY

WHEN ONE HEARS the phrase "parapsychological investigation", images of *The X-Files* probably spring instantly to mind. Sadly, the truth is rather more prosaic; rather than nail-biting chases through abandoned missile silos and similarly exotic locations, real-life parapsychological investigation is more likely to involve a good deal of tedious mucking about with ping-pong balls and large manila envelopes. That said, some of the findings emerging from recent parapsychological experiments have been no less fascinating than the *X-Files* take on the subject – perhaps even more so for being real. Indeed, one or two of the experiments have been interesting in themselves – particularly one involving high fashion. There have also been some intriguing tales of success from less academic sources, with a "psychic detective" featured in *Fortean Times* chalking up another curiously accurate prediction.

The big growth area in parapsycology over the last twelve months or so has been the US government's experiments into so-called 'remote viewing'. The basic concept behind remote viewing is connected with the old idea of astral travel. Essentially, it involves a psychic "leaving" their body and attempting to psychically observe distant events, people or locations. The CIA had been experimenting with remote viewing at its Fort Meade base since 1973, when its set up its inital "Scanate" experiments. "Scanate" was short for 'scanning by co-ordinates'; since then, the programme has gone under a variety of names, including "Grill Flame", "Center Streak" and "Sunstreak". It was revealed at the end of 1995 that the CIA was to recommend to the US government that they discontinue the programme, now called "Star Gate"; prior to this, it had been hoped by many in the intelligence community that the programme might some day become a reliable source of valuable, and otherwise unobtainable, information. Since this information became public, interest in the various programmes has rocketed, particularly among conspiracy researchers, many of whom believe it was linked to secret experiments in mind control.

The programme was assessed for the CIA by the American Institute for Research, under the supervision of statistician Dr Jessica Utts and psychologist Dr Raymond Hyman. Their hefty report reached a few interesting conclusions. Most significantly, they discovered a "statistically significant laboratory effect", whereby "hits" – "good" results – were recorded more often than might be expected. Indeed, Dr Utts subsequently referred to the test as "convincing evidence of a real phenomenon". However, they had a number of reservations. Particularly, they felt unsure that it had been satisfactorily demonstrated that the observed effect actually was due to psychic power, rather than "characteristics of the judges or of the target or some other characteristic of the methods used."

Ultimately, they decided that the effect was of no operational use, for a number of reasons. Firstly, the experiments were being carried out in laboratory conditions, which would be difficult if not impossible to replicate in the field; secondly, although "some accuracy" was noticed with regard to broad characteristics of 'targets', little in the way of specific information was obtained – exactly the sort of information that would be needed in intelligence work. Moreover, what little information was obtained was described as "inconsistent, inaccurate... and required substantial subjective interpretation." Finally, and most damningly in their eyes, "[in] no case had the information ever been used to guide intelligence operations," a clear sign that it had not been producing "actionable intelligence".

Despite this, a number of successes have been claimed over the years by the remote-viewing team at Fort Meade. Amongst these were: the locations of a Soviet submarine project in 1979; the nuclear testing range at Semipalatinsk, where they apparently described equipment unknown to the CIA through conventional means; a radar installation in Tajikistan, in 1987; and, most puzzlingly, the secret location of Saddam Hussein during the Gulf War – puzzling, since press reports added that this information "was never verified by conventional means"...

Given the level of interest in the remote-viewing programme, it was perhaps inevitable that the world's best-known psychic would reveal his involvement to the world, and he did not disappoint. At a press conference in January, Uri Geller mentioned that he had been involved in the early days of the Star Gate programme in the early 1970s. The conference had been called to launch Uri's latest venture, one of the most audacious and public experiments in psi ever carried out: a website where would-be spoon-benders can test their powers, and perhaps enrich themselves to the tune of $1 million

(US dollars, we dearly hope) in the process.

Under the title of "Uri Geller's Internet Challenge", this website is believed to be the first attempt to discover whether telekinetic powers can function over the internet. In the bowels of Geller's Berkshire mansion lies a safe, containing a spoon, a highly sensitive stress gauge, and a video camera linked to the internet. To take the challenge, one must head for **http://www.urigeller.com/**, register (which costs £3), and concentrate. The spoon has been insured for $1 million against bending. If and when it does, the stress meters will record the time, and everybody who was logged on to the site at the time will be summoned to Uri's home. There, they will be asked to put on a repeat performance before Uri himself, along with representatives from the spoon's insurers and David Berglas, President of the Magic Circle. If successful, they will leave $1 million richer.

URI GELLER: Stress his spoon and win $1 million

And what better to spend it on than some of the world's first psychic T-shirts? Noted Manchester fashion house Joe Bloggs has launched a range of 'psychic clothing' in association with none other than Uri Geller. Each shirt will be personally touched by Geller before it reaches the shelves, and on the first of each month, Uri will send out 'positive energy' to all those wearing his shirts. Each shirt comes with a form for reporting anything interesting or out of the ordinary which occurs while wearing it. We at *Fortean Times* are sure that Uri would never dream of abusing this awesome power over Britain's youth.

One of the more curious tales of psychic activity covered by *Fortean Times* during 1996 was the case of Chris Robinson, the 'psychic detective' from Luton profiled by Rob Irving in *FT86*. Chris interprets his symbolic dreams, recorded in a diary, to predict impending terrorist attacks, disasters and spectacular crimes. He can lay claim to a substantial list of successful predictions, including a fatal mid-air collision at an air show and the 1991 IRA attack on 10 Downing Street. The ink on *FT86* was barely dry before he added another notch to his tally – the IRA bombing of Manchester in June.

According to the June 29th issue of *Psychic News*, Chris and psychic collaborator "Jeanette" began to sense the "psychic build-up" to the bombing at the beginning of June; Chris apparently requests his psychic sources to inform him of upcoming IRA bombs on the first of each month. Via an arcane symbolic system not easy to describe here, details began to emerge from his dreams which enabled him to infer that the IRA were planning to attack a major city, using a bomb hidden in a car or van, and that many people would be injured. Unfortunately, because of a confusion over the name Piccadilly – also an area of Manchester – Chris came to the conclusion that the target would be London.

However, Chris and "Jeanette" (her full name was not given by *Psychic News*) saw a number of clues which enabled them to interpret their visions more accurately after the event. For example, "Jeanette" was shown the walkway at the Arndale Centre, devastated in the bombing. She added that she believed London was the original target, with the IRA switching at the last minute because of the police presence in London for Euro '96.

Psychic News also reports the lovely snippet that in the week before the Manchester bomb, Chris was contacted by a German TV crew who wanted to film him around London, at the scenes of previous IRA attacks, on what was to be the fateful Saturday. He refused. "No way," he said, "am I going to any large city on Saturday. I believe that a bomb will go off on Saturday morning. Between the hours of 10.30 and 12.30 I am staying indoors!" Needless to say, the crew was back the day after the bombing...

SUCCESSFUL LOCATIONS AND IDENTIFICATIONS BY THE 'MYSTICS OF FORT MEADE'

 A major Soviet submarine project in 1979.

 A suspected Libyan training facility for PLO terrorists in 1989.

 A radar establishment at Dushanbe, Tajikstan, in 1987.

 The ultra-secret nuclear testing area at Semiplatinsk, including equipment unknown to the CIA through other means.

 The wreckage of a Soviet Tu-95 'Backfire' bomber which had crashed somewhere in Africa (to within several miles).

 How a KGB colonel caught spying in Africa had transmitted his secrets (through a 'calculator').

 The whereabouts of 52 American hostages in Iran after the embassy takeover in 1979.

 The location of Gen. James Dozier, kidnapped in Italy in 1981.

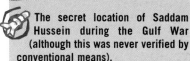 The secret location of Saddam Hussein during the Gulf War (although this was never verified by conventional means).

GOAT'S KIN: Siamese 'kids' delivered in Moyo District, northern Uganda.

In the pages of *The Monitor*, a Kampala newspaper, outrageous tales of the paranormal and uncanny vie for space with more run-of-the-mill political stories. You can probably guess which ones we've collected here. While these tales may push the limits of credibility, they contain pleasing echoes of classic Fortean reports from European and American newspapers around the turn of the century.

IN MARCH 1995, *The Monitor* ran a story under the title "Busia ghost goes wild, burns houses". The trouble began when Ochieno Auma died in Nairobi in December 1994. His father, Sidoro Oyoolo, a resident of Syangu village in the Ugandan province of Busia, refused to perform the traditional burial rites as he was a practising Christian. What sounded like stones began to shower on the Oyoolo's roof, although none was ever found. Whenever Sidoro and his wife went out to investigate, the figure of a naked man was seen running out of Auma's house before vanishing. The stone-throwing eased off, but every morning Oyoolo would find his doors smeared with faeces and doors and windows opened by themselves at night.

Then food which had just been served to Oyoolo started turning into soil. Enraged by Oyoolo's cool response (said *The Monitor's* correspondent, David Musengeri), the ghost began setting fire to nearby thatched roofs. A clan meeting was held on 29 January, but came to an abrupt close when the kitchen caught fire. Two days later, Musengeri and others saw a bicycle riding itself from Oyoolo's house. After about five min-utes wheeling around, it parked itself against the wall. The report stated that "shortly after, cups, plates and sugar bowls sat themselves up on the table and were filled with strange tea."

IN APRIL 1994, Mr Dembere, chairman of Iki-Iki sub-county, encountered a magician, locally referred to as an *omusawo*, putting on a show in the local marketplace, and demanded to know who had given him authority to do this in his area of jurisdiction. The magician responded with mocking laughter and an enraged Dembere went to fetch his colleague, the Defence Secretary Mr Kalupede. Meanwhile, the magician exhibited his 'miracles' to an ever-growing throng. He made plastic mugs disappear into the head of one client, 'cut off' the head of another and even pulled off his own right leg and hopped around on the other one.

Dembere and Kalupede returned and demanded he pack up his bags and leave. The magician refused and warned them to leave him alone, or they would regret it. When Dembere ordered his colleague to fetch some policemen to effect an arrest, the magician picked up a talisman and threw it at Dembere, who 'instantly lost his sexual organs'. He started wailing, "Oo amaka gawoirewo... omusaiza antwaireku amaka!" ("The home is finished. The man has taken my home!")

The *omusawo* advised Dembere to go home and take his first wife to bed in order to restore his lost "home". Dembere's wives got wind of the affair and refused to copulate; when the desperate chairman returned to the market, the magician had gone. Some elders advised him to follow the showman to Pallisa market the following day. This he did and, after shaking hands with the *omusawo*, "[he] regained his penis and testicles. He could not believe it until he went behind some bushes and checked himself."

IN DECEMBER, 1993, Musigi Orena, who had eloped with somebody else's wife, was drinking *ajon nu imumoniwa* (sorghum brew) at his home with some friends. A snake appeared, hissing loudly, with a torch-like light on its head. It demanded, in broken Ateso (the local language) that the woman with whom Orean had eloped return to her previous husband. Perhaps the sorghum brew was stronger than usual; anyway, Orena took to his heels, leaving his friends to kill the snake. The next morning, the dead snake had vanished. "It reappeared at noon and quietly went straight to bite Orena on the knee as he was dressed in shorts. He collapsed and died instantly." How it was known that this was the same snake, risen from the dead, is not made clear.

All stories from The Monitor. (Uganda): Busia ghost, March 10 1995; Mr Dembere, May 1994; Musigi Orena, 11 Jan 1994.

Epidemics

We think we know about diseases, but we cannot control them. Nor, in many cases, can we even begin to understand what causes them. Perhaps in a few centuries people will regard the words "mass hysteria" with the same contempt we give to medieval complaints such as "the King's Evil". Or maybe not.

HAD YOUR CHIMPS

THE EBOLA VIRUS claimed the lives of 13 people in Gabon, West Africa, in February after a dead chimpanzee was eaten at a feast in the remote village of Mayibout. Seven people infected with the virus had been admitted to hospital in Makokou and seven others were under observation. The authorities were trying to trace those who had helped to bring the sick to hospital. A number of dead animals were found near Mayibout and neighbouring villages, including a second chimpanzee, a wild cat, an antelope and two gorillas.

Ebola, which causes extensive internal and external bleeding, kills at least 70 per cent of the people it infects. The virus was named after the River Ebola in northern Zaire, where it first appeared in 1976. There was an outbreak in and around Kikwit, Zaire, in May 1995 which killed 245 people, and another case in the Ivory Coast last December, but the victim survived. [R] 19 Feb 1996.

AFRICAN PLAGUE

A **MENINGITIS EPIDEMIC** has been sweeping western Africa. By the beginning of April, the World Health Organisation estimated that 40,000 people had been affected by the epidemic, with 6,000 deaths. The majority of the cases and deaths came from Nigeria, where 26,000 people were affected, with nearly 4,000 deaths. The land-locked state of Burkina Faso had just fewer than 12,000 cases and 1,000 deaths: health officials there said they needed a further four million doses of vaccine to stem the outbreak.

FASHION FEVER

ON 9 NOVEMBER 1995, staff at a Daks-Simpson clothing factory in Larkhall in Lanarkshire collapsed with skin rashes, nausea and breathlessness, and 42 of the 1600 factory workers were hospitalised. They were soon released with no obvious ill-effects, but the plant was closed for tests. Four days later 25 of the 53 workers at Delta Textiles, a T-shirt factory twelve miles away in Lanark, complained of similar symptoms, although no link could be established between the factories or their processes.

The following day, 20 of the 365 workers at Daks-Simpson's Polbeth factory went down with rashes and sore throats, three of them being sent home. The West Lothian plant makes up men's clothes for Marks & Spencer from material supplied by colleagues at Larkhall.

After thorough micro-biological and chemical tests at all three sites drew a blank, Lanarkshire Health Board, like many puzzled health authorities in similar circumstances, suggested mass-hysteria, although a safety expert later blamed "a minor chemical irritation, colds and anxiety" – which amounts to much the same thing. The initial trigger was supposed to be a reaction to chemicals used to resist fire and creasing in clothing. Why then doesn't the reaction happen wherever these chemicals are used? *Scottish Daily Express, 10 Nov; Edinburgh Eve. News, 14+15+16+17 Nov 1995.*

the natural world

Alien CONTACT and ABDUCTION

by Jenny Randles

SOME MEANINGFUL progress was made in ufology this year. Two aspects in particular stand out; both run counter to the trend of recent times which has seen the reality of alien kidnaps struggle to keep pace with mounting evidence to the contrary. This problem has driven researchers more towards subjectively experienced phenomena – not necessarily mere hallucinations, but experiences which are in some sense hallucinatory in origin.

However, those who believe in a literal invasion by extraterrestrials now have something to shout about. There have been some major omissions amidst the 2000 abduction stories investigated globally to date – chiefly the near-total dearth of 'observed encounters' and any attendant physical evidence to the reports.

It is easiest to see this in comparison with a bank robbery. Should one of these occur, police will collect statements from the bank tellers, of course, but they are unlikely to take the matter seriously if there is no hard evidence that a robbery occurred. Should passers-by outside the bank react with blank expressions when asked to describe the getaway car and the fleeing robbers, it seems probable that the police will file this not as an X-file, but as an ex-file.

In alien abduction terms we have plenty of stories from bank tellers – usually reputed abductees who were on their own in bed or in a car on some lonely road. Occasionally they have had others with them to back up their story, perhaps a husband or wife. But investigators had come to worry about the missing physical evidence and any supporting testimony from uninvolved passers-by.

Support from third-party witnesses would be a good way to strengthen the case for actual physical reality behind an abduction. Alien contact stories are very difficult to attribute as real events; unfortunately, the track record of evidence of this sort is disturbingly one-sided. There are cases from South America, Europe and Australia which emphatically point in one direction – away from actual reality, in which you and I could share in what was seen by the abductee.

One case alone stands out as a potential landmark. A woman called Linda Napolitano claimed she was floated out of her apartment block in Manhattan, New York, by small grey creatures who ensured that her family were and remained unconscious and thus did not see her leave; then brought her aboard the hovering UFO and subsequently returned her after extraterrestrial medical tests. Unfortunately, these usually omnipotent aliens failed to allow for two secret service bodyguards and an international statesman who happened to be parked in the street down below and who saw the whole thing.

The so-called 'Manhattan Transfer' case has been a *cause célèbre* for American ufologist Budd Hopkins since it occurred in 1989. Now – after some difficulties – he has finally pub-

lished his book about the investigation. The case is not without criticism from within ufology, let alone from the sceptics who find it all too good to be true. Doubts about it have been raised by a number of ufologists; it will not change the world, most realise – at least not unless the independent witnesses, particularly the mysterious 'third man' (whose identity is much debated in the UFO world) come out into the open.

The same may be true of the question of physical evidence. To date nothing demonstrably not of this Earth has ever been taken from a UFO by an 'abductee'. One case gained notoriety during May 1996 when MoD investigator Nick Pope published his memoirs about UFO exploits in his government department. This was an incident in the Quantock Hills, in which a man claimed to encounter a UFO and aliens. Despite Nick Pope apparently taking the story seriously, BUFORA spent much time and effort investigating it and were less excited. A green substance found below where the UFO had been reported turned out, according to analysis carried out by the Geological Museum on BUFORA's behalf, to be a fish pond ornament!

The best hope seemed for many to lie in claims of 'implants': objects reputedly put into abductees during their kidnap and left there as some sort of monitoring device – and this is where the second major development of 1996 occurred.

At least a dozen claims are on record of such objects being placed inside a witness, but all efforts to find them by medical searches had failed. One reputedly appeared briefly on a dental X-ray in an Australian case, but vanished when a more sophisticated picture was taken, leading to the speculation that aliens had abducted the witness a second time between these two sessions and thus removed the implant! The more cautious-might prefer to suggest that the first image was just a shadow on the X-ray which vanished on the use of better equipment. But in 1996 implants were allegedly recovered from two patients in the US; see pp94-95 for a fuller report on this case.

Whilst such work has occurred beneath the surface the media's love affair with alien abductions has continued unabated – with TV series from *Nova* to *Strange but True?* presenting specials. Many magazine and newspaper features have told new stories – usually of hypnotically retrieved testimony. UFO groups have been swamped with pleas from witnesses who, having seen this blitz, are sure that they must have been kidnapped and need hypnosis to remember the event. Whilst hypnosis is still used in many countries, the major UFO associations in both Britain and Sweden have banned its use altogether, considering it to be a further complication, and medically unhelpful to the witness.

Whilst all this goes on, ufologists have continued their search for the truth about abductions – which, contrary to expectations, is not all centred around whether aliens are little and grey or tall and blond. Sceptical psychologist Dr Sue Blackmore told a Society for Psychical Research conference in September 1996 that she had investigated abductions and has concluded that they are examples of sleep paralysis and the attendant vivid dreams/ hallucinations.

Meanwhile her counterpart, Dr Serena Roney-Dougal, published in *New UFOlogist* (Number 4) her evidence linking abductions with the pineal gland and chemical reactions occurring within.

In my book *Star Children*, looking at abductees who believe that they are involved in a procreative experiment by aliens, I isolated a series of clues that seemed to link these people together. For example, they were found to be artistic and visually creative and had a phenomenal memory of very early life – often back to just after their birth, whereas most people can only remember events from the age of two or three years old.

Building on such steps, Peter Hough worked with psychiatrist Dr Moysha Kalman in a year-long study into a group of British abductees in an attempt to find a common pattern. Dr Kalman believes he has discovered a link involving phenomena within the temporal lobe of the witness. The book resulting from this work will be published by Cassell in the spring of 1997.

Meanwhile in February this year the American folklore researcher Dr Eddie Bullard published the results of his five-year project – not as a book but as a major scientific treatise. He has studied the individual databases of abduction cases from some of the world's best-known researchers. Most of these people are from the USA, but Australia and Britain were also represented. He wanted to see whether the belief systems, modes of investigation and the ongoing findings of each individual ufologist has any significant influence on the type of evidence that emerges from their case-work and research.

His results were stunning. Although hypnosis is a contaminating factor, it apparently does not significantly alter what is produced. Nor does the belief system or methods of the investigator alter the data. A consistent form of abduction occurs everywhere, with relatively minimal adaptation of the evidence because of the filter through dozens of different investigators with their widely differing approaches. Bullard feels that such research points firmly away from a folkloric or psychological explanation and towards some sort of physical reality, although he wisely keeps his options open.

All this shows that there are major questions still to be answered but that the phenomenon of the alien abduction is one that is receiving very serious investigation – even if the trivialisation by the mass media tends to suggest otherwise.

CITY LIGHTS: Linda Napolitano and the Manhattan apartment block where her abduction by extraterrestrials in 1989 was apparently witnessed by an international statesman and two bodyguards

Tough Shit

Fate clearly has a sense of humour, and a firm understanding of the principle that all comedy has its roots in other people's tragedies. Whether you see these incidents as bizarre coincidences, cosmic karma, or stupidity editing itself out of the gene pool, 1996 has been another bumper year for Destiny jerking humanity's leash to remind it who's in charge.

PASTA KILLER

RICHARD H. ROSENTHAL, 40, an insurance executive living in the posh Boston suburb of Framingham, was recently promoted and became a father; but he behaved out of character on 29 August. On that day a bloody trail led police from his four-bedroom, $300,000 home to the woods nearby where they found the body of Laura Jane, 34, his wife of four years.

She had been slashed from neck to navel and her internal organs were skewered on an 18in (46cm) wooden stake about 30ft (9m) away in a nearby garden. Her face had been pummelled with a large rock, leaving her so disfigured that she was listed as "Jane Doe" on Rosenthal's arrest report.

Under investigation, Rosenthal told police: "I had an argument. I overcooked the ziti [a pasta dish]." He appeared rational, but showed no emotion and referred to his late wife as the "unknown victim". At one point he asked, "Is this a big case?"

The couple had no history of violence. Their baby daughter, Marla, was unharmed and placed in state custody. *New York Post, 30 Aug 1995; Hackensack (NJ) Record, 31 Aug 1995.*

STRONGARMED: Seven Spanish teenagers were hospitalised after trying to mug a defenceless woman in Alicante. Herminia Alvarez, as the boys discovered, is a circus weightlifter, the centrepiece of whose act is supporting eight people on one shoulder. *Guardian, 17 Oct 1995.*

GOODBYEWATCH: Lorenzo Trippi, a lifeguard in Ravenna, lost his job when three people drowned after he had hit them with life-preservers. Police said his aim was too accurate. *Independent on Sunday, 10 Sept 1995.*

KING SIZE: Ireland's tallest man, 7ft 4in Mick Coulter, was unable to launch a non-smoking campaign in Ulster schools after he was sentenced to nine month's jail in the Irish Republic for stealing cigarettes from a petrol station in Lifford, County Donegal. *D. Telegraph, 7 Mar 1995.*

COLOUR BLIND: Police in Rio de Janeiro were baffled when residents of the Parada de Lucas all came out at once on 26 September and painted all the buildings pale green. They suspected that the order came from local drug barons hoping to confuse the police – with obvious success. *D.Telegraph, 28 Sept 1995.*

LIGHT SHOWERS: A production of "Singing in the Rain" starring Paul Nicholas and complete with designer puddles, had to be abandoned on 6th June 1995 after a fault in the sprinkler system poured hundreds of gallons of water into the Edinburgh Playhouse. *Edinburgh Eve. News, Liverpool Echo, 6 June 1995.*

COUP BLIMEY: The star speaker of a British Council seminar on "How Can Democracy Be Sustained?", Brigadier Julius Maada Bio of Sierra Leone, was unable to attend: he had just overthrown his country's government in a military coup. His first degree was to cancel the forthcoming elections. *D. Telegraph, 19 Jan 1996.*

IDLE HAND: Thomas Passmore of Norfolk, Virginia, cut off his hand because he thought it was possessed by the devil, then refused to let surgeons at Sentara Norfolk General Hospital re-attach it. Now he is suing them for $3 million, saying that they should have known he was crazy. *Eve. Standard, 14 May 1996.*

OUT OF SEASON: On Christmas Day 1994, Niyi Owoeye was driving his bus near Akure, capital of Nigeria's Ondo state, when he thought he saw an antelope beside the road. Fancying a snack, he drove at it and killed it. Then he discovered that the "antelope" was Mr Ratimi Alesanmi, a member of the Federal Commission for Road Safety. *Ivoir'Soir [Ivory Coast], 29 Dec 1994.*

DRAINED: PC Terry Chard, 30, was dispatched to guard a black metal "landmine" washed up at Whitecliffe Bay beach on the Isle of Wight. He stood guard for five hours in the pouring rain before being told by bomb disposal experts that it was a drain cover. *Morning Star, Sussex Eve. Argus, 27 Oct 1995.*

FINGERED: Steve Larking, 18, charged with breaking into a nudist camp at Whiston, Merseyside, was arrested after a finger found in a chain-link fence was sent for prints. *Times, 16 Dec 1995.*

LUCKY IN LOVE: Huang Pin-jen, a 27-year-old Tai-wanese soldier, and his 26-year-old transvestite boyfriend Chang Shu-mei decided to commit suicide as both sets of parents were opposed to their relationship. They stuck their heads in plastic bags for an afternoon, but this only made them vomit. Then they drive their car off the Central Cross-Island Highway, but they missed the water and ended up unharmed in a valley.

On 21 April they hired a room on the 12th floor of the Samantha Hotel in Taipei. They tried hanging themselves with nooses made from bedsheets tied to ceiling rods, but when they jumped they brought the ceiling down. So they tried the gas fire, but were sick and passed out. The meter ran out and they woke up with headaches. Then they jumped out of the window hand-in-hand, but crashed through the tin roof of a five-storey restaurant below, wrecking a lobster tank and ending up on a banqueting table. They were hospitalised in Kaohsiung, with fractures but in a stable condition. *[AP], China Post, 23 April 1996.*

MONEY FOR NOTHING: Art dealer John Austin advertised in a Sydney, Australia, newspaper that he would supply "absolutely nothing" for $1; and 489 people replied, enclosing the cash. *News of the World, 12 May 1996.*

BURN RUBBER

WHAT SEEMED like an ingenious way of getting rid of mountains of old tyres has led to major problems in Washington State. Two highways near Ilwako and Spokane, repaired with chunks of rubber, are smoking and oozing an oily, toxic goo that is threatening nearby wetlands. It smells like creosote, with a burned-plastic undertone.

The state used the rubber from one million recycled tyres in place of rock or gravel to provide 7,000 cubic feet of fill when it rebuilt a 140ft (42m) stretch of Route 100 last October. In December the asphalt began to crack and give off noxious smoke, with temperatures up to 160°F (71°C). Some of the rubber had spontaneously combusted, in a process similar to the heating up of a compost heap. The other problem road is in Garfield County, and has been emitting smoke – and even flames – since January.

Both roads have been closed and digging the mess out will cost more than $1 million. *Standard-Examiner, 3 Feb; Idaho Statesman, 25 Mar 1996.*

FLIGHTS OF FANCY

TED JOFFE, general manager of American Minerals Inc., was stopped by Osaka airport police after the crew of his Thai Airways international flight from Manila reported that he had refused his meal, "which could indicate that he swallowed drugs to smuggle into Japan." A bemused Mr Joffe was soon released. "Next time I'll stuff the meal into the seat pocket in front of me," he said. *[AFP] 9 Aug 1995.*

SNAKE MUFFLED

ON 29 JANUARY a distressed resident of Tilehurst, Berkshire, spotted a cobra lurking motionless by the side of an electricity substation in an upright position, as if ready to strike. The RSPCA inspector was not available, so he rang the Ark Animal Sanctuary in Caversham who told him it was probably motionless because the weather was so cold. As the man waited for help, he warned passers-by to keep back.

Bob Andrews of the Sanctuary arrived, kitted out with a net, box and goggles to protect his eyes from the spitting beast. As he approached the cobra, he realized it was an old exhaust pipe. *Reading Evening Post, 1 Feb 1996.*

Medical Bag

Illness, disease and the various workings of the human body fascinate everyone; only the weather provides a more fertile topic of conversation. From deadly plagues to unique natural anomalies, from strange compulsions to obscure afflictions, from hilarious side-effects to inexplicable maladies; it all astonishes us as much as it appals us. Here's a selection of some of the medical stories covered by FT this year.

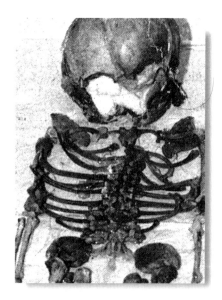

THAT'S NO LADY, THAT'S MY WIFE

THE UNIVERSITY OF UTAH

Signature

LEASA BIBIANNA HERRERA
U585-51-2695

UNDERGRADUATE STUDENT

A MISSING PERSON report filed by Bruce Jensen in Bountiful, Utah, led to the unmasking of his "wife" as a man named Felix Urioste who had defrauded Jensen of $40-60,000 dollars during their marriage of three and a half years.

The deception ended when Urioste, 34, was pulled over for speeding in Nevada and police found 33 credit cards and other identification in 19 different names, as well as keys to four hospitals in Salt Lake City. At the time he was travelling as a man. Police established that he had enrolled as a female student at the University of Utah and had worked as a doctor at the four Salt Lake hospitals, alternating between male and female aliases.

Jensen, 39, was a lab technician at University Hospital, Salt Lake City, when he met Urioste, or "Leasa Bibianna Herrera", a female doctor with a "Cleopatra-style" wig and heavy make-up, in September 1991. According to Urioste's family, he ran away from home at 13 and at 17 told them he had a sex-change operation. Urioste told Jensen that he was an Israeli disowned by his parents for marrying a non-Jew, and had later joined the Mormons. After a single sexual encounter, he said he was pregnant with twins and Jensen felt morally obliged to give the children a father. They were married in December 1991. Several months later, Urioste claimed that the twins had been stillborn, and that he had cancer. He was apparently able to pull off the deception because Jensen never saw him naked and the marriage was essentially celibate.

After the imposture was exposed, Jensen sought an annulment, citing irreconcilable differences. Confused, embarrassed and broke, he planned to return to his native Wyoming and "crawl in a hole for a few years and not let anyone within rifle range." *Ogden (UT) Standard-Examiner, 12+21 July; Meridien (CT) Record-Journal, 14 July; [AP] 14 July 1995.*

URIOSTE after his arrest in Nevada

FOETUS IN FOETU

THIS FOETAL SKELETON was removed from the womb of a Burmese woman after it had been there 19 years. Dr Islam Abdul Moneim said that half of the woman's womb was removed as it was adhered to the colon and intestines. The baby had died just a week before the due delivery date. *Riyadh Daily, 6 April 1995.*

DAPHNE OF THE LIVING DEAD

DAPHNE BANKS, 61, an epileptic, was pronounced dead by Dr David Roberts, called to the family farm in Stonely, Cambridgeshire, at 2am on New Year's Day. Undertakers took her to Hinchingbrooke Hospital, Huntingdon. At 6am, minutes before she was placed in a mortuary refrigerator, undertaker Ken Davidson, a family friend, noticed a vein twitch in her right leg. Then he saw her chest moving up and down and she began to snore.

Mrs Banks was rushed to intensive care, regained consciousness after 24 hours, and four days later was well enough to be transferred to a general ward. It later emerged that she had taken an overdose of epilepsy pills and sleeping tablets which could have lowered her blood pressure, making her pulse hard to find. By 10 January, when she gave a press conference, she was well on her way to recovery. *D. Telegraph, 6, 8, 9 & 11 Jan; S. Telegraph, 7 Jan 1996.*

GETTING THE POINT

IF YOU GO ABROAD, make sure you have medical insurance. Ulrich Schild, a 39-year-old German tourist in the Dominican Republic, didn't. The wonder is that he lived to regret it.

Ulrich and his girlfriend Michelle Sujatta were travelling on a country road at night on a rented motorcycle when it spun out of control. He was flung through the air and impaled on a branch which broke off with the force of the impact. "I could feel the branch sticking out from both sides of me," he said.

Michelle managed to flag down a passing motorist. Still conscious and with nearly 5ft (1.5m) of branch protruding from the top centre of his chest, Ulrich was taken to a nearby clinic. The clinic said they had no facilities to treat him, advising Michelle to take him to the hospital in the city.

Although he was in shock, Ulrich somehow found the strength to continue. "I didn't think I'd be able to get up again, but I told myself to pull myself together or die."

At the hospital, emergency room doctors quickly gave Ulrich a pain-killing injection. However, when they learnt that he did not have any travel

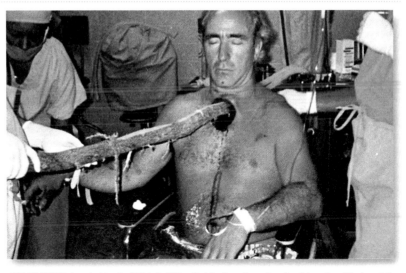

OUT ON A LIMB: Impaled tourist Ulrich Schild waited for three hours in a Dominican Republic hospital while they wrangled over his medical bill – he had no travel insurance – but made a full recovery.

insurance, they refused to operate without cash.

Luckily for Ulrich, a compromise was eventually reached. The hospital demanded a letter from the German embassy confirming that they would cover the cost of the treatment Ulrich needed. He then had to wait for more than three hours, still pierced by the branch, while an embassy official

could be located to sign the letter. Finally, Ulrich, still conscious, was wheeled into an operating theatre where surgeons removed the branch.

He had been very lucky. The stake had missed his heart and emerged to the left of his spine. "When I woke up and found I was not paralysed, I knew I would recover," he said. *Sunday Mirror, 21 Feb 1993.*

RELAT-EYE-VITY: American doctor Harry Abrams has put Albert Einstein's eyes up for sale, for an asking price of $5 million. Abrams removed the physicist's eyes during an autopsy (see *FT79:12*). *D. Record, 14 Mar 1996.*

ELECTRIC BOY STUCK FOR TRANSPORT

Johnathan Rainey from Carrickfergus in County Antrim, Northern Ireland, generates so much static electricity that he causes electronic havoc wherever he goes. He first noticed the phenomenon one day at school when all the numbers on his calculator went crazy. "One of my worst moments came when my mobile phone blew up and the the the car stopped, all within 15 seconds, leaving me totally stranded. I could never guarantee that I would be able to turn up anywhere on time and eventually I lost my job."

His new Rover 100 Kensington broke down repeatedly. After three months when the car spent more time in the garage then it did on the road, mechanics laid the blame on a faulty immobiliser and gave him a replacement; the new vehicle broke down 22 times in just under four months – because of the immobiliser. Johnathan's static was confusing the message from the remote-control hand switch to the car. For the moment, things are all right. He has borrowed a Renault Clio which doesn't have an immobliser. *Belfast Telegraph, 8 Feb 1996.*

SHOCKING: Jonathan Rainey

WIRED FOR WEIRD

Forteans have taken to the internet like the proverbial ducks to water. No matter what your Fortean interests – lake monsters, bigfoot, UFOs, ABCs, ghosts, and just general Weird Stuff, there's a website, newsgroup or mailing list to suit you. On Usenet, there are three Fortean newsgroups (alt.misc.forteana, alt.paranet.forteana and – hey! – alt.paranormal.forteana) along with literally hundreds of groups which deal with matters of interest to forteans - from alt.alien.research and alt.alien.visitors to alt.conspiracy and alt.paranormal, and even the entirely enigmatic alt.cthulhu.cabinet.sombrero.buenos-dias.coffee.slam. For those with e-mail access, there's the Forteana mailing list (send an e-mail with the body text "subscribe forteana" to majordomo@lists.primenet.com to subscribe). And for those out and about on the Web, there's the *Fortean Times* home page at http://www.forteantimes.com. Once you're finished with that lot, you'll have acquired a hunger for much more; here's a smattering of sites from Ian Tresman's monthly "Wired for Weird" column in *Fortean Times*.

THE UFO FILES
Dozen of files, including The Secrets of the Mojave, the Crim-Ram (or Cosmic Conflict) series, Dreamland in the Rockies, UFO Sightings by Astronauts, and some images.
http://linex3.linex.com/ufo/

THE CONSCIOUSNESS RESEARCH LABORATORY
Research into mind-matter interaction and technologies, the effects of lunar, solar, and meterological influences on human performance, and mass "mental coherence".
http://eeyore.lv-hrc.nevada.edu/ ~cogno/cogno.html

THE SOURCEBOOK PROJECT
The most authoritative compilation of objective articles, categorising anomalous phenomena in the fields of biology, archaeology, geophysics, and astronomy. Covers male menstruation, giant skeletons, ball lightning, radiometric dating problems, the red-shift controversy, ancient coins and batteries, and hundreds more.
http://www.knowledge.co.uk/ xxx/cat/sourcebook/

THE WEIRD AND THE GROSS
Not for the faint hearted: "Bodily Functions", "Chaos, Madness, and the Bizarre", and "Horror, Gore, and Freaks on Parade".
http://ezinfo.ucs.indiana.edu/ ~cdmoore/weird.html

AT THE EDGE HOME PAGE
Launched as a 40+ page A4 magazine in February 1996, At the Edge aims to "walk on the cracks" between disciplines, and explore new interpretations of past and place in archaeology, mythology and folklore.
http://www.gmtnet.co.uk/indigo/ edge/atehome.htm

THE "X" CHRONICLES
A new magazine from Canada investigating the "Strange and the Unknown", covering UFOs, Ghosts, Hauntings, ESP, Animal PSI, Alleged Government Conspiracies, Demonic Possession, Alien Abductions, Oujia Boards, Poltergeists, Angels, Dreams, Miracles, The Ancient Astronaut Theory, Skulls from the Triangle of the Ancient Gods, Extraterrestrial Encounters, Dowsing, Altered States of Consciousness.
http://vaxxine.com/xchronicles

ZETATALK
Information relayed by the Zetas through their emissary, Nancy. Covers such subjects as portents of a Pole Shift and how this relates to the coming millennium Transformation the world is about to undergo; how visitors from other Worlds are watched by the Council of Worlds; to what extent the Government is aware of and interacting with the alien presence.
http://www.netis.com/members/ millennium/zetatalk/

THE UNUSAL OR DEEP SITE OF THE DAY
A potpourri of links, such as those to the Institute for the Study of Contact with Non-Human Intelligence, the Mind Uploading Home Page, Anomalous Cognition, Paranormal Belief Survey, Agora Pages (a personal experience of the synchronous, anomalous and paranormal), the Astral Projection Home Page, the Vodoun (or Voodoo) Information Pages, Healing-Energies on Internet, and the Dead People Server.
http://adsint.bc.ca/deepsite/

THE SHROUD OF TURIN HOME PAGE
Examine the Shroud for yourself, keep abreast of current research, and updates on The Shroud of Turin CD Rom Project.
http://www.shroud.com/

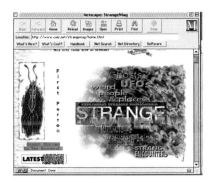

STRANGE MAGAZINE'S "TEN STRANGEST" LIST

In the opinions of the editors, the ten strangest occurrences in the past year include: a rain of slimy globs, the Tianchi Lake Monster, an Invisible Flying Hippo, and a glowing green mist claimed to have been seen over the President Nixon's grave by a night-watchman.
http://www.cais.net/strangemag/home.html

IN SEARCH OF GIANT SQUID

An online exhibition of the creature that has inspired many a fantastic fable. The Giant Squid is among the biggest animals in the sea, but is rarely seen.
http://seawifs.gsfc.nasa.gov/squid.html

SHOCK MEDIA

Shock Media explores the antithesis of information and exposes some "shocking" truths about our societies. Recent articles include "The Mad Cows of Britain", "UFOs Have Arrived", and "The X Files".
http://www.ipgnet.com/~jun/media/

SURVIVAL KIT

An e-zine full of reviews that focus on sources of strange, deviant, cult, bizarre and extreme information: science-fiction, cult movies, serial murder, erotica, horror, body modifications, mind control, strange cults and religions, conspiracy theories, Fortean phenomena, UFOs, occultism and occulture, and more.
http://users.hol.gr/~diceman/

ZINES LITERARY GUIDES

Links to on-line UFO and Skeptic magazines, including The Swamp Gas Journal, The Crop Watcher, The Desert Rat, Schwa; The Rational Enquirer, and Skeptics UFO Newsletter.
http://www.duke.edu/~dpk/zines.html

THE MIRACLES OF URINE THERAPY

...or uropathy to give it its proper term. A serious look at the medicinal applications of the amber nectar.
http://www.dlsu.edu.ph/othersites/health/uro/uro.html

KOESTLER PARAPSYCHOLOGY UNIT

The Chair of Parapsychology at the University of Edinburgh researches parapsychology, extrasensory perception and psychokinesis, and publishes the European Journal of Parapsychology.
http://moebius.psy.ed.ac.uk/

UFOs: A CLOSER LOOK...

The page dedicated to presenting the truth about the UFO phenomenon by trying to verify every fact, as well as the search for government documentation made available under the provisions of the Freedom of Information Act.
http://www.tcet.unt.edu/~chrisl/ufos.htm

X-FILES

Spontaneous Human Combustion, Ball Lightning, Flesh-Eating Bacteria, The Sky is Falling, Alien Abductions, and the TV Show.
http://ourworld.compuserve.com/homepages/Ponder/xfiles.htm

THE OOGA BOOGA PAGE

Vampires, Lycanthropy (Werewolves), Ghosts, Witchcraft, including book-lists and links.
http://star06.atklab.Yorku.ca/~peterpan/index.html

FLYING SAUCER REVIEW (FSR)

A quarterly magazine "recognised as the leading international organ in the world on the subject... we know that Governments have been lying about the UFO problem for more than forty years... take the problem extremely seriously, and we know that the U.S. Government in particular holds a number of crashed craft and a considerable number of preserved bodies of small dead crew members of a certain species about 4ft-4.5ft in height."
http://www.cee.hw.ac.uk/~ceewb/fsr/fsrhome.htm

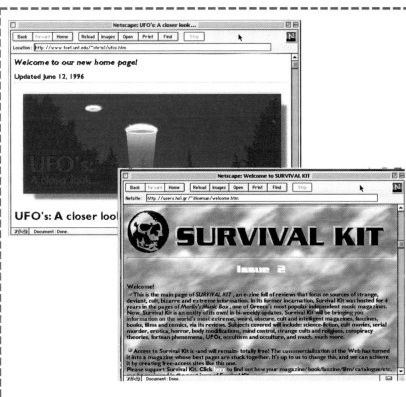

1996 in Contemporary Legend

by Bill Ellis

CHUPACABRAS PHOTO: Posted to the Internet. Real or fake?

FOR THE FOLKLORIST, *any given year's legends are "déjà vu". Legends are ways of talking about the outer fringes of experience, the happenings that, in fancy or reality, challenge our sense of The Way Things Are. Happily, culture's definitions of reality don't change very quickly; unhappily, reality never quite conforms to our definitions. Folklore fills in the slippage, so we find the same kinds of clashes – and the same stories – decade after decade.*

CHURCH FIRES: Kossuth, Mississippi

GOATSUCKERS, HORSE-RIPPERS AND CHURCH-BURNERS

One of the most active areas of legend discussion concerned attacks on domestic livestock by assailants who make no sound and leave odd tracks, or none at all. Late in 1995, a local flap emerged in Puerto Rico, where goats and other small animals were found drained of blood. Media blamed the 'chupacabras' or 'goatsucker', a mystery bipedal animal with hairy arms, glowing eyes, and a row of multi-coloured quills which double as wings down its head and spine.

By March 1996, the creature had become a popular topic in Spanish-language tabloids and talk shows. Livestock deaths in Miami were being linked to the 'chupa', and local zoologists had to hold 'public necropsies' to try to quiet fears. But word of the weird entity spread throughout Hispanic communities in the United States, with incidents and theories being exchanged via Internet websites and e-mail discussion groups. By May, encounters had been reported throughout Mexico and the southwestern border states of the USA, and authorities were even starting to talk about vampire bats as an explanation (see pp52-54).

Though less widely spread, the 'vampire of Moca' flap of 1975 had included many of the same elements. Named after the Puerto Rican town where the scare began, the 'vampire' targeted the same kinds of small domestic animals, leaving them drained of blood through wounds that seemed to have been made by "a sort of punch" that both pierced and removed flesh. Animals were even killed inside locked cages, and witnesses either heard nothing or recalled a kind of screech and the flapping of gigantic wings. Then as now, amateur speculation focused on extraterrestrials who were using the creatures as their servants, while officials blamed vampire bats or psychopaths.

The 'lunatic' theory was also popular in the summer of 1996 along the border of Denmark and Germany. There "horse-rippers" were blamed for "a new crime phenomenon" in which animals were found killed or injured by a small sharp instrument that pierced their head or chest. Danish authorities checked with their German counterparts, who told them that they had also collected 318 such incidents in their country since 1992. A veterinarian, interviewed on TV, said that the horse-ripper wounds were strangely small and neat, and could not be linked to any conventional weapon.

Danish authorities noted that most of the incidents occurred in fields close to roads leading to vacation homes rented by German tourists. So they warned horse breeders to keep close watch over their animals and be alert for cars with German licence plates. Others decried a 'smear campaign' against Germans and instead pointed to sexual perverts as the more obvious culprits. At last word, the German Society for the Prevention of Cruelty to Animals was offering a reward for the arrest of a bona fide horse-rippers. Readers

CHURCH FIRES: Kossuth, Mississippi. Not a conspiracy at all, it seems.

will recall that a similar panic over horse mutilations occurred in England's southern counties in early 1993. One authority blamed the attacks on a group of kooks who "delight in child pornography or get involved in covens and do bizarre sexual things in the night." But despite intense investigation, none was found.

Happily, "covens" or "satanic cults," the most common explanations for US livestock deaths in the 1970s and 1980s, seem to have disbanded... or have they simply exchanged tactics with their Scandinavian counterparts? In 1992, after eight historical churches burned in Norway, authorities and media there blamed cults of youthful devil-worshippers. And in the summer of 1996, the US media worried over what was seen as a pattern of church-burnings in the southern states.

At first linked to racist groups (many of the churches were used by black congregations), the "pattern" led to an official FBI investigation ordered by President Clinton, which turned up no sign of a conspiracy. In fact, church vandalism rates have declined nationally and have always involved more white churches than black ones.

However, old rumours about ritual desecration reappeared, and in both North Carolina and Virginia police blamed teenage cults. Virginia's State Police even prepared a guide on how civic-minded residents can spot and report the danger signs of satanic worship. Included is a list of graffiti "satanic symbols" to watch for, including the "Cross of Nero", better known as the peace symbol.

Cults, foreigners, cryptozoological animals – all are "usual suspects" whenever an apparent pattern emerges of seemingly random violence. Whether the animal attacks in Puerto Rico or in Denmark are eventually explained, whether the culprits in US church burnings are found, conspiracy is always preferable to happenstance.

"HEARD" ON THE INTERNET

As more and more users linked up to the information network known as the internet, the more it became a conduit for stories previously passed on orally or through photocopies. Some well-known contemporary legends have easily made the transition to cyberspace, such as the Outrageously Expensive Recipe (once for the Red Velvet Cake, now for cookies) sold to a customer who is circulating it out of revenge. Craig Shergold, too, is now out on the net, still looking for business cards (or is it postcards? or get-well cards?) along with those seemingly superannuated drug dealers trying to give Your Kids those LSD tattoos.

But a number of anecdotal legends attributed to the NASA space programme clearly appeal to the modern scientist set. One concerns the remark, "Good luck, Mr Gorsky", allegedly made by Neil Armstrong during his moon walk: the "truth" is that when he was little, he overheard Mrs Gorsky yelling through the bedroom window, "I'll give you oral sex when the kid next door walks on the moon!" Another NASA legend tells

of a cryptic message sent to the moon with the astronauts by Navaho Indians in their own language. Long afterward, curious scientists finally managed a translation: "Watch out for these guys, they come to take your land."

But no legend continued to provoke more fear than that of the totally evil, totally brilliant hacker who had managed to create a computer virus that could be communicated through e-mail. If read, it would place your computer's hard drive into "an nth complexity infinite binary loop", which would either destroy it, "wipe" it, or at least make it irritated at the user.

Happily, you could spot it because the phrase "Good times" appeared in the subject header and you could then discard the message unread. More happily, the US Dept. of Energy's "Computer Incident Advisory Capability" (CIAC) whose business it is to detect such beasts, could not locate a single example of such a virus or of a hard drive so affected, suggesting that it never existed.

Unhappily, CIAC then discovered some hacker had obligingly created such a virus and distributed it on the commercial network America Online under the name "AOLGOLD." Happily, it doesn't scrub hard drives, but it does eliminate a number of common directories needed to access basic programs. Unhappily, the e-mail virus will probably be back, in debugged form.

AND JUST FOR FUN

Each summer some new sexual misadventure circulates that "really happened" to a friend of a friend. Previous calamities involved a kinky husband who liked to dress up in a Batman suit, super-glue in the condom, or peanut butter and an affectionate dog.

This summer it was my friend's grandmother who went for her gynecological check-up and was startled to hear the doctor comment: "Fancy... FAN-cy!" Puzzled, she returned home to find that instead of female deodorant, she'd used her granddaughter's hair glitter. Now that story is really true... it happened to my mother's best friend in 1954. Only it was green stamps, see... what really happened was...

Strange Days

Inept Crime

Criminals are normally seen as villainous schemers, planning their work with precision. They're not. In fact, according to our evidence, they're just as likely to make incredibly stupid mistakes or trip over Fate's shoe-laces as the rest of us. And whatever Government ministers may claim about falling crime rates, Fortean crime has definitely been on the rise. Here are the pick of the stories we've reported in the last year.

FOWL THREATS

RODERICK BAKER, a 50-year-old antiques dealer, tried to ward off police by holding 140 chickens hostage at knife-point. The trouble began on 27 June when sanitation workers were sent to clean up Baker's rubbish-filled yard in Uniondale, New York State. Baker produced a large knife and threatened to kill one chicken if the authorities didn't get off his property. He carried out his threat, beheading three birds before the police moved in and arrested him. He was charged with obstruction of government administration and two violations of agriculture and market laws before being released. The surviving chickens were moved to a farm on Long Island to "live a normal chicken life", according to Larry Wallach of the Society for the Prevention of Cruelty to Animals. *Denver Post, 29 June; Philadelphia Inquirer, 1 July; Independent, 6 July 1996.*

MONKEY BUSINESS

ON 12 DECEMBER 1995, a schoolteacher in the Calcutta suburb of Domjur shot a monkey that had entered his garden. The primate hobbled to the adjacent police station compound and lay there, writhing. Local people took the animal to a veterinary clinic but it died. When the monkey's body was brought back to the police station, more than 50 monkeys from the neighbourhood gathered, shrieked loudly and refused to leave for hours.

A local communist Party politician, apparently moved by the monkeys' protest, filed a formal complaint with the police, asking them to arrest the schoolteacher who had shot the monkey. Police did not take any action. *[AP] 15 Dec 1995.*

CRIME OF PASSION

SHANE PATRICK NEHO, 17, and an associate broke into Barbarella's sex shop in Palmerston North, on the south island of New Zealand, early on 3 February this year. They fled on bicycles, pursued by the police, dropping most of their loot which included a blow-up woman, a female mannequin dressed in rubber underwear, a large drinking mug in the shape of a vagina, and an inflatable sheep.

"We have not yet ascertained why a sex-shop would be stocking blow-up sheep," said Sergeant Ollie Outrim, "especially as Palmerston North has a large sheep population." At his trial, Neho said he couldn't remember much as he was drunk at the time. *New Zealand Herald, Eastern Express, 24 Feb 1996.*

THE BODY OF Henry Carlton, 41, was found on 5 February wedged half-way through the basement window of a real-estate agency in Williamsport, Pennsylvania. His legs were inside and his head and arms outside, and a bag of burglary tools were next to him. He apparently believed that he could squeeze through the 15in (38cm)-high, 18in (45cm)-wide window and drop to the floor; but the window was obstructed by a heating duct and Carlton's bulky clothes stopped him. He froze to death. *[AP] 7 Feb 1996.*

LEMON ENTRY: Two bank robbers in Washington DC ditched face masks and rubbed lemon juice into their faces instead because they'd been told it blurred security cameras. It didn't work, of course, and they were arrested and jailed for 24 years. *D.Record, 11 June 1996.*

EAST COAST PHANTOM DARTS BACK

DART MAN, who terrorised women in Manhattan six years ago, may have a suburban cousin on Long Island.

The first new assault was on a jogger in Massapequa on 29 June 1995. Then on 15 August a 15-year-old girl was hit with a dart while riding her bicycle with a friend on Unqua Road, near Burton Lane in Massapequa. The needle portion of the dart was three inches long and had a plastic plug at the back.

The following day, a 44-year-old man was hit while jogging on Sunrise Highway and Riverside Drive at about 9pm. "I felt a sharp pain in my lower back," he said. "I thought I had been stung by a bee. I reached back and there was something on my back, some kind of hunting dart."

All three victims were hit in the back and none was seriously injured, but the Nassau police are not treating the incidents lightly. As a spokesman pointed out: "Aside from the wound itself, the dart could have contaminants like AIDS."

The dart attacks bring back memories of the summer of 1990, when more than 50 women walking in midtown Manhattan reported having their bottoms pierced by home-made darts. The following year another series of dart attacks took place in Penn Station. *NY Daily News, 18 Aug 1995.*

CARD DOG

ROBERT MEIER of Tampa, Fla., has been charged with theft and forgery after he allegedly married his comatose girlfriend hours before she died, then charged $20,000 to her credit cards. But, he says, it wasn't his idea. "He said he was sitting on the couch when Ms. Sewell's dog told him she would want him to go on living, have a better life and it would be OK to use her credit cards," a police spokesman said. An investigator who searched the apartment for evidence couldn't find collaborating evidence. "The dog was in the garage and didn't say anything," he said. *(AP)*

ALIENS TOLD ME TO DO IT

A MAN WHO claimed space aliens forced him to murder two women got what he wanted for his birthday on 29 March: a death sentence. Robert Joe Moody said that he wanted to be executed so that the aliens, or "extrasensory biological entities", would resurrect him and prove their existence.

The one-time financial planner and real-estate agent showed no reaction to the sentence and spent most of the hearing smiling at the packed courtroom in Tucson, Arizona.

Moody was convicted in October of murdering Michelle Malone, 33, and Patricia Magda, 56, in separate attacks in 1993. Malone was shot to death; Magda was bludgeoned. Acting as his own lawyer, Moody argued in his defence that extraterrestrials forced him to kill because they wanted to prove their existence by getting the public's attention.

Prosecutors maintained he killed the women to support a drug habit. The women's stolen cheque-books and bank cards were found in his car. At an earlier hearing, a psychologist testified that Moody suffered from a multiple personality disorder, a diagnosis that was not brought out during the trial. *[AP] 30 Mar 1996.*

LOCKED OUT

A CLASSIC TALE about the August 1980 night raid on a leisure centre in Chichester, Sussex. The gang silently paddled a speedboat across a lake, picked up their gear and paddled back to the office. But they had mistaken welding gear for cutting equipment and sealed the safe shut. The staff had to use a hammer and cold chisel for an hour to get it open again. *D. Mirror, 26 Aug 1980.*

Fires and SHC

Spontaneous human combustion (SHC) is one of the most perplexing and terrifying of Fortean phenomena. Although there have been so many cases that SHC's reality is beyond question – whatever its cause – as Larry Arnold explains below, many orthodox investigators would still prefer to pretend that it doesn't exist.

SPONTANEOUS BLAZES

LARRY ARNOLD has been researching spontaneous human combustion for over 20 years. This year his book Ablaze! *was published by M Evans and Co. Here he gives a quick overview of the subject, and the extent of his finds.*

The phenomenon of spontaneous human combustion has been attested to by observant medical specialists at scenes of atypical localised incinerations of human beings; by firemen who arrive ill-prepared and are befuddled by a mound of human ashes in an otherwise fire-free zone; and by survivors of baffling blazes themselves.

Undeniably, the data is at times disquieting and gruesome (sorry, no way around it). For some it is more than disconcerting. Some fire investigators have refused outright to look at the photographs. One said he'd rather "go out, get drunk and forget about it". Other fire-fighters, sceptical but more open-minded – such as the half-dozen arson investigators I met recently in Southern California – reacted with single-wordedness to the evidence: "bizarre"; "astounding"; awesome"; "dazzling" they exclaimed. But SHC has its humorous side too, whether it be the movie fantasy of over-heated lovers' passion (as in *Pyrates*), drummers who flash away behind unsinged drumkits (*Spinal Tap*), or Peter Jones's real-life nonplussed reaction to twice surviving his spontaneously self-combusting self one day in October 1980.

The non-human side of spontaneous combustion is no less damnable; no less confounding; no less provocative. My research discovered, blazing alphabetically: an accordion; bedding; books; calendars; a cat; chickens; clothing (sometimes damp); a cricket; a crow; a dog; escargot; flowers; groceries; hair; handkerchiefs; headcovering; mops/brooms; a mosquito; newspaper/paper; an opossum; sheep; shoes; a spider; a turtle; and wallpaper.

I await a report of a kitchen sink bursting into flame.

The remains of Dr John Irving Bentley, possibly the most celebrated SHC case. The localised burning typical of SHC is very clear from the picture: one of the rubber feet on his walking frame has not even begun to melt.

SHIRT OFF YOUR BACK

CHRIS WILLIAMS, 20, from Port Talbot, narrowly escaped injury last February when the shirt he was wearing caught fire. He had bought the £60 Timberland shirt from a Swansea shop called Moustache two months earlier. "We were going out to a family evening and so he decided to wear the shirt," said his mother, Geraldine Williams. "People began commenting on bright lights which appeared on it. A couple of seconds later the front and back burst into flames." Chris was saved from serious injury by a T-shirt he was wearing underneath.

Moustache immediately removed from sale all their Timberland shirts and offered a refund. "Timberland sent us a letter claiming the shirt had been subject to a surface flash – suggesting that it had been near a naked flame, which we know wasn't the case," said Mrs Williams. *South Wales Eve. Post, 23 Feb 1996.*

KEEP THE FIRE BURNING

FOR THE PAST four years, Michael Milner has been custodian of the famous fire in the Saltersgate Inn, near Whitby, North Yorkshire, which at the beginning of this year celebrated 200 years of non-stop burning. Tradition says that disaster will strike the 400-year-old pub, which stands on the moors between the Devil's Elbow and the Hole of Horcum, if it ever goes out.

On occasions when the flames have burned low, appliances have switched themselves off and on, pictures have fallen down, and the beer has gone flat. Regulars will not venture into the pub if the fire is not roaring. "I've seen what can happen," said Mr Milner. "A year ago a picture above the fireplace jumped off the wall. There's no way it should have happened. It was a big hook."

The tradition dates from 1796 when a customs officer was killed by smugglers and buried under the hearth. To avert the police's suspicions, a fire was lit and kept burning. Should it ever go out, apparently the officer's spirit will be released to haunt the pub. *D.Telegraph, 17 Dec 1995; Yorkshire Eve. Press, 5 Jan 1996.*

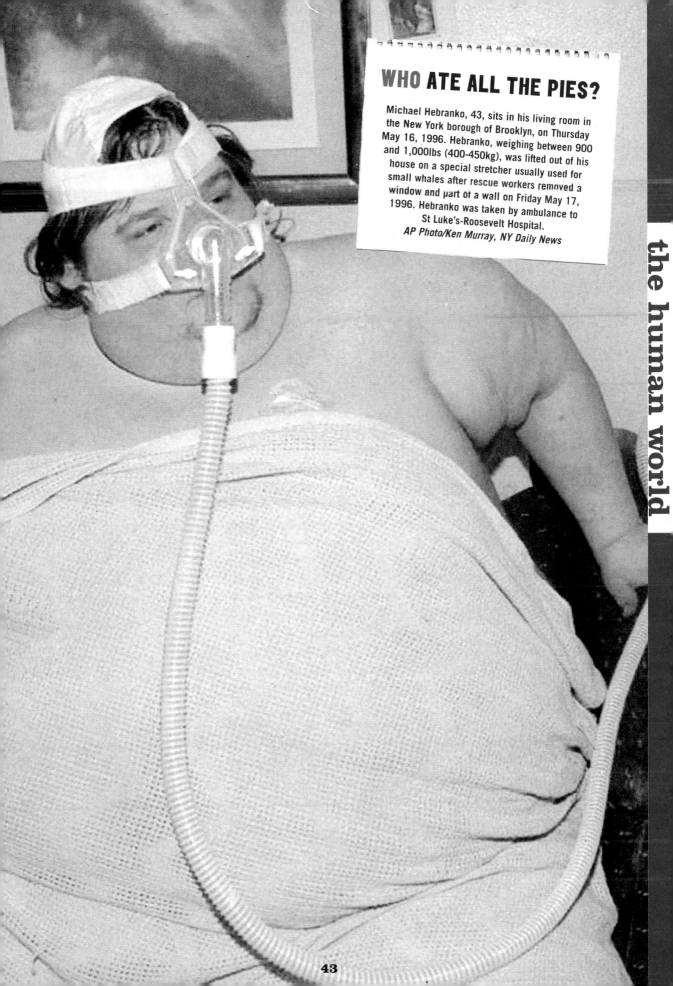

WHO ATE ALL THE PIES?

Michael Hebranko, 43, sits in his living room in the New York borough of Brooklyn, on Thursday May 16, 1996. Hebranko, weighing between 900 and 1,000lbs (400-450kg), was lifted out of his house on a special stretcher usually used for small whales after rescue workers removed a window and part of a wall on Friday May 17, 1996. Hebranko was taken by ambulance to St Luke's-Roosevelt Hospital.
AP Photo/Ken Murray, NY Daily News

the human world

Popobawa

Among all the cryptozoological files, reports of creatures which prey on humans are treated with scepticism - particularly the ones whose appetites are of a carnal nature. Nevertheless, so many reports of such creatures and such attacks come in from all over the world that they cannot be ignored. Whether you see it as a sexual or social phenomenon, the popobawa story puts an interesting new twist on an old tale.

LAST YEAR there was widespread fear on the island of Zanzibar concerning the return of the *popobawa*, a dwarf with a single Cyclopean eye, small pointed ears, bat wings and talons, notorious for swooping into houses at night and raping men. Its name derives from the Swahili words for 'bat' and 'wing'.

One victim was Mjaka Hamad, a quietly spoken peasant farmer aged 55 from the village of Sogea. At first he thought it was a dream, but the stifling force pushing him into his mattress dragged him from his sleep. "I couldn't imagine what was happening to me," he said. "You feel as if you are screaming with no voice. It was just like a dream, but then I was thinking it was this *popobawa* and he had come to do something terrible to me, something sexual. It is worse than what he does to women. I was fighting it."

Reports of the *popobawa* first appeared on Pemba, the smaller of Zanzibar's two main islands, around the time that the country's president was assassinated in 1972. Fear overcame shame as the *popobawa* told its victims that unless they told others of their ordeal it would be back. The island was in pandemonium as men went about announcing that they had been sodomised. After a few weeks the *popobawa* departed.

There was another period of attacks in the 1980s, but nothing more until 1995, when the winged beast swooped on Zanzibar's largest island. Hamad was one of its earliest victims. He knew it was not a dream because when he woke his whole house was in uproar. "I couldn't see it. I could only feel it. But some people in my house could see it. Those who've got the spirits in their heads could

see it. Everybody was terrified. They were outside screaming 'Huyo!' It means the *popobawa* is there. I had this bad pain in my ribs where it crushed me. I don't believe in spirits so maybe that's why it attacked me. Maybe it will attack anybody who doesn't believe."

There is no known protection against attack by the *popobawa* except for seeking safety in numbers. Whole families took to sleeping arm-in-arm in front of their houses. Some said the *popobawa* took human form during the day. Fingers were pointed. A mentally ill man was hacked to death after he inexplicably confessed that he was the *popobawa*. The country's main hospital treated men with bruises, broken ribs and other injuries which the victims blamed on the creature. One month later, the *popobawa* disappeared.

Even sceptics admit that for true believers the attacks are real. Some attribute the return of the beast to times of political tension. Recently the islands have been facing the uncertainty of elections and calls for self-government. The chief minister blamed the opposition for bringing back the *popobawa*, while his opponents responded by wondering if he himself might not be the creature.

Several explanations have been put forward for the *popobawa*. Some see overtones of the story of the *tokoloshe*, a not-dissimilar night-visitor from South Africa, or of other nocturnal terrorists from around the world. Others, including Joe Nickell of CSICOP, see it as "a Zanzibarian version of a psychological phenomenon known as a 'waking dream'" or "hypnogogic hallucination", characterised by feelings of either floating or being weighted or held down, coupled with a very vivid dream, often of extreme terror.

It seems a very rational explanation, but Forteans would ask which really came first: hypnogogic hallucinations or the *popobawa* and its ilk. One way or the other, we await more news of the bat-winged buggerer with bated breath.

Report by Chris McGreal in The Guardian, 2 Oct 1995; CSICOP information and opinions from http://www.csicop.org/sb/9512/i-files.html

Names & Numbers
and
Fortean Folk

The cosmic joker has a special love for the appropriate name and the significant number. Then there are those special few whose lives are somehow more Fortean than the rest of us...

TITLE BOUT: The 1995 winner of *The Bookseller*'s Diagram Prize for the Oddest Title of the Year went to *Reusing Old Graves* by D Davies and A Shaw. Runners-up included: *The Baby Jesus Touch and Feel Book*; *Amputee Management – A Handbook*; *Simply Bursting – A Guide to Bladder Control*; *Searching for Railway Pole Insulators;* and *The History of the Concrete Roofing Tile*.

A memorable previous winner was titled *How to Avoid Huge Ships*.

Guardian, Western Morning News, 3 Nov 1995.

BIRDS OF A FEATHER: Ann Bird, Pam Peacock and Tom Goose have been appointed regional organisers of the Royal Society for the Protection of Birds. *D. Telegraph, 21 Feb 1996.*

WORD GAMES: Questioned by journalists last October about France's South Pacific nuclear testing, the French ambassador to New Zealand, Jacques Le Blanc, said a 110-kiloton device was technically not a bomb because it was exploded underground and did not produce a mushroom cloud. Rather, Le Blanc said, "It is a device which is exploding." *Edmonton Sun, 11 Oct 1995.*

Noun, verb or adjective?

THE NAME of a little town in northern Austria causes endless amusement among English-speaking visitors. In an effort to slow down souvenir hunters, the town council has set up an extra-large signpost. The notice underneath reads: "Please – not so fast!" *Expressen (Sweden), 28 Jan 1996.*

Fortean Folk

Kim Il-Sung/Kim Jong Il

CERTAIN PEOPLE seem to attract the extraordinary or become the focus of bizarre events; and in the annals of Fortean folk there are few who are surrounded by more great stories than the father-and-son partnership of North Korean rulers, Kim Il-Sung and Kim Jong Il.

Kim Il-Sung, the 'Great Ruler', was loved by his country – literally. When he died aged 82, on 8 July 1994, the North Korean Central News Agency (KCNA) reported that around Mount Paekdu, revered as the cradle of North Korean communism: "Lake Chon, that had been calm under a thick fog, suddenly stirred up violent waves. A whirlwind rose and heavy rains fell. It rained uninterruptedly for three days... raging waves beat upon the shore and rose high in whirlwind."

About two weeks later, a swallow flew into a classroom in Nampo and "wept for 10 minutes" in front of Kim's portrait, while wild geese wailed and circled around Kim's statues. All who saw these things, said North Korean radio, immediately pledged loyalty to Kim Jong Il.

The phenomena even began before Kim Il-Sung's death: on 6 July 1994 KCNA reported that rare triple rainbows had loomed above Lake Samji near Mount Paekdu on 17 June. We trust they were reprimanded for their poor time-keeping.

Despite the supernatural blessings given to his father, Kim Jong Il has managed to make his own mark as a Fortean fellow. Always a keen sportsman, in late October it was reported that he had achieved five holes-in-one in a single round of golf. He also completed the 18-hole Pyongyang course in 34 strokes – 25 shots better than the world record.

Woe betide anyone who dares to question Kim's expertise, for he is also a crack shot. As one of his official hagiographies tells us, describing Kim shooting at bottles 100

KOREA BLIMEY: Kim Il-Sung and Kim his son

metres away: "Ten gun reports were heard, but all the bottles remained where they were. One aide, doubting his eyes, went up there to find all the necks of the ten bottles shot off as if cut with a knife. It was divine skill." *[R] 14 Jul; Independent on Sunday, 24 Jul; S. Express 16 Oct 1994; 'Great Leader Kim Jong Il' by Tak Jin et al, Sorinsha, Tokyo, 1986, p259.*

Do Nomads Dream of Electric Worms?

DR KARL SHUKER, one of the world's leading experts on unknown animals, casts a cold eye over recent reports of a deadly 'new' creature from the Gobi Desert.

by
Dr Karl Shuker

WHAT IS UP TO FIVE FEET LONG, worm-like in shape and dark blood-red in colour, with smooth skin and spike-like projections at both ends of its body, but no visible eyes, mouth, or nostrils; what can kill not only by squirting a corrosive lethal poison but also by apparent electrocution; what resembles an animate cow intestine? The answer is a truly bizarre creature that has been sought but never sighted by scientists, yet which seems to be a fearsome reality to the nomadic people inhabiting the stark, arid sandscape of Mongolia's southern Gobi Desert.

The locals call it the *allergorhai-horhai* or *allghoi-khorkhoi*, local terms that translate as 'intestine worm' after its repulsive appearance. Colloquially, however, it is known by an even more apt and chilling name – the Mongolian death worm.

The earliest Western record known to me of this extraordinary cryptozoological creature dates back to the 1920s. It was penned by renowned American palaeontologist Prof. Roy Chapman Andrews in his book *On the Trail of Ancient Man* (1926), documenting the American Museum of Natural History's Central Asiatic Expedition, which he led to the Gobi Desert in 1922. Andrews revealed that during his team's meeting with the Mongolian government in the final stages of arranging the expedition, he was specifically asked by the Mongolian premier to capture, if at all possible, a specimen of the death worm for his government.

The premier and his cabinet members all firmly believed in the reality of this creature which, they stated, is so poisonous that merely to touch it means instant death. They even claimed to know some people who had seen one. Andrews, conversely, seemed rather less convinced, but he soberly promised that if his team should encounter an *allergorhai-horhai*, he would endeavour to seize hold of it using a pair of long steel collecting forceps, in order to distance himself from its deadly effects.

If this is really what he would have done, it is no bad thing that Andrews did not succeed in finding a death worm. Some years later, one of the members of an American team of geologists visiting the Gobi was idly poking a long iron rod into a patch of sand when for no apparent reason he suddenly dropped down dead. As his horrified colleagues rushed towards him, the sand that he had been poking began to churn, and out from its depths writhed a huge fat worm: the dreaded *allergorhai-horhai*.

Andrews's account of the death worm was reiterated in 1931 within an article by Karl Meusburger dealing with another vermiform mystery beast, the Alpine-dwelling tatzelworm. Apart from this, the only pre-1990s account I am aware of is a short item from 1946 in *Doroga Vetrov* ('The Wind's Path'), by Russian palæontologist Ivan Efremov. I have not seen this work, but I understand that Efremov recorded various legends concerning the death worm recounted to him by an elderly man from Dalandzadgad called Tseveng, whom he met during a Russian expedition to the Gobi.

According to Tseveng, the worm lives in the sandy dunes of Khaldzandzakh, roughly 80 miles south-east of Dalandzadgad. It can reputedly kill from a great distance, but remains hidden beneath the sand for most of the year, only emerging during June and July, which are the two hottest months.

After several decades of virtual obscurity, the history of the Mongolian death worm has gained a very significant new chapter during the 1990s, thanks to Czech author-explorer Ivan Mackerle. After casually learning of this creature's existence from a Mongolian student, Mackerle led two expeditions to the southern Gobi, in 1991 and 1993 respectively, to seek its deadly denizen. Mackerle's fellow expedition members included two of his long-standing friends, physician Dr Jarda Prokopec and professional photographer George Skupien.

Unfortunately, the team did not succeed in locating a specimen on either occasion, but they collected a large fund of valuable information regarding this very mystifying creature, which Mackerle has since made available in various articles, a recent telephone conversation with me, and a Czech TV documentary entitled 'The Sand Monster Mystery'.

First and foremost: they learnt that the death worm can kill in two very different ways. The most mysterious of these occurs merely (but instantly) by touch, and even from a distance, without the worm making tangible contact with the victim. It can kill people, horses, and even camels via this invisible but inimical mechanism. According to an old nature ranger from Dalandzadgad called Yanzhingin Mahgalzhav, who was interviewed by Mackerle and his team, a single death worm lurking beneath the desert sands killed an entire herd of camels just south of Noyon during the 1960s.

The team's guide, a local man called Khamgalagu, informed them that a death worm once found its way into a child's box of toys at a native campsite. When the boy reached into his box to fetch out a toy, he touched the worm and died immediately. So too did his parents when they saw what had happened and tried to dispatch the worm.

Combining those testimonies with the dire fate of the geologist who inadvertently prodded one of these creatures with an iron rod, the incredible but inevitable conclusion that must be drawn is that somehow this extraordinary beast can kill by electrocution. After all, how can we explain the incident with the geolo-gist, who did not make direct contact with the worm – unless we assume that he was killed by a powerful electrical discharge generated and emitted by this animal and conducted from its body to his through his rod?

Science has already documented several species of fishes, including the famous electric eel, that can kill in this manner, using specialised organs that have evolved from various types of modified musculature, but the death worm would be the first terrestrial animal to do so. Indeed, as I have discussed in detail elsewhere (*Strange Magazine*, Fall 1995), if it functioned in a manner analogous to a living spark-plug, this amazing creature might even be able to emit a lethal discharge across a small gap physically separating itself from its victim – which in turn could explain the widespread belief among the Gobi people that it can kill from a great distance (fear is a very potent stimulus for exaggeration!)

The second way in which the death worm can kill is slightly less mysterious but no less dramatic – or effective. On the rare occasions when it emerges from the sand, the worm moves over the surface by an odd sideways sweeping or squirming motion, which sounds similar to the method used by the sidewinder rattlesnake to keep as much of its body as possible out of direct contact with the sand's burning heat. But beware of any death worm that rears one half of its body upwards through the sand and begins to inflate. According to an elderly woman called Puret, interviewed by Mackerle and his team, it then produces a bubble-like projection from this exposed, inflated end and spurts forth from the bubble a stream of deadly poison.

Judging from native descriptions, this poison seems to be highly corrosive too, because they claim that anything coming into contact with it, even metal, turns yellow at once and looks as if it has been corroded by acid. If, as the locals affirm, victims do indeed die as soon as they have been sprayed with this poison, then presumably it must be a fast-acting toxin that enters their blood system by searing through their flesh like a powerful acid.

Another notable piece of information gained from the Gobi people concerning the death worm is that it is often seen after a period of rainfall (this is characteristic of many subterranean vermiform creatures), and especially in areas sustaining *Cynomorium songaricum* – a species of cigar-shaped parasitic plant known locally as the *goyo*, which is found on the toxic roots of the saxaul plant. Mackerle has speculated that the worm may even derive its poison (or at least some component of it) from these roots.

Assuming that the death worm really does exist, it is unquestionably so novel a creature that without a specimen to examine, its taxonomic affinities with other major animal groups cannot be predicted. Judging from its description and behaviour (according to Mackerle, it can contract and expand its body) it does not appear to be a snake, limbless lizard or other vermiform vertebrate, but where it should be classified among the heterogeneous assemblage of invertebrate animals loosely termed 'worms' is anyone's guess at present. All that we can say is that somewhere amid the forbidding sandy vista of the Gobi squirms the answer to this question, and if it should one day be captured and submitted for detailed zoological investigation, it may well provide some electrifying revelations – especially if its researchers are using steel forceps!

REFERENCES

Andrews, Roy Chapman, *On the Trail of Ancient Man*, GP Putnam's Sons, London, 1926, pp102-103; Mackerle, Ivan, 'In Search of the Killer Worm of Mongolia', *World Explorer* no. 4 (1993), pp62-65; Mackerle, Ivan, 'In Search of the Killer Worm', *Fate* vol. 49 (June 1996), pp22-27; Mackerle, Ivan, Personal communication, 18 September 1996. Mackerle, Ivan, *Záhada Písecného Netvora (The Sand Monster Mystery)*. Meusburger, Karl, 'Etwas von Tasselwurm', *Der Schlern*, vol. 12 (December 1931), pp458-479; Shuker, Karl P.N., 'Mongolian Death Worm – A Shocking Secret Beneath the Gobi Sands?', *Strange Magazine* no. 16 (fall 1995), pp31-32, 48; Shuker, Karl P N, 'Highly Charged', *Wild About Animals*, vol. 8 (March 1996), p9; Shuker, Karl P N, *The Unexplained: An Illustrated Guide to the World's Natural and Paranormal Mysteries*, Carlton Books, London, 1996, pp118-119.

Antiquities

What's so strange about archaeology? What isn't strange? Every year brings news of finds that force radical reappraisals of our knowledge of the past – civilisations that existed where they couldn't have, objects that turn up where they shouldn't have. And then there are the oddities and incongruities of societies long gone...

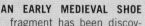

AN EARLY MEDIEVAL SHOE fragment has been discovered in a growing bag bought from a garden centre. The bag of peat was destined for flower pots until Tom and Rona Gibson from Topsham, Devon, came upon the 10in (25cm)-long piece of leather. They took it to the Royal Albert Memorial Museum in Exeter, where it was dated to 800-1200AD. The shoe, found in peat from County Tyrone, was sent to the National Museum of Ireland in Dublin. *Guardian, D. Telegraph, 8 July 1995.*

THE LIVING DEAD OF SAN BERNARDO

SAN BERNARDO is an agricultural town of 12,000 people in the Andes foothills, 40 miles (64km) south-west of the Colombian capital of Bogota. Gravedigger Eduardo Cifuentes was the first to notice that the town's dead defied the normal process of decomposition when he began work 17 years ago. "The burial pit was full of bodies,' he said. "I didn't like stepping on them, so I started organising them." (The custom was to remove mortal remains and transfer them to smaller urns five years after burial.)

Some of the mummies are housed in the underground crypt of the local cemetery. In front of one of the rows of white, box-like tombs is a metal trapdoor, which opens to reveal a flight of steps leading down to a small, dank chamber. A dozen bodies are arranged in a standing position around the walls. The smell of rotted flesh is strong and bags of bones are stacked in a corner. A dozen of the better preserved mummies were moved in late 1994 to a new museum behind the cemetery. Here they are displayed on concrete slabs under glass. Three small children lie huddled together, one still wearing clothes and small white shoes, but with a large hole in the top of the doll-like head. Then there is Prudencia Acosta, dressed in a dark brown shawl and cape, clutching a red carnation in her claw-like hands. Some look peaceful and calm, while others are contorted with the grimaces of painful final moments.

Time has turned the mummies' clothes and skin to an earth-brown colour. A few stand naked, exposing dried-up genitals of uncommon size.

The best preserved body stands neatly attired in a jacket, tie and trousers, with only an oddly pale face and sunken eye sockets to suggest he isn't with us any more.

Scientists have examined the mummies, but cannot explain the lack of decomposition. Local people say the only other site in Latin America with natural mummification is the central Mexican town of Guanajuato, where villagers cite underground gas and soil conditions as the secret. However, in San Bernardo the bodies are entombed above ground and do not come into contact with the earth. The locals offer a variety of explanations: the purity of the local water; the fact that the cemetery attracts solar radiation; the lack of chemical additives in the food; or the fact that people eat a lot of guatila and balu.

Guatila is a dark green fruit about the size of an orange, with small thorns on its skin, used in soups and other dishes after peeling and boiling. Balu looks like a giant green bean pod. Its outsize purple beans are extracted to cook and mash into flour for cakes. San Bernardo onions stay fresh longer than those from other regions. One elderly man said he never eats vegetables so that he can decompose properly after death.

"Some people say they are not going to have a bunch of kids coming along and poking fun at their dead relatives," said Claudia Garcia, a San Bernardo resident. "If they see that the body has mummified when it is disinterred, they ask for it to be chopped up with a machete or an axe and then burnt. Sometimes they watch to make absolutely sure the body is cut up properly." *[R] 9 Dec 1994; [AP] 24 May, 20 July 1995.*

MAMA MIA! Kept under glass, the mummies baffle scientists who can't explain the lack of decomposition

Country File

BRAZIL

Brazil, as *Charlie's Aunt* told us, is where the nuts come from. Although the big Brazilian story of the year, the Varginha 'saucer crash', is covered elsewhere (see UFOs, pp 8-9), there's still plenty of high weirdness to spare.

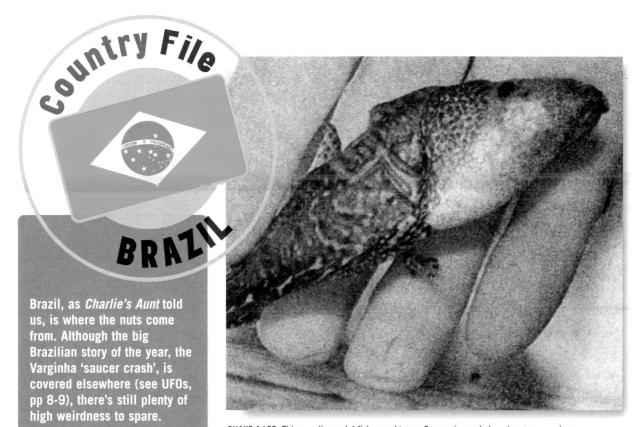

SHAKE A LEG: This peculiar pedal fish, caught near Guaracai, may belong to a new species.

AN UNUSUAL FISH was caught in September 1995 with a rod and line in a lake near the Brazilian city of Guaracai, northwest of São Paolo, by Paulino Clemente. At almost 5 inches (just under 13cm) long, with just one gill, barbels (beard-like appendages near the mouth), a tail and a pair of feet, it caught Paulino's attention because it was the only fish that stayed alive out of the water for more than 15 minutes.

According to the biologist Angela Pereira Garcia, the creature was not a mutant trying to be an amphibian, and did not belong to any known species. She believed it used air to survive as it had to leave the water ever five minutes to breathe. The legs were articulated. "It is not a case of a defective fin," she said, "but of a useful component, since there is a membrane between the toes."

Since then, it has been suggested to *FT* that the 'fish' may actually have been a part-transformed tadpole of the paradoxical frog, which is unique in that its tadpoles are actually larger than the frog itself. The webbed feet, the shape of the creature's tail and the fact that it only has one 'gill' all lend support to this theory; however, one might assume that a Brazilian biologist would be reasonably familiar with an unusual local species. *O Estado de São Paolo (Brazil), 22 Sept 1995.*

RELIGIOUS STRIFE was sparked in Brazil last October when a vocal, evangelical pastor, Sergio von Helder of the fast-growing Universal Church of the Kingdom of God, appeared on a late-night television programme called *The 25th Hour* punching and kicking a three-foot high plaster representation of Our Lady of Aparecida, a black representation of the Virgin Mary that turned up in fishermen's nets in the 18th century and became Brazil's patron saint.

"You see," the pastor shouted, sweating profusely and gesticulating, "she doesn't talk back, she's powerless. This is not a saint or a God, just a piece of worthless plaster. Can God really be compared to this ugly thing?" Catholics all over Brazil revere Aparecida ('revelation' in Portuguese) as a miracle and honour her on October 12 with a national holiday. Von Helder's blasphemy stirred up a religious row in what had been one of the most tolerant countries in the world. Protestors stoned the headquarters of the Universal Church in São Paolo, and pelted another in Rio with tomatoes and eggs. The Universal Church was founded in 1977 in the back yard of a Rio de Janeiro funeral parlour by lapsed Catholic, state lottery official and self-styled 'Bishop' Edir Macedo. The church now has 2,100 temples in 46 countries, takes £476 million a year in donations and owns TV Record, with 47 broadcasting stations and 230 affiliates. The faithful pour into football stadia to witness exorcisms, the lame casting off their crutches and the short-sighted stamping on their glasses.

In the 1980 census, 89 per cent of Brazilians declared themselves Catholic, but by 1990 the figure had fallen to about 70 per cent, and the decline continues. Many have turned to spirit cults such as Umbanda and Candomblé; but the biggest wave of defections has been to the Evangelical churches. In December, the Catholics counter-attacked. Brazil's Attorney-General ordered an investigation into the Universal Church and Macedo, for alleged tax fraud, extortion and links with Colombia's cocaine barons. *D. Telegraph, 31 Oct; S. Telegraph, 6 Nov; Independent on Sunday 31 Oct 1995.*

ROBERTO CARLOS DA SILVA, 21, from a small town in São Paolo state, was inconsolable after the death of his fiancée, Raquel Cristina de Oliviera, in a motorcycle accident a few days before their wedding. Three months later he dug up her body, which had been buried in her wedding gown, and found it had been well preserved by the embalming fluids. On 9 February, he confessed to having sex with the corpse. *Reuter, 11 Feb 1994.*

Images

Spontaneous images and the like are a long-standing Fortean favourite; sometimes they prove to be genuinely inexplicable, sometimes less so. We particularly cherish memories of the face of Jesus appearing on a wall, which was subsequently revealed to be a poster of country and western singer Willie Nelson under a layer of whitewash...

OLD FLAME: Tony O'Rahilly's picture of the face in the Wem blaze

SEX SIMBA

A VIRGINIA-BASED anti-abortion group named the American Life League has called for video cassettes of Disney's cartoon *The Lion King* to be withdrawn from sale. League spokesman Rodney Miller has said that a four-year-old boy had seen the letters "S-E-X" take form one after the other in a cloud of dust raised by Simba, the lion, when he jumps off a cliff. The observation was reported to the League by the boy's aunt. "It's kind of iffy," said Mr Miller. "Some people see a cloud, kind of wavy lines. It's hard to see even if you slow it down."

With a shaky grasp of English, Disney spokesman Rick Rhoades said that what appeared to be a word was "nothing more than a perception" and that there were no plans to withdraw the video. "We can guarantee that there's no symbolism," he blustered.

The League has also alleged that there are risqué scenes in two other Disney feature cartoons: in *Aladdin*, they say, there is an audible message: "Good teenagers, take off your clothes"; and in *The Little Mermaid*, a man at a wedding ceremony is supposed to become visibly sexually aroused. *NY Times, 2 Sept; AP 5 Sept 1995.*

SPECTRE SHOT IN THE FLAMES

IN NOVEMBER 1995, amateur photographer Tony O'Rahilly took some photographs of a blaze which destroyed the town hall of Wem in Shropshire. One photograph, taken with a 200mm zoom lens from across the road, seems to show a girl standing in the doorway of the hall's fire escape. O'Rahilly said he didn't see the figure until the film was developed in March. It has been suggested the figure is the ghost of the girl who started the Great Fire of Wem which virtually destroyed the town in 1677.

Tony Adams, chief photographer of the *Shropshire Star*, examined the strip of negatives including the picture reproduced here, and found no evidence of tampering. Before the photograph was developed, workmen refurbishing the town hall reported seeing a ghostly figure emerge in a swirl of mist, and town councillors were considering calling in paranormal investigators.

Meanwhile, the Association for the Scientific Study of Anomalous Phenomena (ASSAP) had the photograph analysed by their photographic consultant, Dr Vernon Harrison. Dr Harrison's report concluded that although the film and image showed no signs of tampering, the 'figure' was, most likely, a chance image. If the face is obscured, he says, "all resemblance to a human figure vanishes and I am left with the suggestion of a rectangular window in the far wall of the building seen through thick smoke." He suggests that the "face" might be a random burning pattern on the end of a falling beam, as the railing is in fact some three meters in front of the door. The fire service video of the event backs this up; a roof beam on fire can clearly be seen in a position corresponding to the figure's head. *D. Mail, 26 Feb; Wolverhampton Express & Star 25 Feb; ASSAP News, August 1996.*

STELLAR SIMULACRUM

AN APPARENT image of Jesus appeared in a picture from the Hubble Space Telescope. The picture showed a number of vast shapes resembling stalagmites in the Eagle Nebula in the constellation Serpens. The columns of gas and dust are six million million miles high and are 7,000 light-years away, so we are peering into the distant past. The vast cloud is being torn apart by an interstellar hurricane of ultra-violet light and the whitish haze surrounding the nebulae is where hydrogen is being dispersed into interstellar space in a process known as photo-evaporation. In a few million years, the clouds will be blown away and the nebula will become a mass of bright stars.

Our whole solar system would fit easily into one of the tiny illuminated protrusions at the columns' uppermost tips (known to astronomers as evaporation gaseous globules or EGGs).

Each of the 50 or so EGGs in this photograph is made of superdense hydrogen collapsing under its own weight, forming young stars which continue to grow as they accumulate more material from their surroundings. Our own Sun probably did not hatch from such an EGG, as the existence of the planets is evidence that the solar system was not exposed to powerful ultra-violet radiation.

After the picture was shown on CNN, dozens of viewers phoned the TV network in Atlanta to say that they could see the face of Jesus at the end of the leftmost column when the image was turned on its side. Judge for yourself...

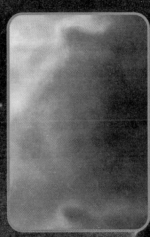

Christ as seen by CNN viewers

Christ as pictured on the holy handkerchief of Genoa (see p4)

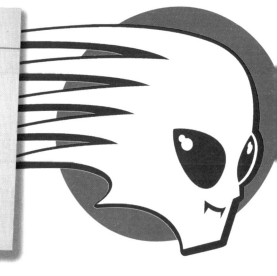

Goatsucker

The punctured corpses of hundreds of animals in Puerto Rico have given rise to fears that a supernatural beast is at large. Witnesses have likened the chupacabras to a demonic alien kangaroo vampire, but could it be nothing but a social panic driven by misidentification?

THE *CHUPACABRAS* PANIC began in March 1995, when residents of the municipalities of Orocovis and Morovis in the mountainous interior of Puerto Rico were confronted with a terrifying reality; an unseen force was slaying small farm animals (goats, chickens, rabbits, etc.) in a manner very different from attacks by wild animals or even humans. The victims were completely exsanguinated; their blood drained through a single, small p u n c t u r e wound. As the number of mutilations reached an almost epidemic level across the island, the small hole was a recurring factor in the killings.

The first actual descriptions of the mysterious creature behind the killings came about six months into the mutilation epidemic. In September, sightings by Madelyne Tolentino, a housewife from Canóvanas, and others gave it a form and a name. Described as a fanged, kangaroo-like entity with bulging red eyes and spines, sightings of the improbable and terrifying *el chupacabras* – Spanish: 'goat-sucker' – became commonplace.

Municipal authorities led 200-strong search parties on nightly forays, and politicians demanded an official investigation. Reports of other *chupacabras* activity remained constant into the early weeks of 1996, when sightings and livestock killings began to dwindle. The unseasonably cold temperatures experienced on the island were thought by some to have sent the predator into hibernation.

ALIEN OR HEDGEHOG: The first depiction of the *chupacabras*, drawn by ufologist Jorge Martín from the descriptions given by Madelyne Tolentino and others, in March 1995.

This lull in activity ended abruptly in early March 1996, when farmer Arturo Rodríguez of Barrio Sumidero, in Aguas Buenas, reported the loss of 30 fighting cocks and hens. The slaughtered birds had puncture marks on their bodies and throats. Agents from the Department of Natural and Environmental Resources allegedly visited the site to conduct further research.

The killings continued in Barrio Sumidero – especially in the La Vega, Capilla and La Araña sectors – where hundreds of 'backyard' animals including chickens, geese, ducks and sheep, and even a few goats, sheep and cows, were drained of blood. At one scene of carnage, whatever killed the animals also tore a 16ft by 14ft (4.8m by 4.2m) galvanised iron gate off its hinges. Such unnatural displays of force only reinforced the fears of local residents.

By the time the *chupacabras* phenomenon spread to the Spanish-speaking areas of Florida and Texas, its social aspect far outstripped the paranormal one. Restaurants started calling themselves 'Chupa Cabras'. Salsa musicians adopted 'Los Chupacabras' as their stage name. So famous has it become that a *chupacabras* display is being planned for New York's Puerto Rico Day parade.

One self-styled psychic, Brother Carmelo, pontificated that the mutilators were 'a race of vampires which feasted on animal blood'. The only way to slay these creatures, he insisted, was "a laser beam or a silver bullet". It was the clairvoyant's learned opinion that the *chupacabras* was not preying on humans because our blood is too full of toxins and fats.

Less benign fantasies began to circulate as well. One UFO cult with the acronym NOVA announced that the *chupacabras* had descended on this world from outer space to conduct experiments on human blood and release fatal viruses such as HIV. NOVA harassed witnesses and researchers, and claimed to have the backing of "a secret government organisation" like something from *The X-Files*.

It was even suggested in some quarters that the creature had been summoned up during a Santeria ritual or some darker form of sorcery. The belief that the *chupacabras* was a demonic creature heralding the "period of confusion" (Greek: *parusia*) foretold in Revelation was also widely accepted. Arguments about one-fanged dogs, rogue apes and genetic engineering were unable to dispel this pervasive, apocalyptic anxiety. When witnesses report that the *chupacabras* was accompanied by "the strong smell of sulphur", a good investigator can but record the testimony.

Typically, Julio Lopez, whose daughter's pet rabbit was allegedly slain by the *chupacabras*, commented: "The shape in which the cage was left was incredible. [It tore] through the metal tubing and barbed wire... took out the rabbit, killed it, and tore out its heart and other entrails... This is the work of a supernatural agency. Neither a dog nor an ape nor a snake could have done such a thing."

To the relief of researchers and law enforcement officers on Puerto Rico, the lurker in the shadows which had feasted on all manner of beasts, domestic and wild, had not turned its attention to the human population. This policy changed, however when it travelled thousands of miles to the Pacific coast of Mexico.

On 1 May, 1996, a report on Mexico's *Primer Impacto* ('First Impact') TV news programme alerted the population to the growing number of animal mutilations in the Sinaloa, Jalisco and Veracruz regions. The latter location had been particularly hard hit, since the towns of Tlaliscoyan, Las Trancas and Nachital subsist mainly on goat livestock.

At first, speculation supposed a new species of giant bat could have migrated from South America. Jose Burria of the Mexican Department of Agriculture dismissed the killings as due to coyote or feline depredation, possibly exacerbated by the drought in the northern part of the country.

However, the situation was electrified by news that humans had

SNAPPED! An alleged photograph of the *chupacabras*, posted to the internet. See page 38 for more infomation

been attacked by the *chupacabras*. Teodora Reyes, a resident of the small village of Alfonso Genaro Calderón, in the Mexican state of Sinaloa, displayed on TV the irregular 'bite marks' – which actually resembled lacerations or burns – resulting from a swipe of the claws of the *chupacabras*. At the same time Angel Pulido, a farmer living hundreds of miles away in the state of Jalisco, showed reporters the twin puncture marks left on his right arm, inflicted, he said, by "a giant bat which looked like a witch".

More people have come forward, telling of "being overcome by shadows", to find a painful puncture wound somewhere on their bodies once they regained consciousness. In the state of Nayarit, the Judicial Police allegedly opened fire on a fleeing *chupacabras*. Apparently it turned to glare at them with crimson eyes before vaulting over a 6ft fence.

Some commentators have noted the role played by Spanish-language media in spreading the *chupacabras* panic to Hispanic communities outside Puerto Rico. In particular, said Tony Zavaleta, an anthropologist at the University of Texas at Brownsville, the news media, with their daily and credulous reports, have transformed the *chupacabras* into a legend. According to Mark Glazer, an anthropologist, at the University of Texas-Pan American in Edinburg, whatever the truth of it, the *chupacabras* story is now as durable and culturally important to Puerto Ricans as, say, Nessie is to Loch Ness.

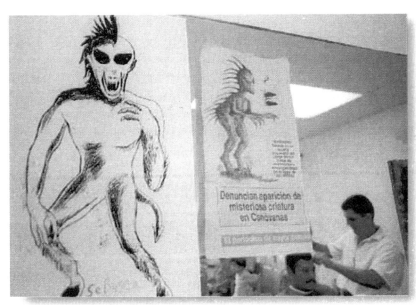

SHORT BACK AND SPIKES: Drawings of the goatsucker in a barbershop window in Puerto Rico

The Chupacabras Song
by Ron Schnell (Tune: 'Copacabana' by Barry Manilow)

His name is Chupa, the Chupacabras,
With ugly spikeys in his hair and a spine exposed to air.
He don't merengue, don't do no cha-cha,
But it's the thing he does the best,
That most people do detest.
He does it all night long, just listen to my song.
One day a goat will be walking by,
Next he's awfully dry.

He's the Chupa (Chup), the Chupacabras (Chupacabras)
His mealtime's a taste of macabre (Yeah?)
Yes, the Chupa (Chup), the Chupacabras (Ooh),
He sucks goat's blood but he still is my bud
Yes he's the Chupa – he strikes at night!

His name was Pico, he was a farmer,
He once had 30 head of goat, now not one darn sheepskin coat,
Because the Chupa, he paid a visit.
And while our Pico slept in bed, Chup enjoyed much blood-a-red,
Pico woke up that day,
Did not know what to say,
There was blood and some thirty goat heads,
He knelt down to pray.

He's the Chupa (Chup), the Chupacabras (Chupacabras),
His mealtime's a taste of macabre (Yeah?)
Yes, the Chupa (Chup), the Chupacabras (Ooh),
He sucks goat's blood but he still is my bud,
Yes he's the Chupa… he fell in love!
Chupa… My Chupacabras… He sucks goat's blood…
    He still is my bud…

His name is Chupa, the Chupacabras,
With ugly spikeys in his hair and a spine exposed
    to air.
Once he went hunting, hunting those *cabras,*
But when he moved in for the kill,
Then he felt a sudden chill,
There she was, so refined, he took her, wined and
    dined.
Her name was Gretta the old vampyress,
She was quite a find.

He's the Chupa (Chup), the Chupacabras
    (Chupacabras),
His mealtime's a taste of macabre (Yeah?)
Yes, the Chupa (Chup), the Chupacabras (Ooh),
He sucks goat's blood but he still is my bud,
Yes he's the Chupa… He lost his blood!

Ron was inspired to write this after reading about our spined friend on one of the many Usenet newsgroups devoted to Forteana.

Poltergeists

Most Fortean phenomena are pretty mind-boggling, but poltergeist activity is downright unbelievable in its sheer defiance of normality. Whatever your theory to explain it – and there are almost as many as there are poltergeist stories – new cases are always fascinating. The spirits have been restless of late, and here are the cream of the cases that FT covered in 1996

ABOVE: The bungalow where poltergeist activity raged for over a year. BELOW RIGHT: Stephen Mera of NARO takes notes on the gravity-defying water.

SHOCKING DRIP: Water started spouting from Guiseppe Galli's walls and electric sockets in Pesaro, Italy. A plumber could find nothing wrong; neither could the fire brigade who suggested poltergeist activity. Galli moved out and called in a priest. *Sunday Express, 13 Aug 1995.*

KNOCK AND RUN: Pensioners in Riverside Close, Cuckney, Nottinghamshire, have been regularly woken by tapping on their windows and ringing on their doorbells; but when they look out nobody is there and no tracks are left in the snow. Police were investigating. *Sheffield Star, 13 Feb 1996.*

POLTS AND VOLTS: Southern Electricity faced a claim that a poltergeist was responsible for Sharon McGrath's £900 electricity bill. It had allegedly turned on lights and electrical equipment, and had shredded telephone directories and bills at her house in Cowes, on the Isle of Wight. *Edinburgh Eve. News, 31 Oct 1995.*

WET WET WET

IN LATE 1994 the Gardener family in Rochdale began to be plagued by water dripping from the ceiling of their prefab bungalow. Jim Gardener, Vera's second husband, explained what had happened: "We noticed a damp patch on the wall of the back bedroom" which was occupied by Vera's grown-up daughter, Jeanette. "It began to seep water and we called the housing department. They examined the loft but couldn't find any leaks. We left it – then it began on the ceiling."

The Gardeners wondered whether the water was due to condensation, but were later astounded when they saw it flash across the ceiling. "It would start dripping in one place then shoot from corner to corner. The edges were jagged like broken glass, and it would finish at a point."

The phenomenon transferred from Jeanette's bedroom to the kitchen. Men from the council re-examined the loft, and an electrician dismantled the light fittings while Mr Gardener watched from beneath an umbrella. The investigations yielded nothing, and the council decided that the only explanations were condensation or fraud – an allegation which the Gardeners angrily deny.

Jeanette moved into the front bedroom, but the dripping followed her there. Then, after a week of quiet, Jim relaid the carpet and Jeanette moved back into her bedroom. Within ten minutes water had started to drip from the ceiling again. When analysed, the mineral content of the water from the ceiling was very different from local tap-water.

Apart from the water there were more phenomena: handles turned, doors opened, and quite often a smell of cigarette smoke pervaded the bedroom. it smelled of liquorice. Jim smoked a pipe but Vera's first husband, Geoffrey, had been fond of cigarettes rolled in liquorice papers. He had been a chronic asthmatic and had died in the house's hall from a massive coronary.

Six investigators from the Northern Anomalies Research Organisation (NARO) conducted a vigil at the bungalow on 5 September 1995, with the Gardeners absent for the evening. In the week before the vigil, several members of the family had been hit by flying objects. Although the team did not witness any dripping water during the vigil, a statuette of a Greek goddess appeared to move or materialise, voices and a wheezing sound were heard, and one team member was "flicked" by something unseen.

In poltergeist cases there is usually a focus or catalyst, and Vera's 33-year-old daughter, Jeanette, was the obvious candidate. The incidents began when Jeanette moved into the bungalow, and she had been at the centre of family problems which had created a rift between her and her deceased father Geoffrey which had never healed. Was he or his spirit the source of the activity manifested there? *(Condensed from Peter Hough's article in FT89).*

the paranormal world

Earth Mysteries

by Joe McNally

"What," you may well be asking yourself, "are Earth Mysteries?" It's a tricky one, and the answer might not be what you expect. So read on...

EARTH MYSTERIES is, in a way, the Cinderella branch of Forteana. While the media are always more than happy to give air-time to the most manic of ufologists, or the latest near-pathological peddler of conspiracy theories, EM (as it is known for brevity's sake) gets rather overlooked. This is an enormous pity, for while research being done by those involved in the field may not be as visually entertaining as tales of alien abduction or New World Order intrigue, it's one of the few areas of Forteana which regularly produces real, quantifiable advances in human knowledge.

Indeed, comparatively few people are even aware of the field, and many of those who are avoid it like the plague, put off by images of faintly wet 'pagans' with a profoundly shaky grasp on history. However, in recent years, most of the serious EM researchers have been quietly dropping any hippyish mantles they may have once worn to reveal an extraordinary gift for keen analysis, carried out over an impressive array of fields. While most EM activity in its early years tended to centre around the simple study of 'leys' – with a somewhat embarrassing smattering of new-agery – it has now blossomed into a vast, multidisciplinary field, taking in sociology, ethnology, psychology, anthropology, musicology, archæology and even pharmacology. Some, such as *At The Edge*'s Bob Trubshawe, have branched out from EM into pure antiquarian research.

At the forefront of this revival, we inevitably find a few cutting edge journals. *The Ley Hunter*, for many years edited by Paul Devereux, has proved central in redefining EM (and will presumably continue to do so under new editor Danny Sullivan). In *FT86*, Peter Brookesmith gleefully reported that *The Ley Hunter*'s researchers "long ago gave up gawking mysticism for asking hard, scholarly, imaginative questions about the meaning of ancient sites", and this is as good a description of the attitude of the new generation of EM researchers as one will get.

As a near-perfect example of the sort of research going on in EM at the moment, the summer/autumn issue of *3rd Stone* featured a lengthy piece on the notorious ithyphallic chalk Giant of Cerne Abbas. This is one of the best-known chalk images in Britain, and is usually accepted without question as an ancient site of some ponderous mystical significance. However, *3rd Stone* featured a substantial, well-researched article by Jeremy Harte which argues convincingly that it is absolutely nothing of the sort.

The Giant is a chalk figure 180ft tall, cut into a hillside near the Dorset town of Cerne Abbas. Its most notable feature is, inevitably, its enormous erection, fully 30 feet from base of scrotum to tip of glans. For many years people had been content to assume that it was an ancient fertility image; or perhaps the extraordinarily obscure local god Helith; or even a representation of Hercules, since the Giant also carries a club (this last theory, it should be noted, dates from a period of the mid-18th century when the Antiquarian movement was systematically attempting to shoehorn every ancient site in Britain into a correspondence with Græco-Roman history and mythology.). There has been little or no significant new research about its origins since Dr William Stukeley's survey of 1764-65.

Harte, however, went back to original sources – and discovered that they were rather hard to come by.

John Hutchins, rector of Wareham and author of *History and Antiquities of Dorset* mentions in his letters that he visited the village vicarage in about 1750, and the conversation naturally turned to the giant. Most of the guests were content to go along with the conventional assumption that it was some pagan monument with its origins lost in obscurity. However, one guest, the steward of the lord of the manor, insisted that it was at most a hundred or so years old, having been cut between 1654 and 1662. He was, naturally, ridiculed by the erudite company.

This is something of a pity, since the man was almost certainly right; Harte's research has been unable to come up with any written evidence of the Giant's existence prior to 1694. In that year, the church wardens of Cerne paid for the Giant to be recut; later records show that it can last around 30 years without needing renewal. It is wholly absent from a detailed survey of the manor carried out in 1617, and from the accounts of a local scholar who passed through Cerne in 1625. From this, Harte infers, not unreasonably, that it more than likely was cut, or at least

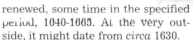

renewed, some time in the specified period, 1040-1065. At the very outside, it might date from *circa* 1630.

Moreover, there was no reference to any association between the Giant and fertility customs prior to 1888. Although it is clearly shown in early surveys, its enormous member is not even alluded to by commentators until 1774, when it was excised from the illustration used in a new edition of the *History of Dorset*. The first direct reference to it comes in John Sydenham's *Baal Durotrigensis*, from 1841. Harte concludes, not unreasonably, that the Giant probably came into being as a calculated insult to the Puritans in the days leading up to the Civil War.

His pure conjectures also bear up well. Most notably, he suggests that the Giant's recent origin makes it likely that other well-known chalk giants are also comparatively recent, and possibly created for similar purposes. "That," he says, "would account for them adjoining, not Romano-Celtic holy places, but two universities and a sea-port." Quite. It is worth noting that the function of a well-placed two-fingers to authority has returned to chalk figures in recent years. A version of the Long Man of Wilmington clad in underpants and bearing a traffic cone on its head was used in 1994 by the *Guardian*'s Steve Bell in a dig at John Major, later reproduced on a hillside near the A27 in Sussex; a group of schoolgirls from Roedean duplicated the Cerne figure in white paint on their playing fields as an end-of-term prank in the same year.

By careful documentary research, and a little creative thinking, Harte essentially reclaims an important part of Britain's social history from the grasp of those who would chuck all of mythology and ancient history into a bran tub and pick out the shinier baubles. And this, you will be glad to hear, is pretty much typical of the leading edge of EM research at the moment.

Of course, it's not all work, work, work. In amongst all the serious, heavy-duty research, attention should be drawn to the activities of the London Psychogeographical Association (East London Section). The LPA share a few of the ideas found in the works of novelists Peter Ackroyd and, more particularly, Ian Sinclair – ideas of how geography, specifically urban geography, affects the human psyche, and can be employed for magickal purposes. However, the tone of their regular communiqués, with their magnificently po-faced, declamatory style, lends everything a pleasing air of the absurd – although I cannot emphasise strongly enough that everything contained therein is completely true.

A recent issue of the LPA's newsletter, for example, featured a lengthy thesis on the true meaning of the London Marathon as a none-too-symbolic sacrificial ritual, designed to build up to the ritual murder of King Charles in the year 2000, near Canary Wharf.

Another issue discoursed at length is about the psychogeographical implications of the Orange Order's troubled marches through the Drumcree Road in Portadown, Northern Ireland in recent years. An all-time classic LPA discourse concerns Derek Beackon's election victory for the British National Party. This, they contend, was due to his acquisition of a house which once belonged to the infamous Elizabethan magician John Dee, and which stood on a ley running through the mystical Omphalos (don't ask) of the British Empire, sited in Greenwich Park. Inevitably, Beackon's sudden rise to power required a sacrifice; in due course, soon after his election, one Ian Donaldson, lead singer of the Nazi rock band Skrewdriver, was killed in an apparent car accident. Coincidence – or something altogether more sinister? The LPA know...

3rd Stone: PO Box 691, Devizes, Wilts SN10 2TS. The Ley Hunter: PO Box 258, Cheltenham, Gloucester GL53 0HR. London Psychogeographical Association: LPA (ELS), Box 15, 138 Kingsland High Street, London E8 2NS.

Falls

Mysterious (and not so mysterious) falls from the sky fascinated Charles Fort. Amongst his many outré theories, he suggested that there might be a sort of Sargasso Sea in the sky, with whirlwinds and tornadoes lifting objects into vast floating clumps, thence to be deposited on unsuspecting ground-dwellers at potentially inconvenient moments. Here we present a round-up of some of the more remarkable falls to appear in our pages in the last year.

KETTLE OF JELLY

A CLEAR JELLY-LIKE SUBSTANCE, cold to the touch, was discovered in a garden in Horley, Oxfordshire, on 23 September. The finder, who wishes to remain anonymous, said, "I don't know what it is, but if I had scraped it all up, there would have been enough to fill a kettle." A friend, Ian Lawson of Banbury, who was visiting at the time, said, "It has obviously come from the sky. Maybe it is some form of refrigeration substance used on aircraft." No more of the material was found in neighbouring gardens. *Banbury Citizen, 29 Sept 1995.*

CRAYFISH

SHIRLEY TOVELL found a freshwater crayfish in the flowerbed of her home at Alexandra Park, near Scarborough. As she lives about two miles from the nearest river or sea, the mystery was how it got there. The consensus of consulted wildlife experts was that it had been dropped by a heron or gull. *Weekend Telegraph 19 Nov 1994.*

FIREBALL

PEOPLE LIVING in central Japan were agog on the afternoon of 7 January as they watched a fireball accompanied by a loud noise and a white plume of smoke. One eyewitness said: "An orange object with sparks following it fell to the south-east and it looked like a huge firework going off." Shortly afterwards, Ryutaro Araki, 19, found what appeared to be a fragment of meteorite in Tsukuba, Ibaraki prefecture, north-east of Tokyo. It landed about 50m ahead of him while he was driving and was still warm when he picked it up. It resembled half an egg measuring 2in (5cm) by more than 1in (2.5cm) and weighing about 2oz (60g). *AFP, Japan Times, Evening Standard, 8 Jan; Guardian 11 Jan 1996*

FROG DROP

WE HAVE NOT HEARD much of the traditional Fortean phenomenon of falling frogs for some time now. The only recent report comes from the TV show "Schofield's Quest" last October, when a woman rang in to describe a shower of frogs her family experienced when they were touring Scotland. Nellie Straw, of Sheffield, said that as they headed for Loch Lomond in their car along the A82, a "terrible storm" caught them between Crianlarich and Glencoe. "All of a sudden frogs began to fall on the car, hundreds of them," she said. "We couldn't believe our eyes." The problem is that Mrs Straw didn't say when this happened, and we have been unable to locate her... *Sunday Mail (Scotland) 22 Oct 1995*

TENNERS

DELIGHTED VILLAGERS grabbed handfuls of money when £10 notes fluttered out of the sky over Kidlington, Oxfordshire, in February 1995. Police admitted they were baffled by the windfall. At 6am on 24 March, a motorist saw clouds of greenbacks floating across the four-lane McClellan Highway in East Boston, Massachusetts. Police recovered $7,070 in various denominations, but had no idea how much was pocketed by the public. By the following morning, no-one had called the police station to claim the money. *Western Morning News, 21 Feb; Boston (MA) Herald, 25 Mar, AP 26 Mar 1995.*

FLYING FISH

A JET WAS forced to make an emergency landing after the captain feared a fish had fallen into the engine. A startled eagle dropped the fish just after the plane took off in Alaska. All that could be found were a few scales. *D. Record, 21 June 1996.*

HITTING THE FANS

A BROWN SHOWER landed on spectators at an East of Scotland tournament at Craiglockheart Tennis Club, Colinton, Edinburgh in August 1995. John Paterson said, "I was sitting on the grass watching the tennis when I heard a loud slap. I looked around and my wife Jane's back and arms were covered in human excrement. Several other people sitting near her were covered too. The smell was unbearable – no one would go near them."

At first, the Edinburgh-to-Birmingham shuttle which was passing overhead at the time, was blamed, but stringent checks of the aircraft's sewage tanks ruled this out. Edinburgh airport said the shower could not have come from an aircraft. Edinburgh District Council, which confirmed that the faeces were human, could offer no alternative explanation and environmental health officers were no nearer a solution more than a month later. *Edinburgh Eve. News, 11 Aug, 16 Sept 1995.*

BOLT FROM THE BLUE

A 3-INCH (7.5CM) METAL ROD, 1 inch (2.5cm) in diameter, came within inches of killing production-line worker John MacGregor when it crashed through the roof of the Symphony Furniture factory in Leeds in March, 1995. "It made a hell of a din as it came through, then another clatter when it hit the floor. It gave me quite a shock. It is certainly big enough to have killed me," said Mr MacGregor.

BOLT FROM THE BLUE: John Macgregor

Symphony's technical manager Donald Abbott thought it must have come from an aeroplane. "There are shear marks on the rod where it had broken off something, and we are on the flight path for Yeadon. It must have been travelling fast when it came through the roof and it came very close to hitting John. It could have been fatal."

Rob Lund, operations director at Yeadon airport, said: "All aircraft... are checked routinely by their captains and engineers and nothing has been found missing." He said it must have come from some other aircraft flying over the factory. *Yorkshire Eve. Post, 8 Mar 1995.*

TEARS OF THE GODS

A HUGE TEARDROP of ice, weighing four pounds, fell out of the sky and landed on a grass verge near stunned commuters at a bus stop in Ecclesfield, near Sheffield. Firemen took it back to Tankersley fire station and preserved it in a freezer. Later, someone took it out and dropped it. *Sheffield Star, 18 Mar 1996.*

NEW BALLS, PLEASE

DOROTHY HAYWOOD was at home in West Knoxville, Tennessee, on 28 August. "I heard noises at about 8.15 or so Monday night, but didn't notice anything until my son ran over a tennis ball in the driveway," she said. "The back yard was full of them." She counted 60 to 70 fuzzy yellow balls in her yard, 10 or so in the alley behind her house and several in neighbouring yards on Denson Avenue.

"The only way I can explain this is that they were somehow dropped from a plane," she said. "They're all numbered – Penn 1, Wilson 4... I thought maybe I'd won some type of contest." Her next-door-neighbour Billie Lenear said that her daughter had picked up about four balls from their yard, but had more to collect.

Police spokesman Foster Arnett Jr suggested: "It sounds like a prank played by kids." No evidence for this was offered in the report sent to *FT* by Bishop Victor Mar Michael Herron, Vicar General of the Antiochian Catholic Church in America. *Knoxville News-Sentinel, 20 Aug 1995.*

Cults & Conspiracies

The sheer gullibility of some people never ceases to amaze, and as the millennium approaches, cults, prophecies and wild conspiracy theories are growing more and more prominent – along with more sinister groups and organisations. Whether any of these groups are on the trail of Ultimate Truth we leave to your own skill and judgement.

BLACK COUNTRY HIGH JINKS

SINCE LAST May police have been investigating claims that smartly dressed men were stripping off their suits and dancing naked in woodland near Penn Common, Sedgeley, on the edge of the Black Country. Local residents had expressed worries about their children who play in the same area.

"We just do not know what these men are up to," said Supt Malcolm Gough. "We do not know whether they are genuine nudists, nature-lovers, or if there are more sinister motives... we have not caught anybody yet. Several local people claim to have seen them."

"It's been going on, off and on, for about a year now, although it seems to stop after November," said resident Judy Bardburn. The latest sighting was on 29 April, she added. "People who have seen them say that all they wear are black shoes and black socks." *Black Country Eve. Mail, 1 May 1996.*

CHANDRASWAMI BUSTED

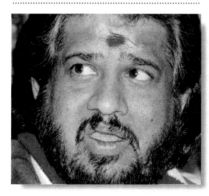

ONE OF INDIA'S most powerful and secretive mystics, the flamboyant Chandraswami, 47, who claimed to have initiated the Ganesh milk-drinking frenzy last September (see pp12-13), was jailed on 3 May this year for a comparatively minor scam. He was charged with cheating Lakhu Bhai Pathak, a senior figure in the Wirral-based Patak pickle dynasty, out of £85,000 on the false promise that he would use his government influence to obtain a newspaper contract, back in 1983.

Disciples of the dubious tantric and faith-healer, "who looks like an over-fed werewolf" according to journalist Tim McGirk, have included Nancy Reagan, Elizabeth Taylor, the Sultan of Brunei, Adnan Khashoggi, Sylvester Stallone and Indian prime ministers Rajiv Ghandi and PV Narasimha Rao, whose Congress Party was voted out of office shortly after the guru's arrest. "Al Capone went down for taxes. If this is what it takes to sink this bad man, then we shall welcome it," said a Delhi investigator. *Independent, 4 May; Sunday Times, 5 May; Times, 7 May 1996.*

WHITE BROTHERHOOD

THE LEADERS of the Ukranian doomsday cult known as the White Brotherhood were jailed in Kiev in February for criminal damage and inciting mass disorder. They had tabled the end of the world for 24 November 1993 and then moved it forward to 14 November. Marina Tsvigun Krivonogova, aka Maria Devi Christos or "the living God" went down for four years; her second husband, 'chief prophet' Yuri Krivonogov, aka Johann Swami, got seven years; and the sect's 'archbishop', Vitaly Kovalchuk, who called himself Pope Peter II, got six years.

Marina apparently realised her divinity following a near-death experience during a hospital operation. The cult attracted thousands of young followers throughout 1993, but when Doomsday arrived, the crowd that gathered in Kiev fell far short of the 14,000 expected by the cult.

Christos and her followers burst into St Sophia's Cathedral chanting, "Cursed is the Beast" before spraying fire-extinguisher foam on priceless icons. There were 570 arrests around the country shortly afterwards. The police only realised they had nabbed "the living God" when people started kissing her feet. *Times, Scotsman, Int. Herald Tribune, 10 Feb 1996.*

VIKINGS FROM HELL

THREE YOUNG men who burned down a church in Gothenburg, Sweden, three years ago because they were 'provoked by Satan' were jailed on 11 January. Two of the men, aged 21 and 22, were sentenced to three-and-a-half years in jail for arson, while the third, a 17-year-old, was given a reduced sentence of two-and-a-half years because of his youth.

Two of the men claimed during the trial that Satanic rock music provoked them to set the Lundby church ablaze, while the third said his Satanic beliefs were responsible for his actions. The three accused were also ordered to pay the sum of 250,000 kronor ($38,460) each in damages by the court. *[AFP] 11 Jan 1996.*

OLD NICK IS UP TO TRICKS

IN THE DAYS leading up to 6 June 1996, the sixth day of the sixth month of a year ending in a six, a pamphlet warned the people of Bogota, Columbia, that the Antichrist (whose number is 666) would claim their unbaptised children on that day. Although the prediction was made by a Protestant fundamentalist group, many Roman Catholics picked up on the rumour, panicked, and rushed to have their children baptised. About 20,000 people were baptised in the city over the weekend of 1-2 June, ten times the average. The emergency baptisms were televised, which led to hysteria spreading across the country.

The rumour took several forms. In one, the Antichrist's birth was expected, a prediction that terrified pregnant women due to give birth in early June. In another, an evil being was expected to possess any unbaptised children and mark them with the Sign of the Beast. And in yet another rumour, closely allied to the familiar folklore tale of kidnapping for the organ trade, it was feared that the Antichrist would steal children from their parents. *New York Times, 6 June; Houston (TX) Chronicle, 8 June 1996.*

ZAL-US LET DOWN

RUMOURS SPREAD that Billy Buchanan, councillor for the UFO hot-spot of Bonnybridge, Scotland, had invited 'Zal-us' of the InterGalactic Council of Nine to address earthlings at Falkirk town hall on 9 November 1995.

At the appointed time about 700 people packed into the hall. There was no obvious sign of Zal-us. Instead, speakers included Geri Rogers ("once rumoured to be Zal-us" according to the *Daily Mail*) and an American channeller who urged people to hug more trees. The audience left baffled and £2 lighter.

In March this year, Buchanan announced that he was quitting as a Bonnybridge councillor, blaming stress for the decision. *Edinburgh Eve. News, Daily Mail, 10 Oct 1995; D.Record, 5 Mar 1996.*

DING-DONG

DO TRUNG KIEN, deputy manager of a Vietnamese bank in Ho Chi Minh City, orchestrated a commando raid on the offices of Hai Yen Co., as the garment company owed six billion dong (£359,000). Sixteen employees armed with high-velocity rifles snipped telephone lines and cordoned off the area. The bankers loaded three trucks with equipment pledged as collateral for the original loan before the police arrived and arrested them. *[AFP] 11 Mar 1996.*

SHOKO ASAHARA, the imprisoned leader of the Japanese Aum doomsday cult, was an avid collector of pubic hair. Asahara, accused of the sarin nerve-gas murders on Tokyo's underground railway system, got the  hair from some of the 30 or 40 women followers with whom he slept, according to the *Nikkan Sports* newspaper. *Northern Echo, 14 Sept 1995.*

EXTRA BODY: Dr David Fieldhouse, the police surgeon at the scene of the Lockerbie aircrash in December 1988, still insists he issued death certificates for 59 bodies, even though the official death toll was only 58. *The Scotsman, 6 Feb 1995.*

CHAD THE PEG: Scientists studying relics of 7th-century Saint Chad in Birmingham found his reliquary contained three legs. Radiocarbon dating suggests that five of the six bones in the casket may be genuine, since they date from the 6th or 7th century. *Hong Kong Standard, 16 June 1996.*

INFERTILITY SEAT: When the Russian psychic and hypnotist Anatoly Kashpirovsky lost his parliamentary seat, he warned that he would use his psychic powers to render impotent anyone trying to evict him from his government flat. *[AP] 28 Jan 1996.*

SATANCALAFRAGILISTIC: Massimo Introvigne, of the Italian Centre for the Study of New Religions, announced that there was a secret agenda in the Walt Disney film *Mary Poppins*, released in 1964. Apparently, behind Mary's sweet-natured mask lay "a troubled creature bordering on the Satanic". *Sunday Express, 17 Sept 1995.*

SF Books of the DAMNED

by David Langford

SCIENCE FICTION WRITERS have always had a soft spot for Charles Fort's iconoclastic suggestions about science and reality. As the proverb goes, "the enemy of my enemy is my friend". SF hacks, while paying lip service to scientific dogma, were just as keen as Fort to locate science's contradictions and loopholes – preferably loopholes wide enough to drive faster-than-light spaceships through, in defiance of Einstein's tiresome speed limits. It made for better stories. Even SF authors who didn't pay much heed to science still found Fort's colourful ideas well worth stealing.

It was the distinguished SF author and critic Damon Knight who wrote the first full-scale biography of Charles Fort: *Prophet of the Unexplained* (1970). A.E. van Vogt's 1940s *Weapon Shops of Isher* series starts with a (fake) newspaper clipping only slightly weirder than some of those Fort collected, and ends with the gnomic and curiously Fortean remark "Here is the race [i.e. humanity] that shall rule the sevagram" – made all the more cryptic because van Vogt never actually told you what a sevagram was. In 1977, Gene DeWeese and Robert Coulson perpetrated an in-jokey SF novel whose best point, I have to admit, was its title: *Charles Fort Never Mentioned Wombats*.

All these writers, including Fort, are mere Americans. (Canadian, in van Vogt's case.) But the SF author who most wholeheartedly took the ball from Charles Fort and ran with it was Britain's own Eric Frank Russell – with his first novel *Sinister Barrier*, published in 1939 in the US fantasy magazine *Unknown*.

Eric Frank Russell was born in 1905, died in 1978, and is best known for later SF works written in a wisecracking American style – cleverly crafted to sell to American magazines. In *Sinister Barrier* the inventive human race gets the short end of the stick. The whole book grew from one of Fort's most inspiredly worrying throwaway lines: "I think we're property."

STARLING SILVER

Specifically, in Russell's story we are herds tended by psychic vampires called Vitons, who ghoulishly feed on our emotions. The book is prefaced by an offbeat but seemingly genuine newspaper clipping about eight dead starlings falling mysteriously and Forteanly out of the sky to land in Fifth Avenue, while another flew madly into a restaurant as though pursued. "What killed the eight starlings? What frightened the ninth? Was there some Presence in the sky...?" This is the tried and tested literary technique known as Unsubtle Foreshadowing.

Sinister Barrier begins with a plague of dying scientists, who pop off from apparently natural causes or seeming suicide while trying to convey some terrible knowledge. Soon the death toll reaches nineteen, with cops puzzled by the fact that all the corpses have painted some part of themselves with tincture of iodine.

Next in the casualty list is an entire town, Silver City, which apparently suffers a nuclear strike... except that there's no radioactivity. And what in fact blew up was a million gallons of innocuous silver nitrate solution at a photographic company. Can such things be? And did Russell really predict atomic mushroom clouds in 1939? No, no: with the incandescent radiance of hindsight, he revised *Sinister Barrier* in 1948.

US government intelligence agent Bill Graham is soon on the trail. The first test of a new photographic emulsion in Silver City had shown strange things like miniature suns in the sky. When Graham takes the iodine treatment, he sees them for himself: the Vitons, our owners. At this point there's a deluge of exposition and Fortean newspaper clippings – Russell had amassed his own research collection of "a thousand press clippings snatched from half a hundred newspapers". You can tell they're authentic, since although the book is set in America in 2015, with gyrocars filling the sky, all the clippings are dated 1942 or earlier.

COO-EE VITON

The secret emerges. For at least 150 years the telepathic, telekinetic and – until now – invisible Vitons have experimented on us. D.D. Home, the nineteenth-century spiritualist, was one of their successes. Kaspar Hauser, "man from nowhere", escaped from a Viton laboratory. Benjamin Bathurst, the British ambassador to Vienna who in 1809 famously walked around his horses and vanished forever, was taken by the Vitons. So were Amelia Earhart, the crew of the Mary Celeste, and lots more.

So far, these flying spheres have concealed their presence on Earth by telepathically spying on people and zapping anyone who catches on. Bill Graham, being tough-minded, manages to think of other things (such as women) until he can spill the beans to a select audience of top officials and world-class scientists. They believe him at once, because of his "complete sincerity".

Despite detonating radio stations (this particular 2015 America lacks television) and large-scale casualties among newspaper staff, the world is told the bad news – also, how to see Vitons. The gospel of Better Eyesight Through Iodine spreads like wildfire. Hastily, the Vitons whip up a distraction by subverting the "Asian Combine", whose superstitious Orientals are easily convinced that these glowing spheres are ancestral spirits who must be obeyed (oh dear), and go fanatically to war against America.

LIGHT CLIPPER

Suddenly, Russell realizes that he has a lot more newspaper clippings and forgets the world war to spend more pages summarizing reports of glowing lights. Did you know that King George V, as a young prince, "described a strange string of floating lights, 'as if of a phantom vessel all aglow'," at 4am on 11 June 1881? Fortunately we are spared the special 2015 edition of the *Herald-Tribune* which pays homage to Tiffany Thayer's celebrated *Fortean Society Magazine* by listing "twenty thousand references to luminosities and glowing spheres culled from four hundred issues of *Doubt*." Russell had contributed enthusiastically to *Doubt* in the early days when it was still called *The Fortean Society Magazine*.

Back to the war! Huge tracts of America have become rubble. We need a good solid *deus ex machina* to fight back – but no known weapon will touch Vitons. Bill Graham, though, has a hunch. Very soon our hero is swivelling an experimental radar installation like a big gun, blasting Viton spheres by the scores, with suitable battle-cries like "You dirty, stinking gobs of parasitic lousery!" The secret weapon specifications are broadcast to the world; humanity can slaughter its capitalist overlords at last; and Graham gets the girl.

Sinister Barrier is not the finest SF novel ever written, even by Eric Frank Russell – it has long been out of print, while Russell's better works do occasionally reappear. But it is the most thoroughly Fortean in its concept. Even the dedication is to Charles Fort, Tiffany Thayer and the Fortean Society of New York (among others).

THIS ASYLUM EARTH

A later Russell novel, *Dreadful Sanctuary* (serialized in *Astounding SF* in 1948; various revisions 1951 to 1967), also used a Fortean notion. One source was Fort's lost book *X*, whose MS was destroyed, though various letters that Fort wrote about it survive. The premise: our civilization is controlled by beings on Mars. Elsewhere, Fort suggested that Earth is a lunatic asylum where advanced races from other worlds dump their rejects; he painted a terrible picture of such visitors going native and sinking into "what their own far-advanced people regard as perhaps unmentionable, or anyway, unprintable, degradations. They would join our churches and wallow in pews. They'd lose all sense of decency and become college professors…"

In *Dreadful Sanctuary*, the wisecracking scientist hero dis-covers that Earth is a vast booby-hatch. Only the Chinese are native Earthfolk, other races being the dregs of the solar system – colour-coded by planet, with blacks hailing from Mercury, browns from Venus and whites from Mars. Supposedly the sane descendants of exiled Martians are running the world and sabotaging space research to keep Earth's lunatics securely confined. In "fact", with proper Fortean scepticism, our hero questions this scenario and finds it's a scam – a deluded but still deadly cult of powerful Earthmen who believe they have extraterrestrial ancestry. The big lie is exploded by flying a rocket to Mars and demonstrating that this planet does not, in fact, harbour a society of white supremacists. Alternatively, in a weird 1963 revision of the book whose US editor reckoned that downbeat endings were more mature, the hero fails and the cult triumphs. Very peculiar.

Eric Frank Russell's SF is still well worth seeking out. Charles Fort himself can have the last word: "I cannot say that truth is stranger than fiction, because I have never had acquaintance with either."

NOW WHERE WAS IT THOSE ALIENS CRASHED?

by William P. Barrett

(reprinted with permission of Crosswinds, New Mexico's largest Alternative Newspaper. ©1996 Crosswinds Inc.)

Illustration by Gary Green

The so-called Roswell 'saucer crash' continues to be a central topic of debate in ufology. An issue which often gets overlooked is the whole question of what, if anything, actually happened on that night in July (perhaps late June) 1947; likewise, if the self-proclaimed Roswell experts can't even agree on the most basic facts of the case, what hope have the rest of us? This special report, from New Mexico underground newspaper Crosswinds, takes a look at the mystery of the amazing moving crash site...

IS ANYONE LEFT on Planet Earth unaware of the Roswell Incident? That's the reported 1947 crash of a saucer-shaped unidentified flying object in south-eastern New Mexico, accompanied by subsequent accounts of alien body sightings.

Years of sensational publicity, numerous books, the dubious 'alien autopsy' film and frequent references to it on the TV show *The X-Files* has made Roswell internationally famous and all but synonymous with UFOs. Now comes this summer's blockbuster movie *Independence Day*, the plot of which turns on the fact that the US actually recovered a functioning flying saucer and its not-so functioning occupants in New Mexico.

It's even fair to say that Roswellian UFO interest resides at the highest level of world leadership. After receiving an inquiring letter from a teenager in Northern Ireland, President Clinton actually told an audience during a 1995 visit to Belfast, "As far as I know, an alien spacecraft did not crash in Roswell."

Indeed, the Roswell Incident – so called because of the 1980 book of the same name by Charles Berlitz and William Moore, assisted by Stanton Friedman – is easily the world's most-investigated UFO happening. It might just live up to the book cover's immodest claim of "the most important UFO encounter of our century."

So why does the crash site keep moving around?

Yes! In spite of all the books and all the alleged investigations and all the attention, veteran UFO researchers cannot agree on the location of the world's most famous UFO incident. Over the years at least six different southern New Mexico crash sites have been identified several hundred miles apart, spanning an area far bigger than the state of Delaware. Four have emerged in the past few years alone.

One site, outlined in a book and video just published in Roswell, is surrounded by questionable paperwork, a changed story, monetary inducement and even sex. It is the one supported by the most prominent UFO museum in Roswell, which stands to profit from it.

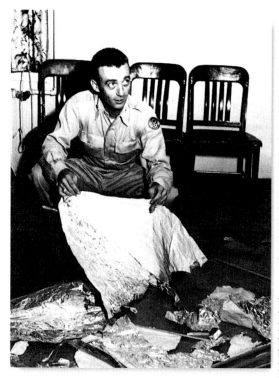

Major Jesse A Marcel with the balloon wreckage in the office of General Roger Ramey, commander of the Eighth Air Force

Surprised there's more than one impact site? Well, Roswell now has three competing UFO museums which draw money from nearly 100,000 tourists annually. Why not competing crash sites?

The frenzy about Roswell started in early July 1947 from a most unlikely source: the Federal Government. A July 8 press release from the Roswell Army Air Field said that it had come into possession of "a flying saucer". The statement was written and hand-carried to local media by Lt Walter Haut, the base's public information officer. Higher-level Army Air Force officials disavowed the statement within hours, saying what actually crashed was a weather balloon hit by lightning. (In 1994 the Air Force said it was really a top-secret balloon helping to monitor Soviet nuclear testing.)

Haut, who today lives in retire-

Veteran UFO researchers cannot agree on the location of the world's most famous UFO incident

ment in Roswell, recently confirmed that his press release referred to a crash site 75 miles north-west of Roswell on a ranch near Corona, New Mexico, just off State Highway 247, managed by W (Mac) Brazel. There is no doubt metallic debris of some kind fell there. Brazel himself was quoted at the time as saying the media and military furore made him sorry he had ever reported seeing anything. That ranch, now owned by the Bogle family of Dexter, New Mexico, is closed to the public.

Call it Site No. 1.

To much of the world, this is the true place of the Roswell Incident. Never mind that the location is almost as near far-bigger Albuquerque as Roswell. However, neither Brazel nor any of the other witnesses ever reported seeing anything at Site No. 1 resembling a craft capable of carrying passengers, much less bodies of dead or dying aliens. This eventually prompted speculation that this location was merely the location of whatever incident disabled the UFO – a lightning strike during a storm, perhaps, or, even more wildly, a collision of two or more UFOs – and that the corpus of one UFO fell to ground elsewhere.

And for a time the main claim was that the actual, final resting spot sat upon the Plains of San Agustin, a grandly named oblong expanse of desert about 200 miles west of Roswell. That's nearly the distance between New York and Washington, a rather wide margin of error. The main evidence buttressing this theory was first outlined in 1980 in *The Roswell Incident*.

It was the hearsay account attributed to one already deceased Grady L (Barney) Barnett. Unfortunately, for the Berlitz/Moore/Friedman theory, it turned out after the book was published that Barney's wife kept an incredibly detailed diary of the couple's doings in 1947. She somehow failed to note the crash of any flying saucer.

Nevertheless, the Plains of San Agustin is Site No. 2.

66

This didn't convince a rival pair of UFO researchers, Kevin Randle of Cedar Rapids, Iowa, and Don Schmitt of Hubertus, Wisconsin, authors of several books about Roswell. They made an interesting pair. Randle has authored dozens of pulp fiction novels under a variety of names as well as nine books about UFOs. Schmitt, who claimed to be a medical illustrator with two college degrees and enrolment in a doctoral programme in criminology, turned out to be a long-time mailman in Wisconsin with no academic credentials. Randle was eventually forced to disown him.

Still, Randle and Schmitt spent a lot of time flopping around Roswell. In 1991 they wrote a book called *The UFO Crash at Roswell*. That book said alien bodies were recovered at a site about 2.5 miles from the afore-mentioned debris field on the Brazel ranch.

Call that Site No. 3.

Photographs taken by William Rhodes over Phoenix, Arizona, on 7 July 1947

Since that book, Randle and Schmitt continued their research. They found retired military people who said they had been involved in a UFO recovery – at a location much closer to Roswell, about 30 miles north by north-west of town off U.S. Highway 285. Tracking down people said to have handled UFO crash debris, they came across the name of a former oil field worker named Jim Ragsdale. Then 66 years old, Ragsdale suffered from lung cancer – he had been on a respirator for years due to a work accident – and his days were clearly numbered.

Schmitt first visited Ragsdale in January 1993. The ailing man told a story beyond his interviewer's wildest dreams and repeated it in an affidavit that he signed the next day before a notary. On that summer night in July 1947, the 22-year-old Ragsdale had been "in the company of a woman" – both "buck naked" in the back of his pick-up truck, he would say later – when they saw a "bright flash" and a "bright light". The next morning they found the crash site and "a number of smaller-bodied beings outside the craft."

Ragsdale's short, two-paragraph affidavit said the site was "approximately 40 miles northwest of Roswell". That was at best an ambiguous geographic description. But Randle and Schmitt had already taken pictures of this new location. In a tape-recorded interview, Ragsdale identified the place from those pictures. (By this time, Ragsdale's lady friend was long deceased.)

In any case, this is the genesis of Site No. 4.

The new home of the famous Roswell Incident sat on a tract that had been purchased in 1976 by farmer Miller (Hub) Corn. Corn's father, grandfather and great-grandfather had worked nearby land flanking Highway 285 in a dynasty reaching back to 1894. Hub Corn had heard UFO tales while growing up. But he said he never heard the stories told in connection with the family farm or environs.

Site No. 4 is reached by driving four miles east from Highway 285 on a county road and then taking a private dirt road across Corn's land for another four miles. Corn's farm house sits 10 miles away, just east of Highway 285.

During early 1994, Corn noticed a number of persons going down that county road and then trespassing upon his property. Soon thereafter, things started hopping

around the Corn homestead. Randle and Schmitt approached the farmer with the big news that he was the proud owner of the renowned Roswell Incident site. About that same time, Corn was invited to a meeting with officials of the International UFO Museum and Research Center, the largest and best known of Roswell's three UFO museums. It sits on North Main Street across from the Chaves County Courthouse.

Among those at the meeting was Walter Haut, the 1947 issuer of the Air Force's most famous press release and the president of the museum. Also present was the museum's secretary/treasurer, Max Littell, a deal-making real estate broker whose business cards exuberantly exclaim, "To Buy or Sell – See Max Littell!!" As it turned out, Littell had notarized Ragsdale's affidavit a year earlier for Randle and Schmitt, although Littell would later deny – somewhat implausibly – that he remembered much about its contents.

Here the versions diverge. Corn – who has been telling his story without change for more than a year – said that museum officials offered to buy Site No. 4 with an eye toward developing a tourist attraction. Corn said he refused to sell but offered to lease them the spot in return for a percentage of the revenues, a proposal that museum officials rejected. Haut and Littell acknowledge that the meeting took place – "We just wanted to know what's going on," Haut said – but deny they made any offers or did anything that would amount to implicit recognition of the site's validity.

Still, the Corns quickly realized they had a new source of revenue to help them weather the periodic New Mexico droughts. Sheila Corn started taking tourists out to the site – at $15 a head. Last month, she had 300 paying customers during the July 4 weekend UFO Encounter Festival alone, and expects at least 650 visitors for the year. The ability to collect good money from people for merely

They found the
crash site and
'a number of
smaller-bodied
beings outside the craft'

visiting a farm has brought Hub Corn considerable envy from many Roswellites.

In mid-1994 Randle and Schmitt published their new book *The Truth About the UFO Crash at Roswell*, which relied heavily on the Ragsdale material and reproduced his affidavit concerning Site No. 4.

End of story? Far from it. Although growing weaker, Ragsdale was still alive. Max Littell had further discussions with him. And soon Ragsdale had profound second thoughts about that amorous night in the pickup truck in 1947.

In September 1994 Littell wrote a memorandum of understanding, saying that Ragsdale had identified a new location for the well-traveled Roswell Incident. This fresh venue was about 55 driving miles west by northwest of Roswell on the edge of the Capitan Mountains a few miles south of State Highway 248, also known as Pine Lodge Road. The spot, off a jeep path in Lincoln County, is owned and controlled by the US Forest Service. As the crow flies, it's about 30 miles south-west of Site No. 4 on Hub Corn's land.

Welcome to Site No. 5.

It eventually emerged that Ragsdale, though dying, had sold his new account, including "any designation of the impact site", to something called Ragsdale Productions Inc. This can be reasonably characterized as a Littell family business. According to corporation records in Santa Fe, the state capital, the president and registered agent is Danny Boswell, Littell's son-in-law. The vice president is Max Littell himself. The secretary is Lana Boswell, Littell's daughter. Also on the board is Ragsdale's daughter, Judy Lott of Crescent, Oklahoma. In an interview Littell said all profits will be split between Ragsdale's

Above: the UFO Museum and Research Centre, one of several such museums and tourist centres in Roswell. Below: This sign, beside one of the roads leading out of Corona, clearly indicates how desolate the area around Roswell is

heirs and the UFO Museum once the corporation's expenses are recouped.

Sometime in 1995, Ragsdale's signature appeared on a second, much-longer, first-person statement containing additional – and different – detail. Besides firmly identifying Site No. 5, he recounted for the first time how the bodies were four feet tall and that "I tried to remove one of the helmets, but was unable to do so." He changed the time of his examination from "at sunrise" in the first affidavit to the middle of the night using flashlights.

In addition to the varying detail, Ragsdale's second statement had another problem. The document carried the seal of notary Kathy Weaver of Logan County, Oklahoma – home of Ragsdale's daughter, Judy Lott – along with Weaver's written declaration that the two-page document was "subscribed and sworn to before me this 15th day of April, 1995." Weaver, an accountant with a local business,

> He changed the time of his examination from "at sunrise" in the first affidavit to the middle of the night

recently admitted that Ragsdale did not actually sign the statement in her presence. "I swear to God he did not," she said.

Faxed a copy of the statement, Weaver recalled that she added her signature and embossed notarial seal after Judy Lott, a co-employee of the same firm, brought the document already signed to Weaver's office. The notary said she was familiar with the Lott family and was quite sure she had never met Ragsdale. Weaver readily agreed that it's bad practice for notaries to attest to a signature not written while they're watching but that "we do it all the time."

In fact, under legal precedent, such a procedure invalidates the force of the notarization. All that remains is an unsworn statement – a mere piece of paper, really – without the added credibility that it has been rendered in the presence of Almighty God subject to the laws of false swearing and even perjury.

Contacted by telephone about this, Judy Lott first denied Ragsdale had signed the affidavit *sans* notary. "We had a notary come to our home because Dad was too ill and couldn't leave the house," she said. But after being informed that the notary had denied ever meeting Ragsdale, let alone witnessing his signature, Lott finally acknowledged that her father "did not" sign in the presence of the notary.

Lott insisted that she herself had typed up the statement from what her father had told her. However, Littell, a fellow board member of Ragsdale Productions Inc., said he prepared the statement himself. (The 80-year-old Littell, by the way, also said he had been unaware of any problems with the Ragsdale notarization.)

In any event Ragsdale died on July 1, 1995, his 70 years ended but definitely not forgotten. This spring Ragsdale Productions Inc. issued a video, for $29.95, and a book, for $14.95, both titled *The Jim Ragsdale Story*. The book reproduces the April 1995 Ragsdale statement, including the false claim that he signed it before a notary. The video more properly should be called *The Judy Lott Story*, since she does far more talking than her dad, especially about the juicy stuff concerning alien bodies.

Both on the video and in the book Lott says that her dad often took the family camping out near Site No. 5, and that when she asked why, he said there had once been a plane crash in the area, with no survivors. "I had no idea it was a UFO crash he was referring to then," she wrote. In fact, long-time residents said there have actually been at least three plane crashes in that immediate area since the end of World War II. Judy Lott said she was unaware of these other incidents.

Given the conflicting evidence that seems to attach to any element of the Roswell Incident, it's fair to ask what kind of detailed research Ragsdale Productions Inc. undertook to bolster Ragsdale's credibility concerning the newly revealed Site No. 5. This is especially so since Littell's UFO museum, the spiffiest in Roswell, is now subtly pushing the Ragsdale site over Hub Corn's Site No. 4 as the true home of the Roswell Incident.

The Ragsdale tale turns out to be pretty thin gruel. For example, it's reasonable to assume that a genuine UFO crash would be accompanied by a lot of notable occurrences. Among them: a massive military operation including the closing of the only road through the area, the movement of many military vehicles, some kind of flat-bed truck to remove what has been described as an alien craft 20 feet in diameter, the presence of military and civilian big-shots, and lingering local gossip like you'd never believe.

Although the Capitan Mountains area is thinly populated, perhaps several dozen homes sit within a 10-mile radius of the new crash site, many occupied by long-time residents. Max Littell freely acknowledged that Ragsdale Productions Inc. never tried to find or talk to any of these people. "As far as we were concerned, this story of Ragsdale was valid," Littell said. "What am I trying to prove he's lying for? We're not going to do that. You go ahead and prove he's lying. I'm just telling you what the man said."

It was not difficult to locate credible people who say the crash didn't happen in the Capitan Mountains and that no one has bothered to check with them. Examples:

- Bill Edgar, who moved to Pine Lodge Road as a farm hand in 1945 or 1946, was there in July 1947 and remained until 1991. "Never happened," he said from his room at a Roswell rest home just a few blocks from the UFO Museum. "I never heard about saucers or soldiers moving around." And no, nobody has ever queried him before, either.
- Kenny Schear, manager of the large Armstrong Ranch, just three miles north, arrived in 1955. "No way," he said. "I've talked to all the old-timers over the years. I think it's the biggest damned joke I've ever heard."
- Dorothy Epps, 82, whose family has owned the closest private land to the new site, a mere half-mile away, since 1907. "I don't think so," she said. "I'm quite sure we would have heard about it if it were true. It's all a hoax."
- Sam Tobias, official with the

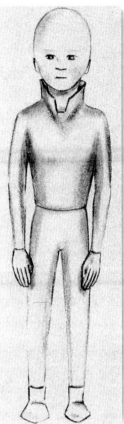

A drawing of one of the Roswell aliens, by Donald Schmitt, based on first-hand testimony

Ruidoso office of the US Forest Service, which owns Site No. 4. "This is the first we've ever heard about it," he said.

Kevin Randle's arch-rival UFO researcher, Stanton Friedman – who previously endorsed the faraway Plains of San Agustin site as well as the two Brazel Ranch sites – finds Ragsdale's new account "believable", if for no other reason than it amounted to a death-bed statement; Ragsdale was said to have been videotaped talking about alien bodies just five days before his death. However, in a Roswell UFO book Friedman authored entitled *TOP SECRET/ MAJIC*, now hitting stores, he does not pass explicit judgment on Site. No. 5. The book does attack the bona fides of Site No. 4 while re-endorsing Sites Nos 1, 2 and 3.

Enough sites? Well, even Europeans are getting into the New Mexico act. Last year, in conferences and subsequent Internet postings, German UFO researcher Michael Hesemann identified a 1947 crash venue near Socorro, New Mexico – 150 miles west of Roswell.

Site No. 6.

Badly embarrassed by Ragsdale's seeming about-face, Randle is sticking by his second book's and Ragsdale's original identification of Site No. 4. And Randle may be getting a late laugh, too, at least at the bank. Testor Corp., the Rockford, Ill., maker of model replicas, is about to release 'The Roswell UFO'. The $15 (suggested retail) kit will consist of a flying saucer miniature based exclusively, according to the model's designer, Bill McDonald, on descriptions of witnesses at Hub Corn's Site No. 4. Randle and Schmitt – but not Corn – will get part of the royalties. Testor Corp. spokesperson Nancy Rainwater said the packaging will probably carry a disclaimer that the company can't confirm the veracity of anything.

"I've talked to all the old-timers over the years. I think it's the biggest damned joke I've ever heard."

Another person with an understandably strong view is Vennie Scott, Ragsdale's former wife. Asked whether she believes his tale about a UFO encounter at any location, she replied, "You want me to be honest with you? No I do not." In more than 40 years together – they were married in 1953, six years after the supposed crash, and were finally divorced in 1994 – she said Ragsdale never talked about seeing any bodies until Schmitt came calling in 1993. Before that, she said she had heard Ragsdale mention witnessing any kind of UFO crash "one time" in the 1960s – while "he was drunk" with a friend.

Having just read the printed version of *The Jim Ragsdale Story*, Vennie Scott scoffed at the claim that damaged trees around Site No. 5 – where her family did in fact camp and hunt deer for decades – was evidence of a UFO crash in 1947. The trees were injured, she insisted, in 1969 or 1970 by a fire she witnessed that was caused by nearby inebriated campers. "These drunks let their fire get away from them," she said. "That fire just burnt a circle and quit. And that's the place that he's saying he saw the spaceship land ... That burnt spot is not what the spaceship made because I was about 400 feet from where the drunks set the fire... We helped them put the fire out."

Retorted Judy Lott, who is estranged from her mother: "If my mother's lips are moving, she's lying."

The sliding around of the crash site is actually in perfect harmony with the overall tenor of the Roswell Incident. Although die-hard UFO researchers would disagree with this conclusion, there is virtually no piece of evidence proving an extraterrestrial event thereabouts that is totally undisputed and would stand up in a court of law. Besides Ragsdale, a number of other key witnesses have either contradicted themselves or embellished their tales decades after the fact, calling their credibility into serious question. Known, proven artifacts from

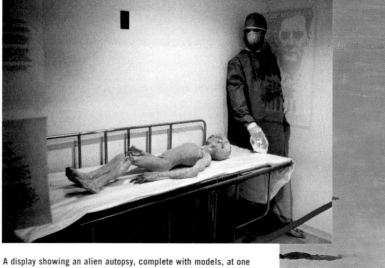

A display showing an alien autopsy, complete with models, at one of the UFO museums in Roswell.

the crash are non-existent. Much of this has been entertainingly and meticulously chronicled over the years in the bi-monthly *Skeptics UFO Newsletter*, edited in Washington by veteran aviation journalist Philip J. Klass.

From conversations around Roswell, it's clear that generally the locals are quite skeptical about any extraterrestrial claims. One of the most ardent UFO proponents, Deon Crosby, the UFO Museum's executive director, admitted that a huge majority of Roswellites – who support 106 churches, one for every 472 residents – dismiss the whole UFO tale: saucers, bodies and sites. Even Roswell business leaders, whose increased tourism marketing efforts has adroitly turned little green men into big green dollars, appear a little leery. Acknowledged Chamber of Commerce president Don Cox, "There are still fears here that by promoting the incident, Roswell will be viewed as Kook City."

WILLIAM P. BARRETT, who lives in Albuquerque, is a veteran journalist for national publications. This article was adapted from Crosswinds, New Mexico's largest alternative newspaper.

2.30

Dr Yu is a dentist with a mission. To fight decay in Quingan County, China, he has built a 2.5m-high pagoda out of 28,000 rotten teeth.
Each of the sections is made from a different type: the foundation is molars, rising through bicuspids, with incisors at its crown. Best of all, it glows in the dark, thanks to the pink lights built into its core.

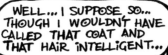

Good Luck/Bad Luck

Is there such a thing as destiny or karma, or is life just a sequence of random chances? Every so often one of those billion-to-one chances comes up, and Fortean Times chronicles as many of these freakish events as it can. On this page we feature this year's reports of cases where the cosmic toast landed butter-side-up, and on the next page the ones where the cosmic dog ate it.

DESCENT OF MAN

PAT DOLAN, 38, from West Yorkshire, wasn't kidding when he recently said he was the luckiest man in the world. He was speaking from his hospital bed after falling more than a mile, landing on his feet and surviving.

He had been paragliding over the Dolomite Mountains in Italy as part of an international competition, when he hit an 'asymmetric tuck' which caused his parachute to collapse and his reserve 'chute to wrap around his body. He fell from a height of 6,500ft (2km) in a standing position, with both arms strapped to his side by the 'chute. He hit the ground at an estimated 100mph (160km/h), crushing three vertebrae and fracturing his right leg and heel. He had the good fortune to land in a small snowdrift on an otherwise bare mountainside; he even fell into the recovery position, which assured his safety when he blacked out after the impact.

The various specialists who dealt with his injuries were astonished both at how mild they were, given the circumstances, and at how quickly Dolan was healing. Dr Enzo DiStefano, whose team in Italy treated him, expected he would need months of treatment, but said that he had made a "tremendous" recovery. Dr Yahya Ahmed, who treated him at Wakefield's Pinderfields Hospital, said that Dolan is expected to walk again. *D. Telegraph, Times, 17 Apr 1996.*

RAINING CATS

HERE'S ONE from the archives that bears repeating. An enterprising vicar, whose cat had got stuck up a tree, was unable to reach it by ladder. So he attached one end of a rope to the bough on which the cat was stuck, and the other end to his car bumper, and drove away slowly, thus lowering the bough so the cat could jump to the ground. But the rope snapped and the unlucky cat was suddenly propelled heavenwards.

Meanwhile, a mother and daughter were picnicking on their lawn nearby. The girl said, "Mummy, I'd like to have a cat."

"You'll have to ask Jesus for one," said her mother. At this point the flying feline came hurtling through the air and landed on the lawn. It has stayed with them ever since.

If this yarn sounds far-fetched, it should be pointed out that it has a very respectable pedigree indeed. It comes from the church magazine of St John with St Michael in Bournemouth, via the *Poole Advertiser. Weekend Telegraph, 24 Sept 1994.*

WATCH OUT: Joshua, a golden retriever from Royston in Hertfordshire, surprised its owner, Sally Whitby, by coughing up a watch she had lost two months before. The strap was missing, presumed digested, but the watch still kept good time. *Independent, 16 Jan 1996.*

THE BEST A MAN CAN GET: A fire broke out in a bathroom extractor fan at a house in Wolverhampton on 2 November last year. Heat from the fire burnt through the fan's plastic surround, causing the motor to fall out and hit an aerosol can of shaving foam which exploded, spraying foam everywhere and putting the fire out. Householder Jeff Crooks slept right through the crisis. *Wolverhampton Express & Star, 3 Nov 1995.*

TIT-ELATION: Dora Oberling, a stripper from Tampa, Florida, cheated death when a bullet fired at her by an irate 75-year-old member of the audience bounced off her silicone breast implants. *Independent on Sunday, 28 April 1996.*

PISSED OFF: A stray dog urinated on a Semtex bomb in a shop doorway in the Czech town of Domazlice and saved the lives of five people. The pee-soaked hammer kept the bomb from exploding. *Las Provincias (Spain), 14 Sept 1995.*

GOLDEN HANDSHAKE: Office worker Frederick Baum found a blank football pools coupon when he cleared out his desk in Munich after he was made redundant. He filled it in and won £400,000. *D. Record, 27 Nov 1995.*

CELL MATES: A robber jailed for eight years in Argentina hired a detective to trace the father he had never met, and found it was the warder of his prison. *D. Mirror, 28 Sept 1995.*

PHONEY: A disappointed sex-line caller complained to trading standards watchdogs when he got a woman nagging her husband instead of a panting girl. They said they couldn't take any action as the line was titled "Hear me moan". *D. Record, 16 Jan 1996.*

POLICE POUNCED on an elderly man when they raided a pub in Loughborough, Lincolnshire, after a tip-off about a drug dealer. The elderly suspect had to explain that his bag of white powder was the ashes of his late wife Alice, which he carried everywhere. *D. Mirror, 1 Mar; Sunday Telegraph, 10 Mar 1996.*

NO WAY OUT: Last July, German factory worker Peter Ditert failed in his tenth suicide attempt when he was discovered after swallowing 60 sleeping pills. Previous attempts included rat poison (he vomited it up), a gun to the head (it jammed) and a hair-drier in the bath (the fuse blew). He was either the luckiest or unluckiest man in the world. *Guardian, 11 July 1996.*

BULL LOVE: A police car taking a drunkard to a lock-up in Kolsva, Sweden, was suddenly surrounded by 20 lovesick bulls who had escaped from a nearby farm. One bull mounted the bonnet, while others rubbed against the doors or caressed the boot.

"Under the circumstances, we did not find it urgent to leave our car until the rutting horde was distracted by a lorry,' said one constable. Although we do not know what happened to the distracting lorry or its driver, farm workers finally managed to lead the runaways back to their field. *Expressen, 31 May; Sydsvenska Dagbladet, 7 June 1996.*

STOWAWAY AWAY

THE BODY of a young man, 18 to 25 years old, was found floating in the Harbor Isle marina in Island Park, Long Island, in the flight path to Kennedy Airport, on 21 May. A homeowner reported hearing a loud boom, then a splash in the water, at 9.25pm.

The victim was carrying Dominican currency and was wearing jeans that were not manufactured in the US. An American Airlines jet touched down at Kennedy just three minutes after the splash and would have been at 2000ft, lowering its landing gear.

Two days later, at 6.35am, a boy cycling to school found a mangled body of a man in the middle of a suburban street about 8.5 miles (14km) west-southwest of Miami International Airport.

Neighbours had heard a thump, but had not investigated. The body was covered in grease stains, suggesting that the man had stowed away in the nosewheel well of an airliner. *NY Post, Houston (TX) Chronicle, 24 May 1996.*

TASTY BIRD

LAST YEAR, in a forest glade near a remote village in the north of Edo state, Nigeria, ornithologist Philip Hall caught a fleeting glimpse of a Rufous Fishing Owl (*Scotopelia ussheri*), one of the rarest birds on earth. There had been only about 30 sightings since the species was first described in 1871 by Richard Bowdler Sharpe.

This year, Mr Hall (who emigrated to Nigeria 24 years ago) made the long trip back to Agenbode, on the banks of the river Niger. He gathered the villagers and asked if they had seen the owl. Yes, they had seen it. They had heard it calling only the night before, and had gone out to find it. But no, they couldn't let him photograph it. They had killed, cooked and eaten it that morning.

All that remained of the owl in the cooking pot was one of its yellow legs, the decomposing head which showed the tell-tale cere (a waxy membrane) on the bill, and several primary wing feathers. *D. Telegraph, Times, 23 Mar 1996.*

Cassock **commotion**

A VICAR continued praying when a ferret disappeared up his cassock during a communion service. The Rev. Stephen Grey, of St Michael's Church, Bamford, near Rochdale, Greater Manchester, was alerted to the interloper when a woman worshipper screamed and jumped up on a pew.

"I looked up and there it was, staring at me," he said. "It went three times around my cassock and then stuck its head underneath." Eventually the ferret, believed to be a pet, was ejected from the church after biting a parishioner's thumb. "I was trained to carry on regardless, but I must admit the prayers speeded up a bit towards the end,' said Grey. *The Electronic Telegraph, Home News, 3 May 1996.*

The humble telephone can be as terrifying as a close encounter, American UFO researcher Martin Cannon learns – when you play

The Numbers Game

OCCASIONALLY, I write about UFOs.

Occasionally, I speak to folks who claim to have seen them or met their pilots. And occasionally I get the chance to relate what I've heard before a radio or lecture-hall audience. Which means, of course, that occasionally someone will ask me: "Has anything weird ever happened to you?"

I always reply, "No." But that's not quite true. I can bear witness to one minor but maddening enigma – one which veteran outer limits researcher John Keel (and a very few other authors) connect to the UFO controversy.

In *The Mothman Prophecies*, Keel writes of a United Nations public relations officer named Don Estrella, who survived a head-on automotive encounter with an invisible and impenetrable something-or-other that accordioned the front end of his car. Shortly after this bizarre accident, a friend of Estrella's in Long Island received an odd phone call. The U.N. officer reported that: "A voice that sounded very distant said, 'Hello, Don.' My friend told him that I hadn't arrived yet. The voice then began to recite a series of numbers meaninglessly."

Keel knew of many similar incidents. In

1961, a telephone conversation between two women in Oregon was rudely interrupted by the voice of a mysterious man who shouted, "Wake up down there!" According to Keel, "The voice started to rattle on in a rapid-fire language that sounded like Spanish." After this odd locution ceased, the women could speak together normally once more. At the same time next day, the women spoke on the phone again, only to earwitness a repeat performance by the oddball voice. After the audio interloper speed-shouted something in a foreign tongue, it began reciting the numbers 40 and 25 continually.

Stranger still: Keel claims to have investigated many instances

of numbers mysteriously read out over television sets during UFO flaps. These interruptions could not be explained away as shortwave or CB interference. Keel even collected a number of stories from individuals who claimed to hear these numbers in their heads.

In 1967, during West Virginia's great "Mothman" wave of UFO-oriented oddities, Keel encountered the phenomenon again. Every night, a young lady in the area was called by a strange man who would speak to her in an accelerated speech that sounded "something like Spanish... yet I don't think it is Spanish."

Brad Steiger's *Mysteries of Time and Space* refers to a similar inci-

> In 1961, a telephone conversation between two women in Oregon was rudely interrupted by the voice of a mysterious man who shouted, *"Wake up down there!"*

dent. A female informant was speaking to a friend on the telephone when their conversation was interrupted by an unusual male voice repeating meaningless two-digit numbers. Thinking quickly, one of the women identified herself to the voice as one of the numbers whereupon the intruder plunged into the rapid-fire pseudo-Spanish noted by Keel's sources. Like Keel, Steiger connects such incidents with UFOs and similar other-worldly phenomena.

Now, to paraphrase an old Bill Cosby line, I told you those stories to tell you this one.

Because, you see, it happened to me.

The story begins sometime in the early Reagan era, when the homeless multiplied like cancer and I came parlously close to joining their ranks. Those were the days when I faced that queasy interregnum between exiting college and finding a niche within one's chosen profession, and since I had chosen the field of art and illustration, the interregnum threatened to last a lifetime.

As it happened, this transition period lingered for nearly three astonishingly miserable years, which I spent sequestered in a dank "bachelor pad" roughly the size of a medium-sized household appliance. I sustained myself with a succession of stultifying employments, punctuated by the occasional art assignment.

Generally, I worked the graveyard shift. It fit my mood. One thing you have to understand about graveyard: the worst aspect of working those hours is not working those hours. What do you do during those nights when the job's not there but caffeine and a chronic insomnia still keep you alert at three, four, five in the morning?

My brother suggested loop lines.

He had learned of these from a computer bulletin board. I spent an evening at his house (he was prosperous, having opted for fast-food management instead of higher education), and received a guided tour of the board's database – which, for some reason, contained an introductory course in "phone phreaking".

Phreaks, as they like to call themselves, are techno-pranksters

Like the stereotypical trained dog, Number-Man wouldn't perform his best trick for others.

who enjoy tweaking the nose of "Bitch Bell", and loop lines are a major weapon in the phreak armory. The telephone company invented loops to serve some arcane testing purpose which need not concern us here. The important point is that 99.9999% of the time the lines lie dormant – officially. Unofficially, they're a phreak phantasia.

Imagine phone lines connected to no telephone, lines that "float" somewhere in the central office of the Telco (if you'll forgive the lapse into phreak-speak). Loops come in matched pairs, and the numbers usually occur in the upper strata of an exchange. Thus, if you dial (212) XXX-9977, you'll speak to whoever might be waiting on (212) XXX-9978.

Why do this? Basically, it's networking for nerds: The loops serve as a sort of lonely-heart's club, whereby individuals in widely separated cities can compare notes in the safety of telephonic anonymity. Occasionally, opposite-sex phreaks loop into each other, resulting in long-distance romances.

What's the advantage of linking on the loops, as opposed to direct dialling? According to my pseudonymous bulletin-board informant, by using loops one could "avoid long distance charges". In other words: free calls. Phreak samsara.

Well, I considered all this info interesting, but not compelling. One had to be a very lonely guy indeed to dial dolts in far-off locales just to hear human vocalizations. And, hey, I wasn't that far gone.

Cut to: three weeks later.

2:30am. I had finished the night's assignment. My eyes remained wide open, my ancient and rather persnickety television set suddenly became obsessed with snowscapes, my car refused to budge and there was nowhere to drive to anyway because the town was pretty thoroughly shut. The only unread book in the apartment was Samuelson's *Economics*. I considered mugging someone – not for the profit motive, but as a conversation-starter.

Nights like this can drive the best of us to "loopy" behaviour.

I got out my list of numbers, and started dialling.

I had numbers for New York, Chicago, and other points east. Most of these connected me to silence. Occasionally, I got odd, repetitive electronic tones – curious, but (since I had not yet acquired a taste for Philip Glass) unsatisfactory.

The Montreal lines were livelier. Here, I encountered actual people, or the closest approximations thereof Canada had to offer. Alas, most of these phreaks made me wonder why I was ignoring Samuelson.

Then I heard The Voice.

Actually, The Voice was preceded by The Tone, a subtle electric buzz somewhat akin to the sound you hear when you hold a seashell to your ear. This faded away, gradually replaced by a young, male Voice reading numbers:

"27... 28... 29... 27... 28... 29... 27..."

During the next few weeks, I heard The Voice many times; after awhile, it seemed to take over the entire loop universe. Roughly every second or third call would connect me to the same tenor orator, constantly repeating a series of two-digit numbers. As I recall, the numbers never dipped below 20 or above 60.

The Voice did not acknowledge anything I said to it. Was it a machine? Perhaps – although this was no simple tape loop. Every so often, the voice would interrupt its strange soliloquy and shout:

'Wake up out there!'

Then more numbers. (Keel's informants recall the statement as "Wake up down there!" Since I never achieved a clear-as-a-bell connection, I suppose that either reading is possible.)

More rarely, I heard gibberish sessions – the odd, sped-up instructions in a strangely familiar foreign language. Imagine a sound like Alvin the Chipmunk on amphetamines delivering a lecture in Spanish.

At least, it sounded like Spanish. While I've never studied this language, I am a native of Los Angeles, which has the largest Mexican population outside of Mexico City; anyone raised under these circumstances should instantly recognize such a commonly heard tongue. I felt no such recognition here: "Spanish" is not an identification, merely the best available analogy. (Portuguese, perhaps?)

Part of the problem resulted from the rapid-fire delivery during the "Spanish" lessons. My telephonic narrator never paused for punctuation. Even if you play a dialogue tape at faster-than-nor-mal speed, you'll usually hear some conversational caesura. Why none here?

I had to know what was going on.

Thereafter, whenever the gods of loopdom connected me with a seasoned phone phreak, I would inquire about the "Number-Man." After all, the Telco used loops to test new exchanges; wasn't it possible that these strange mono-logues constituted some part of the test?

Negative, the experts told me. The Bell brigade came on-line during only normal working hours, and my loop activity occurred earlier (even accounting for the difference in time zones between Montreal and L.A.). Moreover, Telco employees had pretty much stopped using those particular lines. And when official phone folk did use loop lines, they most assuredly did not spout meaning-less numbers or jazzed-up quasi-Spanish.

Had other phreaks also heard these strange messages? A few had. They were just as puzzled as I. Moreover, the telephone company couldn't provide any official explanation – it doesn't even like to admit that loop lines exist. So if anyone was going to solve the enigma, it had to be me.

Fortunately, my brother had loaned me a creaky, barely functional telephone answering machine, which, when used not quite properly, could also record conversations. The solution was obvious: Preserve on oxide the lightning-fast snatches of pseudo-Spanish – and try to have it translated, examined, and possibly explained.

I became a furious looper. Whereas once I regarded the Number-Man as an annoyance, now I demanded an audience. He wasn't hard to reach, and I actually got a bit of his routine on tape. It was Number-Man's greatest hit: "35... 37... 35... 37..." (Unfortunately, I no longer have the cassette.) But nothing I could do or say goaded him into delivering his gibberish arias in ersatz espagnol – like the stereotypical trained dog, Number-Man wouldn't perform his best trick for others. Brad Steiger's informant seems to have hit upon a method of "cueing" the performance, but, alas, I never managed to do so.

One morning I was awakened by a telephone call. I blearily said, "Hello."

Short-wave enthusiasts had triangulated the broadcasts to their most probable origin point: the state of Virginia.

And Number-Man answered: "Wake up out there!" Followed by numbers. He may even have slipped me a bit of the Speedy Gonzales material; I can't recall at this date. But, as you can imagine, the situation struck me as très freaky. Apparently, Number-Man had my number.

One night shortly thereafter, following a few unsuccessful encounters with my numerically obsessed

strikes me as deeply mystifying. Was she really just a lonely ecdysiast? Perhaps – but there was something oddly theatrical about the episode, which seemed designed to fulfil every aspect of a lonely-guy's most outlandish fantasy. Joanne was too good. Was I really so charming a fellow that this pretty thing felt compelled to meet me after I had burped out no more than a hazy half-sentence or two?

One thing's for sure: She almost received a great deal of information about me. Maybe that was the point.

At any rate, my experiments with loop lines ended soon thereafter. I got the bill.

Seems I had misunderstood my original instructions on matters phreakish: Loop lines do not come free. (Later, I discovered where I went wrong. Using loops to beat the system requires strategy: you arrange with a friend in a distant city to use a loop that's local for him at a certain time, then you ask the operator to place a collect call to the other side of the loop. The operator will ring up the number and talk to your comrade, who will happily accept the charges – after all, he's not going to pay a cent. Fiendishly clever, no?)

nemesis, I looped into someone even more interesting – who, I now suspect, may also have played a role in this enigmatic drama. Her name was Joanne, and her voice was so agonizingly sexy I felt tempted to propose to her the moment she whispered my name.

Dig it: Joanne told me she worked as a stripper in Montreal. She enjoyed her work, sashaying her voluptuous assets for all and sundry to goggle. Still, most of the guys she met annoyed her; they assumed she was all body and no mind. Joanne could tell that I was of a higher calibre than her lumpenprole clientele: She just knew that I was intelligent, articulate, and possessed of a rare sensitivity. How she knew this I knew not, since I had Porky-pigged fewer than ten words to her.

Nevertheless, she informed me that she was considering flying out to L.A. to meet me! First, though, I had to write her a long letter, describing myself, detailing my history, interests, aspirations...

She gave me an address. I kept it for years. But I never responded, fearing that her invitation contained the seeds of a nightmarish embarrassment. Suppose I composed a message of de Bergeracian eloquence, and cajoled her to make the trek westward: What kind of date could I offer? A chance to make out in the rusting corpse of my '72 Torino? No. In this case, wimpitude was wisdom.

Nearly a decade later, Joanne's (admittedly delightful) intrusion

Paying Bitch Bell her ton of flesh proved crushing; I considered it a penance for the sin of phreakery, and resolved never to commit such an error again. Nevertheless, a year later I again briefly experimented with the loops. Number-Man, as far as I could tell, had taken his act elsewhere.

Years passed; I segued from being a starving artist to being a lower-middle-class artist. Eventually, I rationalized Number-Man as "one of those things", although no one I met who was learned in the telecommunicative arts could ever explain to me just what kind of thing I had encountered. Then I read Keel and Steiger.

They knew about Number-Man, and they tied him in with UFOs.

Indeed, UFO abduction lore contains a few

incidents. For example, Budd Hopkins's *Intruders* notes that well-known abductee "Kathie Davis" received a series of odd telephone calls in 1980. Repeatedly, a voice spoke to her in an indecipherable language, and when she changed to an unlisted number, the voice continued to ring her up.

An abductee of my acquaintance once received a series of "empty" telephone calls during which she heard nothing but the fuzzy, seashell-like electronic tone that preceded all of my encounters with Number-Man. Like some of Keel's contactees, she also heard numbers in her head. Somehow, she even got the impression that

One document unequivocally asserts that telephonic induction of a deep hypnotic trance was successfully tested in the early 1950s.

she was to perform certain actions in conjunction with certain numbers. She also heard (both 'telepathically" and during abduction episodes) rapid-fire instructions which she felt she would comprehend, and act out, at a later date.

And yet: I don't think the answer lies with UFOs. I think we're dealing with spies.

My encounters with Number-Man call to mind the mysterious "number readers" which afflict the short-wave band. For many years, on various frequencies, female and male announcers have broadcast four- and five-figure numbers in several different languages. In his 1983 book *Big Secrets*, William Poundstone speculated that these transmissions involve codes used by drug-runners, or perhaps by the Cubans. But a few years later, appearing on a local tabloid-TV programme called "Eye on L.A.", Poundstone revealed that shortwave enthusiasts had triangulated the broadcasts to their most probable origin point: the state of Virginia.

Which pretty much gives the game away.

In his book *Without Cloak or Dagger*, ex-spook Miles Copeland reveals that clandestine short-

wave messages sometimes take the form of "screech" broadcasts. The information is sped up, making it incomprehensible to outsiders. One can retrieve the data only by recording the message and replaying the tape slowly.

Consider the loop line as an espionage tool. You can check the telephone records of anyone calling the lines and you'll never learn who his contact is. A trace will turn up nothing: Even the telephone company will be forever mystified. Loops are the last bastion of telephone privacy, and would therefore prove enormously helpful to an operative seeking secure communications.

Consider, in this light, my contact with the sweet striptease

Joanne. Was she a ploy, designed to ferret out background information from someone who had stumbled onto the operation?

Finally, consider an even stranger possibility indeed, a possibility so thoroughly bizarre that I raise the issue with some trepidation: the telephonic induction of hypnosis.

Many researchers in hypnosis will tell you that there ain't no such animal as a telephone trance. But I have examined the released CIA documents on ARTICHOKE, BLUEBIRD, MK-ULTRA and similar "mind control" programmes, and one document unequivocally asserts that telephonic induction of a deep hypnotic trance was successfully tested in the early 1950s.

(If you doubt that the government's efforts to create a "Manchurian Candidate" met with greater success than has ever been officially admitted, consult Walter Bowart's excellent – albeit difficult-to-find – *Operation Mind Control*.)

Some years ago, I began annoying/intriguing the UFO community with a research paper entitled "The Controllers", exploring the possibility that some "UFO abductions" may actually be disguised continuances of the clandestine mind-control projects referenced above. Although I doubt that John Keel would endorse this explanation, he does strongly affirm (in *The Mothman Prophecies*, in *Operation Trojan Horse*, and elsewhere) that some form of post-hypnotic suggestion seems to affect selected UFO percipients.

Is it possible that the rapid-fire "Spanish" actually constitutes some form of hypnotic suggestion, incomprehensible to the normal listener but subconsciously understandable by a properly "trained" individual? If so, we may discover here some explanation as to why number readers and similar telephonic annoyances crop up in UFO flap areas, and why these calls seem to herald odd phenomena and odd behaviour. The Tone itself may also act as a hypnotic cue (provided the listener has been previously conditioned).

Now, I freely admit that the above suggestions are highly speculative. But this minor-key mystery must have some sort of solution. Granted, this conundrum can hardly be considered an earth-shaking matter; still, it has haunted me for years, rather like one of those stray pups that won't stop trailing you. I invite other suggestions and comments. (Of course, I also invite Joanne of Montreal to offer her side of the story: If you're a spook, all is forgiven; if not, forgive me. Whatever the circumstances, you gave a lonely lad something mighty interesting to ponder during one sleepless night.) Additional examples and alternative explanations would be most welcome.

If anyone has alternative explanations...

Does anyone?

Wake up out there!

Ghosts

Ghosts are one of the staples of Forteana: a phenomenon which still defies any kind of rational explanation. This year has seen, among many other stories in the magazine, reports of ghosts in war-zones, ghosts in bedrooms and a recurrence of a classic type of spooky encounter on the road.

HIT-AND-GONE SPECTRE

DAVID BINGHAM, 30, thought that he had run over a pedestrian outside Whitton Cemetery in Moor Lane, Birmingham, at 12.50am on the morning of 2 January. Mr Bingham, a plumber with Forward Drains in Tyseley, was convinced he had seen a figure in the road, but there was no damage to his van or any sign of blood or an injured person. Badly shaken, he reported the incident to Queens Road police station; but officers were unable to find any trace of an accident. According to a police-woman, "This isn't the first time that ghost sightings have been made in the area." *Birmingham Eve. Mail, 2 Jan 1996.*

LEGLESS GHOST IN MORTAR SQUARE

THE MORTAR SHELLS have stopped falling in Bosnia, but still no one drives by Kapija Square in Tuzla's old town after midnight. The square has been deserted since word spread that the ghost of one of the 71 young people killed in a Bosnian Serb mortar attack on 25 May 1995 has been seen at the blast site, searching in vain for her missing legs.

The ghost was spotted last December by a military police officer, Mustafa Piric, who afterwards told friends he had stopped a girl with long, blonde hair after curfew to ask for her identification papers. When she turned around, he saw that she had no face, and then he heard her cry: "Give me back my legs!"

"A lot of people here believe in ghosts and spirits,' said Alma Ahmedbegovic, a 20-year-old radio reporter who helped to pull dying friends from the rubble in the square. "They believe this girl's spirit can't rest because she was buried without her legs."

Maida Hamzic, a 19-year-old nurse, said the ghost was seen by three police officers on patrol. "The fact that they all saw the same thing means the story is true," she said. "I believe the stories about people hearing strange sounds and moans coming from there late at night." Hamzic suffered minor injuries and great mental anguish in the attack. Many lost their legs or arms, or were decapitated. Some bodies were impossible to identify. The mass funeral was held secretly in the middle of the night for fear of another attack.

A flower-covered memorial has been erected and the impact hole in the cobblestones explodes out like a star towards distant walls scarred by shrapnel. The incident had great emotional impact on the town as virtually everyone knew someone who had been killed. Many people have awoken from nightmares to see their dead friends standing in front of them as if they were real. *Hartford (CT) Courant, 14 Jan; Guardian, 30 Jan 1996.*

Ghost stories

THAT REDOUBTABLE VOLUME, 'The Encyclopaedia of Unusual Sex Practices', lists among its many paraphilias the practice of spectrophilia – sexual arousal by intercourse with ghosts. It appears that some of those who have passed over to the spirit world are unwilling to be kept from the pleasures of the flesh by anything as simple as the lack of glands, hormones or flesh itself.

In 1994, Blackpool woman Jill Cook called in a priest, two psychics and even a Mormon missionary to try to help her get rid of a ghost which she claimed regularly sexually attacked her. The attacks began in early 1994, when she felt something climb into bed beside her and pull off the towel which she was wearing wrapped around her head. She heard a voice saying it was going to make love to her, and felt a "vile" sensation as it did so – "like tiny needles trying to pierce my skin". While she continued her quest to be rid of the haunting, she found that placing an ioniser in her room moved the ghost from one room to another.

Meanwhile, a Kent couple, Sue and Ian Davies from Broadstairs, are plagued with a sex-hating phantom. The ghost apparently causes a racket every time they attempt intimacy, distracting them by groaning and banging on the walls. They believe the ghost is that of a former deep-sea diver whose friend used to live in their house, and that his campaign of disruption is aimed at preserving his peace and quiet – they think he hates the noise their children make and wants to prevent them from having any more. They haven't yet managed to get rid of their unwelcome visitor, but have managed to find a temporary solution: a tent in the back garden. "It's chilly, but we have our love to keep us warm," said Ian. "The ghost is a real passion-killer – and a better contraceptive than the Pill." *The Sun, 15 Mar; News of the World, 27 Feb; Western Daily Press, 2 June; The People, 5 June 1994.*

IN THE PAST few months, ghostly phenomena have been noted at the Ilchester Arms, near Yeovil in Somerset. These include the sound of heavy beer barrels being rolled across stone flagstones, although the flags were removed long ago; and the sound of someone typing close to midnight every evening in a room next to that of the barman, Wesley Green.

After cleaning a bedroom in the empty hotel, a cleaner was astonished to find the following morning that it had been slept in. The staff said that there was no way that anyone could have got in.

"Staff have noticed that glasses have disappeared and suddenly reappeared two days later," said the hotel's owner, Tom Finlay. "A little while ago, 30 glasses vanished and then 26 turned up again. On one occasion we all looked everywhere for a waistcoat that had disappeared. It turned up three days later."

Yeovil medium Flo Essex, a Christian Spiritualist minister, identified the spirit as a mischievous girl called Tizzy, aged 12-14 years, who possibly died of rheumatic fever. "Tizzy is very pretty with long hair and blue eyes, a dark dress and white pinafore," said Mrs Essex. "It was her home and I do not think she has realised she has passed. She is not here to hurt anyone." *Yeovil Weekly News, 7 Feb; Yeovil Express & Star, 14 Mar 1996.*

SIGHTINGS OF a spectral young woman with fair hair, dressed in modern casual clothes, have been unnerving early morning cleaners at Bo'ness Academy, West Lothian. One of the women, Mary Cunningham, said, "I felt someone behind me, and turned and saw her. She reached out to touch me and when I let out a squeal she just disappeared... I felt sick with fear and was off work for a couple of days." Workmate Maisie King, 62, also saw the ghost and their supervisor, Diane Prow, had "felt a presence". *Scottish Daily Record, 3 Feb 1996.*

MARY JOHNSON and fellow actor Robert LeBrecht were lurking in the shadows to scare tourists on an Isle of Wight ghost walk when they heard footsteps crunching on the gravel behind them, but there was nobody in sight. They were at a famous local haunt in Newport where a monk was murdered and Ms Johnson suggested the monk's ghost was annoyed because she was dressed as a friar. *Daily Echo, 28 Oct 1995.*

ARMAGEDDON COULD THREATEN UNITED'S PROMOTION PUSH

West Cumbria News and Star, 4 Jan 1995.

DAMP PATCHES DISCOVERED ON SUN

New Scientist, 3 June 1995.

HUSBAND BITES WIFE'S 'THING'

The Monitor (Uganda), 1 Feb 1995.

MICE TO BE BOMBED

Today, 15 August 1995.

UNICORN SAFE THANKS TO CASH

The Stage, 14 Sept 1995.

RIBENA OFFER TO BLOOD SERVICE

Guardian, 21 Sept 1995.

MAN ORDERED TO MARRY COW

The Monitor (Uganda), 2-4 Oct 1995.

MAN FINED FOR QUACKING

Hong Kong Standard, 12 Oct 1995.

DOGS ARE BEING TAUGHT TO DO HOUSEWORK FOR THE DISABLED

Dublin Evening Herald, 21 Oct 1995.

ALADDIN'S CAVE IS FOUND IN PUB

East London Advertiser, 9 Nov 1995.

GOD 'THROWS DICE INTO BLACK HOLE'

Daily Telegraph, 23 Nov 1995.

NANNY CALM AS TROOPS CLOSE IN

Daily Telegraph, 20 Nov 1995.

THREE WISE MEN REFUSED VISAS BY SAUDI ARABIA

Sunday Telegraph, 10 Dec 1995.

New Phyla, species etc

One of the great vindications of the field of cryptozoology - the study of unknown animals - is the discovery of a new species. 1996 proved particularly fruitful in this respect, with several new animals making their debuts.

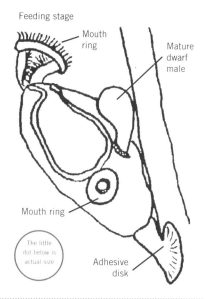

Feeding stage

Mouth ring

Mature dwarf male

Mouth ring

The little dot below is actual size

Adhesive disk

LIFE – BUT NOT AS WE KNOW IT

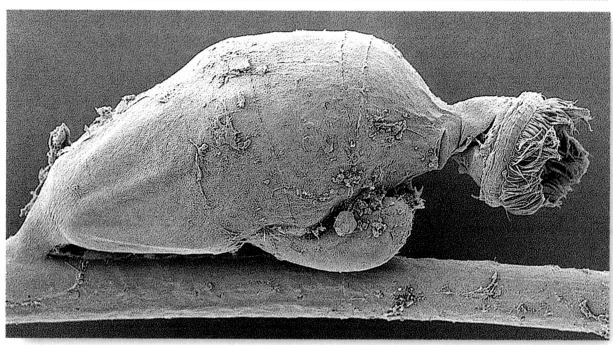

LIP-STUCK: *Symbion pandora*, a completely new type of creature

TINY CREATURES found clinging to the mouths of Norway lobsters have been awarded the ultimate taxonomic accolade – a phylum to themselves. The new phylum, the Cycliophora, is only the 36th ever described for all 30-100 million species. The single species discovered so far, *Symbion pandora*, behaves like an animated cold sore. The name Cycliophora is Greek for "carrying a small wheel". This is because the creature has a circular feeding funnel coated with fine fronds, located right next to its anus.

The larva develops inside the adult by a process of asexual budding, which makes it a genetic clone of its parent. Periodically the parent sheds its upper half which includes the nervous system as well as a disintegrating mouth and gut, and like the objects that flew out of Pandora's Box – hence its name – the larva escapes. Meanwhile, the adult's lost organs are replaced by new ones that were forming inside it well before they were needed.

Symbion pandora has an alternative sexual reproductive cycle in which a dwarf, nonfeeding male, possibly with two penises, lives attached to the female, waiting for her to release a miniature female without a brain but bearing a single ovum, which he fertilises. Before releasing her clone, the host female dissolves from the inside, becoming a sort of soup held together by a bag of skin.

Asexual adults are bottle-shaped and 347 micrometres (about one-third of a millimetre) long. These bizarre creatures were described in *Nature* (Dec 1995, v378: p 709) by Peter Funch and Reinhadt Mobjerg Kristensen, invertebrate zoologists at the University of Copenhagen.

It was, in fact, Kristensen who described the previous new phylum, the *Locifera*, discovered in Roscoff, Brittany, in 1983. These tiny creatures live between sand grains and have a retractable head and thorax. *Guardian, D. Telegraph, Austin American Statesman, 14 Dec; D. Mail, 15 Dec; New Scientist, 16 Dec 1996.*

NEW MAMMAL

AN UNKNOWN MAMMAL species, a nocturnal, squirrel-like rodent, has been discovered on the island of Panay in the central Philippines.

Called the Panay cloudrunner or *Crateromys heaneyi*, it was found as scientists race the chainsaw in the island's rapidly shrinking forests. It is a tree-climber, weighs a little over 2lbs (1kg), has a tail longer than its body and, according to local hunters, rarely leaves its den during the day. Its vocalisations include a shrill, almost insect-like cry.

"The cloudrunner is very similar in size, appearence and habits to our North American fox squirrel," said Dr Robert Kennedy, a researcher at the Cincinnati Museum of Natural History and Science, "but the fox squirrel is diurnal, eats nuts instead of fruit, and it has a somewhat bushier tail." Three cloudrunners, two males and a female, are now on display in Cincinnati zoo.
NY Times, 20 Feb; Int. Herald Tribune, 22 Feb 1996.

DWARF LEMUR

GERMAN SCIENTISTS have rediscovered a dwarf maki (lemur) weighing just over 1oz (31g). This nocturnal and mouse-sized creature, the world's smallest primate, was first described in 1852, but was then forgotten. Only about a dozen have ever been seen. *Ivoir' Soir, 29 Dec 1994.*

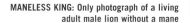

BORN FREE... OF A MANE

DAVID FEATHERBE, a biochemist at Imperial College, London, went on safari at the Hwange National Park in Zimbabwe and took the only known photograph of a living adult male lion without a mane. The animal is at least four years old, according to Doug Richardson, Keeper of Mammals at London Zoo. At the turn of the century, maneless lions terrorised Sabo, near Mombasa in Kenya. "They were picking off railway workers," said Richardson. A photograph was taken of one, but it was dead. The exact purpose of a lion's mane remains unknown, although it is thought by some that it could be used for display in courting. *New Scientist, 24 Feb 1996.*

MANELESS KING: Only photograph of a living adult male lion without a mane

GOING BATTY

A BAT, about to be eaten by two cats in Wallasey, Merseyside, was found to be of a foreign species which has been recorded only once before in Britain. Wallace, as the bat was named, was rescued from an untimely death by a woman who saw the cats tormenting it in her backyard. Clemency Fisher, the chief bat person at the Liverpool Museum, identified it as a Savi's pipistrelle, quite common across the Mediterranean. "Just what it was doing in Wallasey is a bit of a puzzle," said Mrs Fisher. *Times, 13 March 1996.*

IF THERE WAS AN AWARD for most new species from a single country, Vietnam would win hands down. In the last five years alone, some ten unknown animals have been identified. These include: the Vu Quang ox, a deer the size of a buffalo; the Giant Muntjac, the largest known member of the species; the handlebar-horned Holy Goat; the goatlike (probably – the only known specimen was eaten before it could be examined!) Tuoa; the Slow-Running Deer; the Black Deer; a small primate called the Giant Cream Loris; the Laotian Black Muntjac; the Kthing Voar or 'vine-eating cow', which local hunters believe has poisonous horns; Schomburgk's Deer, which was thought to have become extinct in the 1930s; and the gloriously-named Vietnamese Warty Pig. Not bad!

BATTERED: Wallace the Mediterranean bat

PILTDOWN HOAX
SOLVED (MAYBE)
by Paul Sieveking

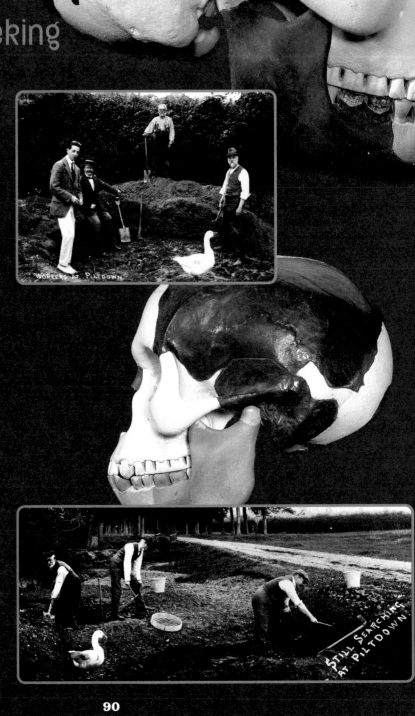

WORKERS AT PILTDOWN

STILL SEARCHING AT PILTDOWN.

IN HIS PRESIDENTIAL address to the Linnean Society on 24 May 1996, Brian Gardiner, professor of palæontology at King's College, London, appears unequivocally to have nailed the Piltdown hoaxer.

Few deceptions have warped science so dramatically as the remains of 'Dawn Man' dug out of a Sussex gravel pit in 1908-12. The pieces of *homo sapiens* cranium, orang utan jaw and Pleistocene 'cricket bat' fashioned from the leg bone of an extinct elephant fooled the academic establishment for over 40 years.

Fluorine dating of the bones in 1949 showed that they were of wildly differing ages, but it was the inspiration of South African anatomist Joseph Weiner one July night in 1953 that led to the debunking of 'the First Englishman'. He showed that the bones had been artificially stained and the 'cricket bat' shaped with a steel knife. Furthermore, the gravel pit was not fossiliferous and all the finds had been planted.

The identity of the hoaxer became an academic parlour game. Charles Dawson, the lawyer and antiquary who unearthed the bones, was long the prime suspect, with opportunity and motive (he had a desperate desire to be elected to the Royal Society). Fingers were also pointed at Professor William Sollas, Sir Arthur Keith, Teilhard de Chardin, Sir Arthur Conan Doyle and the famous practical joker Horace de Vere Cole, among many others [see *FT62·24-30*].

In the 1970s, a canvas travelling trunk belonging to Dr Martin Hinton (1883-1961) came to light in a loft of the Natural History Museum during roof maintenance. Dr Andrew Currant, a researcher specialising (like Hinton) in fossil rodents, examined the trunk's contents.

Underneath hundreds of vials of rodent dissections, he discovered carved pieces of fossil hippopotamus and elephant teeth and assorted bones stained with iron oxide, manganese and potassium dichromate in the same proportions as the Piltdown specimens. In 1899, aged 16, Hinton had published a paper showing how fossils in river gravels would be impregnated with oxides of iron and manganese, staining them chocolate brown.

In 1910 Hinton became a 'voluntary worker' in the Natural History Museum and fell out with his boss Arthur Smith Woodward over funding for a catalogue of rodent remains. "Hinton was well-known for his elaborate practical jokes," according to Dr Henry Gee, who wrote the report on Currant's discoveries in *Nature* (Vol. 381:261-2). Hinton's autobiographical entry in *Who's Who* stated that he had "studied many hoaxes including the Loch Ness Monster".

Other evidence unearthed by Dr Currant and Professor Gardiner appeared to strengthen the case against Hinton; but a tiny window of doubt must remain. Perhaps the real hoaxer planted the stained specimens in the trunk purely to frame Hinton...

I remember Martin Hinton with long white hair and baggy trousers, sitting in his study at Glaisters in Wrington, near Bristol, surrounded by monkey skulls and other macabre objects. After his death, his daughter gave me many of these – including a Romano-British skull, Neolithic axes and a piece of linen unrolled from the mummy of Bak-Ren by Wallace Budge in 1889 – which have pride of place in my collection. I wish I could recall Dr Hinton from the grave for a confidential *téte-à-téte*.

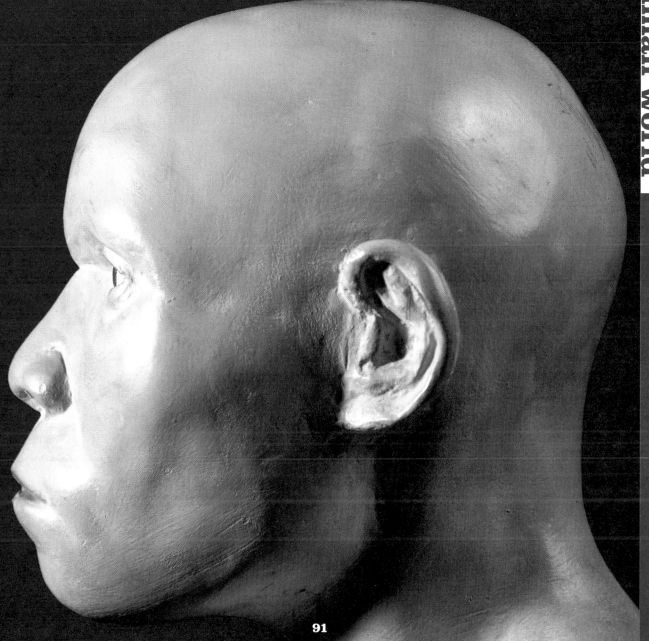

Water monsters

The Loch Ness monster is not alone. There are hundreds of other lakes (including almost a dozen in the Highlands alone) with similar traditions of giant denizens, not to mention anything up to nine species of sea serpents awaiting discovery. In fact the main problem confronting researchers is this very embarrassment of riches: surely there can't really be that many water monsters around?

Five fabulous lake monsters

1. Nessie
The monster of Loch Ness, Scotland, has been seen nearly 1,000 times since the first reports began coming in back in 1933, and helped set the standard for many-humped, long-necked lake critters.

2. Ogopogo
One of the few monsters with a history that goes further back than Nessie's, Ogopogo is supposed to live in Okanagan Lake in British Columbia. It has recently been suggested the monster may be a prehistoric whale.

3. Migo
A new entry from the Pacific Rim. Migo, the monster of Lake Dakatua in New Britain (an island north of New Guinea) is the subject of the longest video of a supposed lake monster yet shot. The footage shows several long, low humps moving through the water.

4. Lake Tianchi
China's answer to Loch Ness is this volcanic crater-lake near the border with Korea. Reports are said to go back 100 years, and the first video was shot in 1994. The monster is said to be as large as a bull, with a dragon-like body

5. Monsters of Achanalt
Highland author RM Cassie penned a bizarre contribution to lake monster lore in the 1930s with a book about his sightings of families of monsters up to 900 feet long in tiny Loch Achanalt and nearby lakes. No one knows if he was telling the truth as he saw it – or just joking.

BIG MOUTH: Dragon, whale, or something else?

BONE BONER

SUB-AQUA DIVER Cameron Turner, 27, from Darlington, County Durham, discovered six bones 60ft (18m) down at Loch Morar, Scotland, during an expedition to the remote 1,017ft (310m)-deep loch. It was suggested they might be the remains of Morag, the monster reputed to live in the loch and first seen in 1895; but they were later identified as deer bones.

"When I saw the bones poking through the silt on the loch bottom, I was sure they were from the tail of a water beast," said a disappointed Turner. The bones are probably the remains of a deer that drowned while swimming in the lake. *[PA News] 2 Aug 1996.*

DRAGON AHOY!

Malaysian fishermen hauled in the 25ft (7.5m) carcass of an unidentified creature on 27 May. They allegedly feared it was a dragon, but took it ashore to a local market in Kedah state, where thousands of people gathered to view it.

Perhaps surprisingly, nothing seems to have been preserved for scientific study. Instead, traditional healer Jefri Ahmed, 39, took the carcass home, doused it with bleach to get rid of the stench, and then extracted seven litres of oil which he made into 'magic potions'.

The discovery was made in water 175ft (53m) deep off the northern island resort of Langkawi and it took half an hour to lift the remains aboard a fishing trawler. Malaysian Fisheries Department officials were said to have "never seen anything like it".

An unnamed Malaysian scientist is said to have studied photos of the body and identified it as a killer whale. We got this photograph from the *New Straits Times* in Kuala Lumpar and showed it to cryptozoologist Dr Karl Shuker. Baffled by the seemingly contradictory characteristics of the corpse, he could not make a positive identification without more information. "The teeth and vertebrae seem mammalian," he said, "yet the head seems reptilian. If it's a whale, the mouth seems unusually large. The remains would allow a marine biologist to identify it clearly had one studied it, but the detail in the photo is ambiguous. For example, if that is a flipper near the head, it is most probably a type of whale."

In August, we heard of a similar find in the Outer Hebrides, where Northumbrian nanny Louise Whitts had discovered the decomposing remains of a 12-ft sea creature on a beach. "It had a small head, a curved back and what looked like furry skin," she said, "but the weird thing was that it had shapes like fins along its back, like a dinosaur or something." Louise took a photograph of her find to the Hancock Museum in Newcastle, where staff admitted they could not identify it – but mention of 'furry skin' reminds us strongly of several earlier strandings which turned out to be dead sharks, whose flesh often decomposes into white, fibrous tufts. *Shropshire Star, Eve. Standard, 28 May, AFP, 30 May; Newcastle Journal, 21 Aug 1996.*

1996 WAS a good year for monster sightings at Loch Ness.

The picture above was taken at about 4pm on 11 August by schoolmaster Austin Hepburn. He was standing on a hillside near Dores when he noticed a U-shaped wake ploughing north up the loch, and shot several frames using a telephoto lens from about 3/4 mile away. The results are suggestive of a boat wake – a common source of monster sightings on the loch – but Hepburn is sure he caught a solid black object in his zoom lens.

On 1 March John Northcote of Fort Augustus, at the south end of the loch, spotted a 'moving brown mass' in the water.

Coach driver Jimmy Burnett claimed on 8 March that he and two bus-loads of pupils saw the Loch Ness monster on school runs 20 minutes apart. Burnett, who had driven the route for 30 years, noticed ripples and a hump, and jumped from the bus with the nine pupils from Dochgarren primary school. Eilidh Barr, 11, said, "We saw a hump in the middle of the ripples, but we didn't see a head."

On 16 April, Nessie was seen by Lancashire disc-jockey Bill Kinder, and his wife and two children. He said, "It was shiny black, with a 30ft-long trail in the water."

On 13 June, Mrs Kate Munro, who runs the Craigcarroch House Hotel beside Loch Ness with her husband, was walking with her daughter-in-law when at about 10pm their attention was drawn to the water. "We saw a frothy disturbance on the loch, with a wake trailing behind it," she said. "It would have been something large and it zig-zagged quite a few times as an animal would do."

She went into the hotel and continued to watch it, joined by her husband Dave and 14 guests. The sightings lasted 5-10 minutes (reports differ), but nothing was seen on the surface. "There was no traffic on the loch at all,' said witness David Neeld, "yet here was a wake as big as comes from a cruiser. I do not think there is any explanation other than it was the Loch Ness monster." *Press release from Ken Macpherson Photography, Inverness; Nottingham Evening Star, 26 Sept 1995; Aberdeen Even. Express, D.Mirror, 9 Mar; Glasgow Herald, 17 April; [R] Dundee Eve. Telegraph, 15 June 1996.*

'FOOTPRINT' MYSTERY

A few years ago, we heard of the discovery of a bizarre line of 'footprints' on the flat, muddy bottom of Loch Ness. Sonar readings taken from a boat about a quarter of a mile out in the loch showed a line of small circular contacts – more than 30 in all – running parallel to the shore.

There was speculation that the strange contacts might have something to do with mines that were rumoured to have been sown in the loch during the First World War – but it was also said that the objects might be new, as nothing similar had shown up during Operation Deepscan's 1987 echo-sounder search of the lake.

Recently scientists working for Project Urquhart, the ongoing biological and limnological survey of the loch, re-investigated the contacts with a sophisticated underwater camera. The Project's remote-control Sea Owl minisub swooped down on a sample contact to discover... the remains of a wheelbarrow, apparently dumped over the side of a passing trawler. Could all 30 objects be similar junk? *Thanks to Yorkshire TV for the footage.*

WHEELBARROW: The sonar chart and the solution

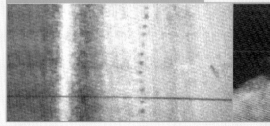

HOT SWEDISH VIDEO

SWEDEN'S MOST famous monster, the Storsjoodjuret (monster of Lake Storsjon) may have been recorded on video by Gun-Britt Widmark, 67, while boating on the lake off Ostersund with a party of old-age pensioners [left]. Whatever it was had humps and was 33-39ft (10-12m) long. "Every year we hear of people who have seen this beast," said Sten Rentzhog, president of the Ostersund Society for the Scientific Investigation of Lake Storsjon, who has collected hundreds of sighting accounts dating back to 1635. "There are probably a lot of witnesses who never tell anybody, for fear of ridicule." The previous winter, the society obtained some detailed descriptions. "There are even people who have seen the beast while they were diving," said Rentzhog. "Storsjoodjuret has been 'explained' in a number of ways – as ripples, gas bubbles, logs or misidentification of known animals – but none cover witnesses' descriptions adequately." *Expressen, 21 July 1996.*

Alien Implants

by Joe McNally

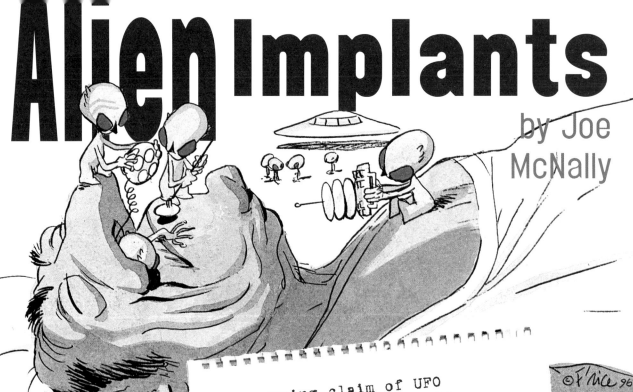

A recurring claim of UFO 'abductees' is that their captors have placed implants of some sort in their bodies for unknown purposes. Early in 1996, Fortean Times reported on an alleged recovery of some implants by a Californian doctor. Since then, the doctor involved has revealed more details about the curious history of what could prove to be the most important ufological event of the decade.

IN MARCH, 1995, the UFO magazine *ISCNI*Flash*, produced by the Institute for the Study of Contact with Non-human Intelligence, published details of what is potentially a major step in the study of alleged alien abductions. A Californian medic, Dr Roger Leir, claimed to have extracted three 'implants' from patients referred to him by a UFO researcher. Dr Leir has subsequently appeared at the July 1996 conference organised by the Mutual UFO Network (MUFON) and delivered an interim report on his research into the nature of the implants.

Alien abductees have claimed for many years that, among the many surgical indignities inflicted upon them by their alien captors, they have been implanted with small objects. Some believe that their purpose is the same as the rings, tags and similar marking systems used by earthly researchers to track animals which they have examined. Others suggest a more sinister purpose, hinting that the aliens may be implementing mind control technology.

Dr Leir, a podiatrist, was introduced to two patients, a man and a woman, by Houston abduction researcher Derrel Sims. They had been dealing with Sims because it was believed that they had a history of abductions. Leir, according to Philip Klass's *Skeptic's UFO Newsletter*, has been interested in UFOs since childhood. He and Sims had briefly shared a platform at a MUFON meeting in 1995, and he occasionally acted as a medical advisor to MUFON, but his introduction to the patients was apparently unconnected with UFO matters.

When Leir X-rayed the pair, he discovered that they both appeared to have foreign objects in their bodies. The woman had two in her big toe, on either side of the bone, and the man had one in his left hand, near the web of skin between his thumb and forefinger. Neither patient had previously claimed to have 'implants', or had complained of any associated pain. In both cases, there was no 'entry wound' or scar to mark the implants' site.

Sims interviewed Leir's patients about the implants, then ordered copies of their medical records; sadly, my sources make no mention of whether the mystery objects had any history in these records. Leir decided to press ahead with surgery, after more precisely locating the male patient's implant with a stud finder and a gauss meter, an instrument used to measure electromagnetic fields. This latter 'went crazy' when put near the implant, while the stud finder lit up brightly. The electromagnetic effect is reported to have disapperared once the implants

94

were removed, although the objects behaved as though they were magnetic during surgery, sticking to the scalpel blades.

Local anæsthetic was used for both patients' operations. Normally the type of anæsthetic used would numb the affected area for a period of six hours; however, Leir reported that while he was searching the woman's toe for the first 'implant' to be removed, he accidentally touched the object, and the woman "almost jumped off the table". According to Leir, this degree of reaction is normally only enountered under anæsthesia when something directly stimulates a nerve; a similar effect was observed in all three implant

MRI scan showing a large white area next to nose-bone of 'abductee'

sites on the two patients' bodies. When each 'implant' was extracted, both patients suffered a degree of pain in response, but felt 'liberated' afterwards. This led Dr Leir to conclude the objects had been somehow connected directly to nerves.

The first object removed from the woman's foot is described as roughly triangular, measuring about half a centimetre on each side. The object removed from the man's hand was "around the size of a cantaloupe seed". The extraction of all three objects was reported to have been filmed in front of witnesses.

Although they appeared to be metallic, the objects were surrounded by a tough membrane. This is normal for objects which have spent long periods of time embedded in body tissue; however, Leir found this membrane to be unusually tough – he was unable to cut it with a scalpel – while subsequent analysis suggested an unusual makeup. It eventually turned out to contain nothing more than blood, with flecks of hæmoglobin and an amount of keratin, the substance which makes up nails, hair and the epidermis. A great many nerve endings were reported to be present in the membrane, although none of the researchers has been able to say what significance this might have. In each case, the tissue and blood matched that of the subject; Dr Leir has suggested that the membranes were used to encase the implants before their insertion, in order to prevent rejection.

Sims then swung into action. He took the objects to Houston, where he exposed them to ultraviolet light, discovering that they glowed green. Derrel believes from his work with abductees that this can be indicative of alien involvement: he has found his subjects often have patches on their bodies which glow green under ultraviolet light. He ascribes this to physical contact between abductee and abductor, so it was no surprise that the implants proved to glow.

He then dried out the objects. The membrane surrounding them went brittle, and Derrel was able to scrape off a small sample and send it for analysis, yielding the results above. The first object, once the membrane was removed, was shiny, black and metallic. On removal it appeared triangular, but without the membrane it was found to be made of two pieces of metal tightly joined in a 'T' shape. The metal is also said to have glowed green under ultraviolet light.

In April, noted UFO author and abductee Whitley Streiber gave some details on the implants at the 'Day of Abductions' conference held in Sheffield. He spoke of the recording of the procedure, adding a couple of details not mentioned in the original ISCNI bulletin: "Everything in the surgery was [recorded] on video. What's interesting is that local anæsthetic wasn't enough, and the patients were also put under anæsthetic hypnosis." Anæsthetic hypnosis, as luck would have it, is a speciality of Derrel Sims.

Also featured at the conference was a hypnotic regressionist, Pauline Delcour-Min, who provided an explanation of why so many reported implants fail to show up under medical examination. Using a diagram showing different dimensions of existence, she explained that "many implants are in the astral body" – that implants may exist in a level above average human perception. This, we are told, drew a certain amount of flak from the floor.

Others are similarly disinclined to accept Leir and Sims' findings at face value. The well-known sceptical ufologist Philip J. Klass has devoted a good deal of time to their claims, and has come up with a number of objections. Firstly, there seems to be some inconsistency in the various accounts. For example, neither patient is said to have been aware of any 'implant'; however, the male patient – identified by Klass as Pat Parrinello – is reported to have been aware of the presence of the lump in his hand for over twenty years, and to have observed that it set off a stud finder in 1984. Less convincingly, Klass also objects that the 'implants' do not show any evidence of "having been fabricated by intelligent creatures for any useful purpose".

Whatever Klass's arguments, the fact remains that the analysis results, as they currently stand, offer no hard evidence either way. Nothing in the implants necessarily implies an alien origin. Moreover, Leir's reaction to the news that the membrane tissues matched those of the subjects might be taken as implying a too-well developed willingness to believe. Whatever the truth of the matter, it looks like we'll have to wait and see what develops.

SOURCES: ISCNI*Flash vol 1, no. 24; Skeptics UFO Newsletter no 41; report by Neil Nixon, FT90:8

the paranormal world

OOPs

Out Of Place animals (OOPs) are actually more common than the name implies, and older; we've all heard about alien big cats and wallabies in remote parts of Britain, but few appreciate that similar stories have been told for centuries. For example, enormous black swine were said, in Victorian times, to infest the sewers of Hampstead; mystery kangaroos have been seen over much of the USA for most of this century. Here are a few of the more interesting out-of-place and rare animals we've heard of this year.

SEE YOU LATER, ALLIGATOR

VALUABLE HUNTING DOGS had been disappearing in the Blackwater River State Forest near Pensecola, Florida, for nearly 20 years and owners had assumed thieves had taken then for resale. Then last August Rufus Godwin's hunting dog, Flojo, vanished near Coldwater Creek and he followed signals from the electronic tracking device on her collar.

James Sauls, who was with Godwin, also received signals from a collar worn by a dog he had last seen several weeks earlier. There was another response from a third collar that had been on a friend's dog. Their signals lead them to a 500lb alligator lurking in a hole. The 11ft reptile, which had turned a secluded game trail into its private fast-food restaurant, was captured on 15 August.

During the struggle, it spat out Flojo's tracking collar. Half of the dog was found in the stomach, which also contained six other collars including one from a dog that disappeared 14 years ago. One hunter estimated that up to 25 hunting dogs had disappeared in the swamp in the last two decades. The alligator was thought to be about 50 years old. *(R)* *29 Aug; D. Telegraph, 30 Aug 1995.*

FROM HULL OR HELL?

A RARELY SEEN sail-finned rough shark, 2½ feet long, black with large pointed teeth and a sandpaper feel to its skin, was dredged up by Scottish fishermen and bought at a Hull fishing market. It usually lives 800ft down, out of reach of most nets. The University of Hull plans to preserve the ugly creature. *D. Mail, 6 Oct 1995.*

BLUE REDFISH

Trawlerman Mattiasson holds the freak fish

AN UNPRECEDENTED blue Norway haddock or Redfish (*Sebastes marinus*) –'karfi' in Icelandic – was caught in deep water off Skejadyp, Iceland, in February 1995.

Kristján Egilsson, a member of staff at the Vestmannaeyjar museum of natural history, could find nothing about blue Redfish in any reference work. He examined the freak find and declared that he suspected fraud, but the trawlermen who caught it deny any imposture.

Oskar Matthíasson, one of the crew, said that they had been fishing with a very big net slung between two trawlers, the *Bylgjan* and the *Thórunn Sveinsdóttie*.

They often caught strange fish at such a depth, they said, and on this trip there had been very many. The Redfish was going to be stuffed. *Morgunbladid (Iceland), 25 Feb 1996.*

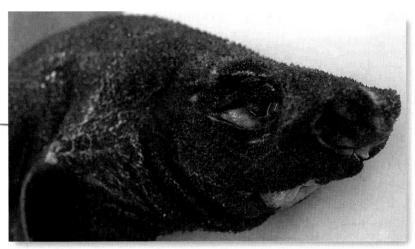

Space Update

Space, as Douglas Adams observed, is big. Given the Earth's status as a grain of sand in the Sahara of the galaxy, it's surprising that so little Fortean research looks beyond the circumference of our planet. The dramatic events of 1996, including the discovery of what might be life from Mars (see pp112-113), seem set to rekindle interest in what might lie above and beyond.

X-crescents

COMET HYAKUTAKE developed a bizarre, crescent-shaped, X-ray glow extending some 30,000 miles on 4 April. It was the first time X-rays have been detected coming from a comet, and scientists are at a loss to explain the observation

The comet, which last visited Earth 9,000-15,000 years ago, made its closest approach to our planet on 25 March, when it was 9.3 million miles away. Two days later there were signs that chunks had broken loose from its nucleus. *D. Telegraph, 9 Feb; NY Times 16+27 Mar; Sunday Telegraph 31 Mar 1996.*

LUNAR ARTEFACTS REPORTED

ON 21 MARCH 1996, Richard Hoagland called a press conference at the National Press Club in Washington DC. In what was billed "the announcement of the century" he promised to reveal startling photographs (suppressed by NASA for thirty years) of astronauts walking amid ancient ruins on the moon and fantastic structures to which he was given names like the Shard, the Castle and the City.

The speakers comprised former NASA scientists, engineers and other researchers who, under the aegis of The Mars Mission – renamed, at the eleventh hour, 'The Enterprise Mission' – issued a challenge to the White House to open up NASA files on "alien artefacts" and other lunar enigmas.

Some of their intriguing claims, hinting at an alien technology of incomprehensible scale, are:

THE SHARD – a 1.5-mile (2.5km)-tall, possibly helical, spire of meteorite-eroded glass.

THE CASTLE – "a geometric, glittering glass object hanging more than 9 miles (14.4km) above the surface of the Moon."

THE CUBE – a complex "megacube" on top of a 7-mile (11km)-high tower.

THE SPIRE – a 20-mile (32km)-tall intact version of the Shard, in the Mare Crisium.

THE CITY – A Los Angeles-sized city-block grid pattern in the north-east Ukert region with a peculiar square crater.

A NUMBER of "glass-like, highly complex domes" in various locations and states of ruin.

Richard Hoagland has no doubt that the purpose of President Kennedy's all-out Apollo Program was to get American astronauts to the lunar ruins first and to bring back any physical evidence they could find. "We are 30 years behind were we would have been – if NASA had been allowed to tell us what they found, at the time the photographs were taken," he says. "It's time for

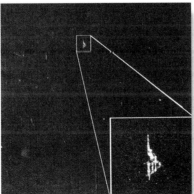

the President to bite the bullet, to open NASA's files on all of this, and come clean."

Establishment forces resist Hoagland's ideas vigorously, putting up experts such as geologist Paul Lowman of the Goddard Spaceflight Center against him. "Hoagland is seeing some kind of processing effect," Lowman told the *Washington Post*. However, if the Lovecraftian shattered domes and floating castles seen by the Enterprise Mission are errors of misidentification and misinterpretation, then they are remarkably persistent ones, presenting themselves consistently for four years to extremely close scrutiny, using every known method of optical analysis. Hoagland remains convinced that, as with the Cydonian enigmas of Mars, the only solution is an un-manned survey expedition. *Sources: Enterprise Mission news releases, and their web site **http://www.enterprisemission.com/**. Washington Post, 22 Mar; Dallas (TX) Morning News, 1 April 1996. Special thanks to Matthew Porter.*

LUNAR PICS: Clockwise from top: a 'shattered crystalline city'; a castle hanging miles above the lunar surface; and 'the shard' (below cross), 1.5 miles high and made of glass. Apparently.

the natural world

Weird People

No matter how weird the stories of aliens, manimals and lake monsters in FT are, it seems the human race is always able to come up with something weirder. Some people just seem determined to push the envelope of odd behaviour. Not for them mere fumblings, mutterings and twitches of the simply eccentric; they prefer the wilder shores of out and out incomprehensibility.

POLICE IN NEW ZEALAND have been baffled by an apparent trend among early-risers in the city of Christchurch for walking domestic appliances instead of dogs. On 7 May, a man walking his dog in the Parklands saw two fellow peregrinators apparently trying to 'walk' a wall oven. Two days later, a woman answered loud knocking at her door at 5.15am to be confronted by a man holding a colour television set. He said he was having difficulty finding his way off her property and appealed for help. She obliged and then checked that the television set was not hers.

Ten minutes later, the police – who had been called to a neighbouring property on an unrelated matter – found the man still clutching the television. Inquiries revealed that the TV did indeed belong to the man, but he could not explain why he was wandering around in the dark with it. "It has left us wondering if there are not enough dogs to go round," said a bemused Senior Sergeant Kortegast. *NZPA, 11 May 1996.*

DAVID GRIFFITHS was expelled from the Conservative Association in Twickenham, west London, after making a speech to an audience of two people in York House in August 1995. Among other outrageous views, he had urged that all criminals should be killed, all homosexuals should commit suicide, and those claiming social security benefit should gun each other down in the streets.

In January 1996, he announced that he would be standing as the Antichrist in the next General Election. Griffiths, 35, who admits he was given a suspended sentence for assaulting a friend, claims to have known he was the Antichrist for some time, but kept it to himself for fear it would damage his political career. His campaign for the Twickenham seat – currently held by Conservative MP Toby Jessel – is being financed by a £37,000 legacy left to him in his parents' will. He is circulating a 44-page manifesto in an attempt to woo voters. *Richmond & Twickenham Times, 19 Jan 1996.*

CHRIS P. CARROT'S plan to campaign against animal cruelty dressed as a 7ft (2.1m) carrot backfired when he visited a Texas school. The headmaster told children he was an example of why they must not talk to strangers. *S. Express, 17 Sept 1995.*

IN 1993, Judge Leslie Isaiah Gaines saw the face of Jesus on a marble pillar in Hamilton County Courthouse, Cincinnati. In February 1996, he left the bench to become an evangelist and 'motivational speaker'. Gaines, a man known for his orotund style, also hosts a weekly radio show, composes blues songs, and once wrote a rap extolling the Cincinnati quarterback Jeff Blake. *Las Vegas Review-Journal, 3 Jan 1996*

IT WAS the perfect disguise. Balding and pale with thick glasses, no-one would have believed that 59-year-old Barry Briskman was an extraterrestrial – except for three young girls. He was, however, a very earthy man with a mission, or rather an obsession, to have sex with underage girls, and he had hit upon the ruse of pretending to be from another planet.

Briskman, from planet Los Angeles, was already serving a 10-year sentence in Nevada for seducing a 12-year-old girl with this trick when he was sentenced to a further 20 years for assaulting two 13-year-old girls in the Tropicana Hotel, Las Vegas. Briskman told the girls, all runaways, that he was from Cablell, an all-Caucasian planet ruled by Queen Hiternia, and was currently ensconced at the Tropicana, having

parked his spaceship at Lake Tahoe. He painted a picture of a wonderful world where the unhappy girls could do what they wanted. He allowed the girls a great deal of freedom. "He would let them drink and smoke cigarettes – they thought he was cool," said prosecutor Steven Ipsen.

Briskman's story was that he had to recruit a team of females of superior beauty and intelligence to take back to Cablell; but first, he told the girls, he had to break down their 'sub-cons' (subconscious intelligence barriers) in order to double their IQs. This involved a superior Hiternian process that would appear to earthlings to be very similar to a game of strip poker after a few drinks.

The girls were still not ready for space travel; they had to acquire special immunities (which he called IRFs) to space diseases – and the quickest way known to wise space folk of acquiring these IRFs was through sexual intercourse. After each session of 'injections', Briskman would appear to phone 'Andy', the Cablellian master computer, Andrak 4000, which confirmed the girls' new IRF rating.

The offences occurred in 1990, and came to light when the family of one of the girls went to police. "He's a classic paedophile," said Det. John Vannerson of the LA Police Department's unit investigating the sexual exploitation of children. "He spins a magical, seductive tale."

One victim, a former child actress who is now 18, conceded, "He led me to believe many things. I wanted to believe them. He manipulated us... I didn't know I was going to have sex with him when I started. He started out gradually. It was a team. We were going to be the best of friends."

The US trial system allows victims to make statements in court about the impact of the crime on their lives. One girl said she wanted to forget and move on, admitting, "He's a gross, perverted, hairy old man and he makes me sick. I trusted him as a father figure and he betrayed our trust." *Los Angeles Times, 16 Sept 1995.*

NEW YORK POLICE are hunting for a burglar who breaks into homes and makes porridge. He (or she) has struck ten times and never steals anything. *D. Record, 15 Sept 1995.*

ACCORDING TO the Manchester Metro News (2 Jan 1996), "Police called to arrest a naked man on the platform at Piccadilly station on New Year's Eve released their suspect after he produced a valid ticket."

SEAN GALE, 33, stopped for erratic driving outside Clonmel, in the Republic of Ireland, was found to be steering with a pair of pliers. "The steering wheel came off when we were visiting the mother-in-law," he told police. *D. Record, 10 July 1995.*

POLICE IN EUREKA, California, are hunting a woman who has been grabbing babies from total strangers and breast-feeding them. "Every child needs lactate nourishment," she told a shocked mother during the latest incident. *AP, 23 Apr 1996.*

AN ANIMAL rights group has tried to get an American village to change its name. It says that the name of Fishkill, in New York State, should change its name to something more compassionate, like Fishsave. Mayor George Carter isn't having it. "I'm not going to change the name of Fishkill. It's been such a long, outstanding name," he told reporters. Animal rights group People for the Ethical Treatment of Animals asked Carter to consider changing the name in a letter in August. The mayor, however, says the name has stood since the late 1600s. Fishkill, 65 miles north of New York City, traces its name to the original Dutch settlers; 'kill' means 'stream' in Dutch. *AP, 6 Sept 1996.*

OBITUARY

KARL WATKINS

KARL WATKINS, a stalwart of *FT*'s weird sex pages in the past, is dead. Karl first came to our attention in 1993, when he appeared at Hereford Crown Court on five counts of outraging public decency – specifically, making love to pavements and, on one occasion, an underpass. Two years later, in February 1995, he was back in court charged with simulating sex with several black plastic dustbin liners in front of a group of schoolgirls. This time, he was given probation on condition that he seek psychiatric help. This apparently didn't work; he was convicted of gross indecency and jailed for six years by Wolverhampton Crown Court in April after a similar performance. It was announced in the *Walsall Observer* on September 6th that he had been found dead in his cell at Wandsworth Prison.

KILLER LAKE STRIKES AGAIN

A LAKE associated with a double child-murder has claimed seven more lives. Susan Smith drowned her two young sons by letting her car roll into John D Long Lake, South Carolina, on 25 October 1994. On 31 August 1996 a party of ten people had parked near the memorials to the two boys when their car, containing an adult and four children, somehow rolled into deep water. All the occupants were drowned, as well as two other adults who attempted a rescue. *[AP] Austin (TX) American-Statesman, Dallas Morning News, 2 Sept; Daily Yomiuri, 3 Sept; Times, 4 Sept 1996.*

JOHN D LONG LAKE: Two multiple drownings in cars in as many years.

While other countries may corner the market in sheer out-and-out supernatural and paranormal weirdness, there seems to be a vein of surrealism in US society which gives its citizens a particular gift for strange behaviour. Perhaps it's something in the water...

THE SAGA of the white buffalo calf continued in 1996. The calf was born in Wisconsin in August 1994, and was hailed as the return of the White Buffalo Woman, a figure from native American folklore, and thus a major religious event. Since then, the calf has grown a permanent, darker coat, especially round her face, neck and legs. Many native Americans continue to regard the calf as a sacred messenger, symbolising impending unity and prosperity. Some commentators have claimed that the buffalo's white coat will return, heralding immense changes in the world. Shades of the ghost dance. *Philadelphia Enquirer, 2 Dec 1994.*

SOME WEEKS AFTER the Oklahoma bomb of 1995, a leg was found in the rubble. Officials released a statement claiming that it did not belong to any of the 168 known victims of the blast. This immediately led to speculation that the leg, clad in a military boot, belongs to the 'real bomber'. However, in February, the leg was identified as belonging to a previously identified female victim, meaning the death toll returned to 168. The FBI used DNA and footprints to match the leg to Airwoman Lakesha Levy, 21, who had been buried with the wrong left leg. *Denver Post, 24 Feb 1996.*

CALIFORNIAN NATURALISTS were baffled by the cause of hundreds of deaths among female sea-lions. Every year, the bodies of around 40 crushed females were found littering a cove near San Miguel island off the Californian cost. At first fishermen were suspected of shooting them, but then Robert DeLong, a National Marine Fisheries biologist, spotted a massive bull sea-lion mating with a female. She was gasping, and died within a minute.

The bull is a cross between a California and a Stellar's sea-lion, and he seems confused about everything from the time he should breed to the way to go about it. Male California sea-lions usually weigh about 900lb (400kg), but the hybrid weighs around 1,800lb (725kg), eight times the weight of an average female. This year, wardens decided to shoot the hybrid, dubbed 'the Marauder of San Miguel Island', if he showed up again, but hoped he would have met his end while wintering in the Antarctic. *D. Telegraph, 17 Oct 1995; the CNN Website (http://www.cnn.com), 3 June 1996.*

BODYBUILDER LOU FERRIGNO, who played the Incredible Hulk on television, lost his rag when a Los Angeles traffic warden gave him a parking ticket. Barnadine Morgan says Ferrigno smashed the windscreen with his fists, and is suing for emotional distress. Ferrigno, meanwhile, insists that it happened accidentally when he threw up his hands in frustration. *D. Mail, 23 Oct 1995.*

TWENTY-SIX YEARS after he disappeared without trace in Vietnam and 17 years after the Army declared him dead, Master Sergeant Mateo Sabog has turned up alive. And the 70-year-old is still in the Army. His name is on the Vietnam Veterans' Memorial, and in April 1995 the Vietnamese government returned human remains they said were his. Sabog showed up at a Social Security Administration office in Rossville, Georgia, in late February to apply for benefits. It remains unclear how he managed to remain institutionally invisible until now, or why he suddenly chose to reappear. He was unable to produce any papers to prove his identity, but a fingerprint examination showed that he was indeed the missing veteran. "This is all a shock to us," said his sister-in-law, Kay Sabog, in Hawaii. "We assumed he was dead and gone." Where had he been? We await further news. *New York Times, 7 Mar 1996.*

DAVID LYNN JUSTICE, 21, was jailed for 30 years last June for abducting two women at gunpoint outside a Houston restaurant in December 1993, making them buy Twinkie snack cakes and caffeine pills, then forcing them on a tour of Christmas lights. "He was depressed and wanted company," apparently. *AP, 22 Jun 1995.*

He Lost His Head

In February, Britain played host to an unusual overseas visitor - Chief Nicholas Gcalecka, a South African 'witchdoctor' in search of the head of a glorious ancestor. How did he get on?

PRACTITIONERS OF MAGIC and shamanism the world over have always believed that a human head or skull, whether of an ancestor or a defeated enemy, is a potent object which links the dead with the living; but to Westerners the very idea of any part of the human body being used or tampered with after death is something which is deeply abhorrent and inherently pagan in nature. When these two viewpoints are brought face to face, the results can reflect interestingly on both cultural views.

On 15 February, Chief Nicholas Tilana Gcalecka flew into Britain from South Africa on a quest for the magical skull of his great-great uncle, King Hintsa of the Xhosa people, who had been killed in 1835 during the Sixth Frontier War.

A certain George Southey had shot the king as be tried to escape the battlefield. An inquiry determined that Hintsa's corpse had been mutilated; it did not say how or by whom. The king's remains were left on the banks of the Nqabara river, and according to Xhosa tradition, his head was missing.

Chief Gcalecka, a businessman turned *sangoma* (traditional healer or 'witchdoctor') explained: "I was submerged in a river for 40 days and during that time I was told by the great snake [an ancestral ghost] that the head was in Scotland," after having been taken there as a war trophy. The king's headless spirit meanwhile was wandering South Africa, causing crime and violence. The skull's return would put an end to this, and it would also help Gcalecka's bid to inherit his ancestor's title and estates.

The media made great play of the chief's theatrical costume – beaded hair, leopardskin, fly whisk and dodgy-looking spear – and he became a talk-show celebrity for a few days. He maintained the skull was in Fort George, near Inverness, but he had no luck there. Several other regimental museums denied all knowledge. Captain Frank Ward of Army HQ Scotland said that George Southey's brother William had cut off 'only' the king's ears.

Undeterred, the chief kept dreaming. He said the spirit of the hurricane told him the skull lay buried in a field containing a white pony beside a river. And sure enough, as is the way of these things, on 23 February a skull duly materialised. Landowner Charles Brooke from Argay, Easter Ross, came forward with a skull which had been dug up 130 years ago in a field next to the Dornoch Fifth in which the family used to keep two white ponies. It even appeared to have a bullet hole.

Chief Gcalecka was overwhelmed. "I have never been so happy in all my life," he said. "This is the moment I have been waiting for. I woke today singing and jumping with joy because I knew this was going to be the day the dream brought by the spirits came true." He later told reporters that meditation with his tribal spirits confirmed the head was his great-great uncle's.

Shortly after the chief's triumphant return to South Africa clutching the head, the Xhosa King Xolilizwe Sigcau declared that the head was not that of his ancestor and refused to let it be reburied. Sadly, genetic and anthropological testing carried out on behalf of the Xhosa Royal Council has proved that this is the case. The skull in fact belonged to a European woman.

It had already been pointed out that the 'bullet wound' was clearly nothing of the sort; the fracture patterns were apparently more consistent with trepanning, leading one expert to speculate that the skull may have been of a trepanned Scottish monk. In July, Chief Gcalecka was contemplating legal action for the return of the skull.

Aberdeen Press & Journal, 1 Mar; *D. Telegraph*, 15 Jan, 16+22+24 Feb, 2 Mar, 26 Aug; *Guardian*. 22+24 Feb; *Independent on Sunday*, 25 Aug; *Independent*, 8 Feb; *Observer*, 7 Jan; *Reuters* 8 Mar; *S. Times* 25 Aug; *Star & SA Times International*, 3 July; *Times*, 24 Feb, 26 Aug; *Yorkshire Post*, 15 Feb 1996.

UNDER THE INFLUENCE: Spirits led Chief Nicholas Gcalecka to the Scottish highlands and this skull, supposedly that of his great-great uncle, King Hintsa. It wasn't.

the human world

Swarms

Swarms and invasions of animals are another perennial topic of Fortean interest. While not obviously weird or inexplicable, occasionally a group of animals will do something so out of the ordinary, funny or even inconvenient that it begs to be classed as Fortean. Naturally, we are happy to oblige.

NEXT TIME you find yourself cursing a train delayed because of leaves on the line, or the wrong sort of snow, spare a thought for travellers on the Casablanca-Fez line in Morocco. In May, an express train was brought to a slippery halt by a horde of snails which had slithered on to the track. The line was blocked for several hours, 87 miles (140km) north of Rabat, near the town of Meknes. Heavy rain had enticed the snails from under cover and, mysteriously, they often congregated at that spot on the railway track. *AP 16 May 1996.*

THE CELEBRATED MONARCH BUTTERFLY migration in northern California was down to a sad trickle this year, with the numbers of butterflies down to the lowest in living memory. Arthur Shapiro, an entomologist at the University of California at Davis, said he had never seen so few butterflies. He estimated populations were down 10 per cent.

The decline may be of disaster proportions; at the heart of the Athe area where the monarchs winter, naturalist Jan Southworth found that the usual count of around 12,000 was down to just one per cent. Naturalists agree that the large number of storms during the winter of 1994/95 was to blame. Drenched vegetation bred fungal and bacterial diseases at the time the pupae were developing. Of the few that hatched, most couldn't fly, mate or lay eggs before the next storm put an end to them. *NY Times, 1 April 1995.*

HUNDREDS OF VIEWERS on the Scottish island of Iona, a television black spot, lost their picture after a swarm of earwigs broke into the island's transmitter box and ate some of the components. *News of the World, 14 Jan 1996.*

A HERD OF SHEEP committed mass suicide in a lake in Inner Mongolia on 17 July last year, refusing to return to shore despite frantic efforts by their Chinese shepherd to save them. Two goats jumped into the 1.5m-deep water, prompting the rest to follow. After a three-hour rescue aided by 20 herdsmen, 281 sheep were rescued, while the other 249 animals, including 206 goats, drowned. Some of the rescued animals tried to jump back in. Veterinary experts had no explanation for this unusual behaviour. An enquiry was planned. *Daily Yomiuri (Japan), Le Matin (Benin), 4 August 1995.*

POLICE RAIDED the home of an elderly woman in Toulouse, southern France, on 26 March and found she was living with 1,000 rats, which she fed with 33lb of grain every day. She slept on the floor, surrounded by cats who were tormented and bitten by the rats, although they had apparently not bitten the woman. Officials planned to kill the colony of rodents. In May 1994, a woman feeding cereal to rats in her New York apartment and singing to them had also surrendered her bed to them while she slept in a chair.

Pamela Drew, an eccentric recluse, died of blood poisoning in her Bournemouth flat on 20 January 1995. She had dozens of cages containing domestic white rats and an unknown number had escaped and were living in the wall cavities and furniture. *AP 27 Mar 1996; Boston Globe May 1994; Western Daily Press 29 Mar 1995.*

SOME YEARS AGO *Fortean Times* reported on the menace of the New Zealand flatworm, an invader to British shores with no natural predators native to the islands. It seems we were too hasty in proclaiming it free of predators; hopes for containing the problem are being pinned on the larvae of some common British beetles. The unlikely Home Guard was discovered by accident during a study of the flatworms.

Worms stained red and green were released into a controlled allotment by scientists at the Institute of Cell, Animal and Population Biology at Edinburch University. Dr Derek Cosens commented: "We were surprised to find beetle larvae which had also turned red and green, which meant they must have eaten the flatworms." Andrew Halstead, chief entomologist of the Royal Horticultural Society's garden at Wisley in Surrey, greeted the news cautiously. "We do not know how effective the beetle will be. It will have a choice of many other things to eat." *Times, 9 June 1995.*

Paranormal

The paranormal is an area of study which many people immediately associate with Fortean Times. In fact, actual paranormal events - ghosts, curses, possession and the like - account for a surprisingly small percentage of our postbag. That's not to say that it never piques our interest; here's a spooky selection of the year's highlights...

KNEECAPS

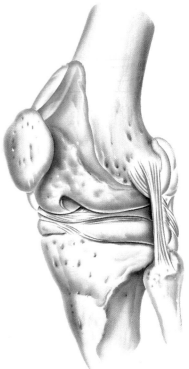

CULTISTS raided dozens of tombs in a southern Philippine province and stole kneecaps in the belief that they could be turned into amulets that protect against bullets. The raiders destroyed 25 tombs in two towns in Agusan del Sur on Easter Day in 1994. According to a former cultist, the kneecaps have to be removed at the stroke of midnight on Easter Day to maximise their effectiveness. The raiders were said to belong to two cults that police had enlisted in the fight against communist insurgency. One of these cults is known as Tadtad ("Chop") after its reputation for chopping up and beheading some of its victims.

Kneecap thieves were at it again in August 1995, but this time their presumed motive was quite different. Police in the central town of Bacolod investigated when residents in nearby Bago complained of hearing nocturnal hammering in a cemetary. Kneecaps were missing from 12 tombs. It was believed they were ground into powder and burned like incense near a house earmarked for robbery. The smoke is supposed to make the occupants fall asleep long enough for the looting to take place. *Reuter, 12 Apr 1994, 7 Aug 1995.*

GHOSTLY FACE IN OFFICIAL PHOTO

THE PHOTOGRAPH below, of the Maintenance Group of *HMS Daedalus*, was taken on the runway at Cranwell in Lincolnshire in 1919. The man half-concealed in the back row, Freddy Jackson, had actually been killed three days earlier, on the same tarmac strip, after stumbling into a whirling propeller. Some of those in the picture, taken by Bassano's Photographic Company to commemorate the disbanding of the transport yard at the base, had marched behind his coffin at the military funeral.

Bobbie Capel, 97, widow of Air Vice Marshal Arthur Capel, was a Wren driver at the base and has no doubt that the face peeping out from the back row is Jackson. She recalls the general astonishment when the photo was pinned up. Her neighbours in the Somerset village of Chipstable recently persuaded her to send the photograph to the *Navy*

News with a plea for other witnesses to come forward.

The photo had been mentioned in *Flight Towards Reality* by Air Marshal Sir Victor Goddard, one of the founders of the RAF. "What is somewhat unusual, to say the least, is that this is an official photograph... also the certainty that there had been no hanky-panky in the dark-room. Not only would Bassano's not have dared to fake it; the negative was scrutinised for faking and was found to be untouched."

Capel said: "I cannot entertain the idea that this was a deliberate fake. For one, the photographer came from outside the base. He didn't know any of us, and once he had taken his picture he left immediately. He just would not have known about the accident... I can think of no other explanation other than that it is the picture of a ghost." *Navy News, May; D. Mail, 1 July 1996.*

DEAD MAN IN THE CREW: Freddy Jackson's ghostly face (to the right in inset) in the official photograph

the paranormal world

Country File AUSTRALIA

TROUT SUIT

ON NOVEMBER 29TH, 1995, the corpse of Neil Wilson was found in a field nearly a kilometre from the nearest body of water, Toolondo Lake, in the semi-arid western regions of Victoria, Australia. His body was completely encased in a fish costume. "Mr Wilson was wearing a heavy, green plastic body suit which he had made from old waterbed material from the tip," according to police.

Toolondo has only about 10 houses and most of these are holiday homes, vacant for most of the year. Wilson had had a house in Toolondo for the past 20 years. The isolation and lack of human contact seemed to appeal to him; he was known locally as a person who liked to keep himself to himself. His first love was the lake, where, encased in his fish suit, he would while away the hours in fishy meditations, supported only by a rope from an overhanging tree while he swung and swam in the cool waters.

Police Officer Allen, who found the body, was guarded in his comments to *FT*'s intrepid investigator Richard Gwynn-Seary, but he did describe the fish suit. "It had round holes for eyes, but no holes for the nose or mouth and no other ventilation. It covered the hands and feet. Both legs fitted into the one 'leg' and the suit zipped up the back with a single large zipper. If you got a bandage and wrapped a person up like a mummy, that's what it was like. He had sewn the suit together himself and he must have put a lot of work into it."

Wilson's body was found a fair distance from the lake, apparently heading for his home some 640ft (200m) away. There were no vehicle tracks nearby, no signs of any other human contact, and no sign of any 'track' that Wilson might have been expected to leave if he had wriggled from the lake. If he had left the lake in his suit, it would have taken him some 14 hours to reach the spot where he was found. He certainly couldn't walk in the suit, and at best could only hop. One is almost led to the conclusion that he was somehow teleported from the lake. Police suspect, but this is by no means certain or an 'official' explanation, that Wilson may have committed a 'bizarre form of suicide'. How Wilson even managed to breathe in the tight-fitting suit is something of a mystery.

An autopsy was performed on his badly decomposed body, but the cause of death has not been established. The body may have lain in the field for up to a week before being discovered, and a corpse encased in plastic in hot and humid weather soon rots.

After the body's discovery, police searched Wilson's home and found another fish suit, this time made of orange plastic. *From reports by Richard Gwynn-Seary aided by Paul Cropper, John Standing and Heather Kennedy.*

KILLER: Does the fierce Tasmanian Tiger still survive 5,000 years after its supposed extinction on the Australian mainland?

TIGER, TIGER

AT LEAST FIFTEEN sightings in the past eight years of a mysterious striped dog-like animal have raised hopes that *Thylacine cynocephalus* is alive and well in Queensland. Although the beast is popularly known as the Tasmanian Tiger, Aboriginal rock paintings on the mainland indicate that it once roamed Australia too.

Dr Lance Mesh, 56, a dentist, had a sighting while driving along the southern slopes of the Buderim rainforest one evening last spring with his daughter. "It was striped and like a combination of a goldy, brindly cat and a dog," he said. "It was medium-sized and had a prominent bump above the eyes. My headlights froze him, he arched his back and crouched before running off the road into the rainforest."

The description matched that of a creature seen one afternoon in July 1983 by artist Leone Dennis while driving with her husband Greg along the Coolum-Yandina road. It had dark stripes on its rump and was brindled. Other recent witnesses to a similar striped creature include Ron and Mandy West of Buderim.

Meanwhile, the other famous crypto-beast of the Queensland forest, the so-called Queensland marsupial tiger, continues to be glimpsed in remote areas. A team of local naturalists plans a high-tech expedition to the Gainsborough Valley, south of Cairns, where it has been heard if not seen.

Typical of the experiences of Valley residents is that of 'Wharfie' Mark Campion, whose dog was terrified by a weird growling. "I was watching TV on the back verandah," he said. "Rusty's afraid of nothing, but all of a sudden, his hair was standing up along his back and he was staring out into the night, shaking like mad."

As similar reports circulated about the 'night growler', hopes are high once again of spotting a beast many consider long extinct. *Brisbane Sunday Mail, 18+25 June 1995.*

Discoveries

There's nothing new under the sun, St Paul said several centuries ago. Whether by new developments in science, or ancient remains turned up, he's been proved wrong on a regular basis ever since... Here's a round-up of this year's most unusual discoveries.

THE DIVER BIRDS

VIVID PICTURES of a sleek black-and-white bird transmitted from a camera surveying 292ft (89m) down in the North Sea have surprised scientists, who identified it as a common guillemot. These birds have paddle-like wings so they can 'fly' underwater. They dive to catch small fish and sand eels. However, no bird has ever been observed diving so deeply into the North Sea.

The camera operator on the Ocean Nomad oil rig, 100 miles (160km) east of Aberdeen in Shell's Guillemot field (appropriately!) thought at first he had seen a penguin, but his colleagues pointed out that the oil rig was thousands of miles from any penguin habitat.

The bird can be seen quite clearly on the video for about 30 seconds, swimming round in circles. Ian Bainbridge of the Royal Society for the Protection of Birds said, "This is amazing. The deepest we have ever known a guillemot to dive is 197ft (60m). Humans at that same depth have to hide in diving bells or reinforced suits."

Sarah Wanless, who studies seabird diving, said there was evidence of guillemots reaching depths of 630ft (192m) while a razorbill was seen from a submarine at 430ft (131m). She said guillemots probably dived to great depths, but recording them doing so was difficult. How such comparatively small creatures – about 16in (40cm) long – evolved the ability to carry out such diving feats is unknown. *Glasgow Herald, Scotsman, Guardian, 9 May 1996.*

COLONY FOUND

THE SITE of the first post-Columbus European colony in the USA may have been found. Pieces of 16th-century French pottery are said to prove that the colony of Charlesfort (!) lies beneath a golf course on the US Marine base at Parris Island, near Beaufort, South Carolina.

The colony was built by an expedition of 150 Huguenots, led by Jean Ribaut, which landed in May 1562, about 20 years before the first English settlement at Roanoke, Virginia. As soon as the tiny fort was built, Ribaut returned to France for fresh supplies and more settlers, leaving behind a garrison of 27 men. He promised to be back within six months, but was diverted to England by civil war in France and was jailed as a Huguenot spy. At Charlesfort, fire destroyed most of the supplies, the men rebelled and killed their commanding officer, and about 11 months after the settlement was started, the mutineers sailed for France. The colony was recorded by both the French and the Spanish, but disappeared without trace.

The Spanish estabished their first colony at St Augustine, Florida, in 1565 and a year later built Santa Elana in South Carolina. Dr Chester DePlatter and Stanley South, archæologists at the University of South Carolina, were excavating Santa Elena when they realised that evidence pointed to Charlesfort being on the same site.

After the French abandoned Charlesfort, only a servant boy called Ruffi, who had taken refuge with the local Indians, stayed behind. It was he who led the Spanish to the site, where they used the moat and foundation to start their own settlement. *D. Telegraph, Guardian, 7 June 1996.*

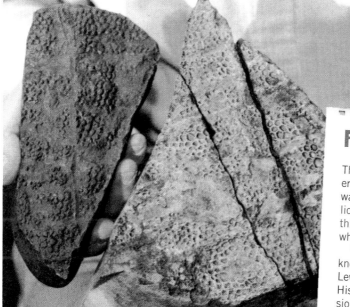

Fossil skin with knobs on

The fossilised skin of a duck-billed dinosaur was discovered in 1991 near Deming in southern New Mexico, and was at first thought to be fossil tree bark. The 70-million-year-old fossil is 10ft (3m) long and 2ft (60cm) thick. The skin is rough, thick and bumpy, with somewhat symmetrical clumps of little crimped-edged knobs.

"It's so weird that as a trained palæontologist I didn't know what the hell it was for five years," said Spencer Lewis, who works at the New Mexico Museum of Natural History and Science. About a dozen such skin impressions have been discovered around the world. *AP, 1 April 1996.*

Attacks by Animals

We've all seen the disaster movies where nature turns against mankind. Usually, the movies give us giant sharks, killer bees and even enormous murderous caterpillars. In real life, attacks tend to come from more prosaic quarters, but remain baffling nonetheless...

IN EMERGENCY, BEAK GLASS

Our correspondent Carl Pendle told us of a small country house near Chichester, West Sussex, which was beseiged by rooks for two days. The blitz started at 4am on Sunday, 9 June, when the birds started to hurl themselves against the windows, pecking at the glass.

Rosemarie Dunnatt, who lives in the house with her husband and three-year-old daughter Charlotte, said the experience was terrifying. Charlotte was the first to be disturbed by a tapping noise on her window. Pulling back the curtains, she was shocked to see a yellow-eyed feathered fiend flapping against the frame and pecking at the double-glazing.

The converted barn is named Owl House, but no owls or other birds had caused any problems since the family moved in a year ago. However, Mrs Dunnatt said: "This is not the first time we have been attacked by birds. At our other house we had some problems with magpies." During the latest attack, Mrs Dunnatt attached pieces of string and paper to the windows and hung models of other birds from the frames, but nothing worked. A spokesman for the RSPCA said the phenomenon was unusual, but not paranormal; it was often caused by rooks mistaking their reflection for other rooks which they then try to drive away. A local farmer has suggested that, if it happens again, they should capture a rook with a rat trap and hang its body upside-down for the other birds to see.

Screaming Gulls

A HIGH-PITCHED RECORDING of a bird in distress was set up to scare off the resident seagulls in Staithes in North Yorkshire. However, the wailing attracted hundreds of other gulls who swooped in to see what was wrong. Tourists dived for cover and locals prepared for a major clean-up as a screeching black cloud descended on the village. Scarborough Council soon abandoned the scheme and began examining other ways of dispersing the birds. *Wolverhampton Express & Star, D. Mirror, D. Telegraph, 5 Aug 1995.*

ROAD HOGS

FARM WORKER JAMIE EASTWOOD, 25, drove two pigs for treatment at a farm in Elmsham, South Humberside, and had the porkers sitting next to him in the cab of the JCB. As he carried the first pig inside, the second pig moved to the driving seat and nudged the gear lever. The vehicle rolled forwards and Eastwood was knocked over and trapped by the leg. He was stuck for ten minutes until a woman passing by heard his shouts for help, bundled the pig back into the passenger seat and put the digger into reverse. Eastwood was not seriously hurt, but was off work for several days. Farm owners R.J. and A.E. Godfrey were subsequently fined £2,500 on March 13th after safety inspectors found that the digger's handbrake was out of order. *Sun, 14 Mar; Weekend Telegraph 13 Apr 1996.*

WOBURNT

STEVE AND JANE Marshall from Cambridge took their two children and Mrs Marshall's mother for a day-trip to Woburn Safari Park in Bedfordshire on 7 August last year. In the tiger reserve, smoke started to pour from the engine of their Renault Espace. Rangers placed Land Rovers beside the car to protect them from the nine tigers. The engine finally burst into flames just as they got out. *D. Telegraph, 8 Aug 1995.*

VALENTIN GRIMALDO, 40, was out walking with his brother near Encino, Texas, when he was bitten on the hand by a coral snake. He bit its head off, skinned it and used it as a tourniquet to keep the venom from spreading. He is expected to recover. *AP, 11 May 1996.*

Hoaxes and Panics

Certain Fortean phenomena are often explained as 'mass hysteria', a supposedly medical condition with very little evidence to back up its existence. There is no doubt that sometimes a story can cause hysteria and panic among those who hear it, often because it has been created to do just that; but there are many other occurrences which cannot be explained away so easily.

Roll-over abuse

JIM PHILLIPS, a child abuse counsellor from Birmingham, has said that three of his clients mentioned incidents at the Rollright stones in Oxfordshire (see 'Secret Country', pp114-115), and claimed to have witnessed people killed and buried in a field nearby. Local police at Chipping Norton dismissed the claims. *Oxford Times, 22 Dec 1995.*

GLORIA MIASMA

DESPITE BEING only two years old, the Riverside Miasma case has become one of the best-known of recent Fortean events. Gloria Ramirez died at the Riverside Hospital, California, in February 1994. There was a strange oily sheen on her skin, and emergency-room staff near the body were felled by 'invisible fumes'. Dr Julie Gorchynski suffered liver and lung damage and bone necrosis; 23 other people were also affected. Two theories predominated: either the mass collapse was due to 'hysteria' or cancer-stricken Ramirez had taken a cocktail of medicines which had combined to make a nerve gas.

To prove the nerve-gas theory, proposed by Patrick Grant at Lawrence Livermore Laboratories, an experiment was filmed to show how the chemical DMSO (sometimes used to carry other drugs) might be oxygenated in the bloodstream and converted into the nerve-gas dimethylsulphoxide. The experiment failed. Until Channel 4 tried to replicate the process, most people – including Riverside County Coroner Scotty Hill – had bowed to Grant's authority and rejected the 'mass hysteria' explanation. In particular, it offered a scientific alternative for the feminist lobby supporting the female emergency-room team in their protest at being 'derogatorily' labelled as 'hysterics'.

Now hysteria (or 'mass sociogenic illness') is the only explanation, the hospital was able to reject a million-dollar negligence lawsuit against it. In the end we still don't know why Ramirez exhibited such bizarre symptoms and why 23 people were so badly affected. *San Jose (CA) Mercury News, 9 Aug; Channel 4, 'Equinox', 26 Nov 1995.*

DUNBONKIN IN DUNGARVAN

WE ALL KNOW the urban legend: a man goes out on the town, gets drunk, picks up a woman and takes her home. He wakes up in the morning, and there on his mirror in lipstick are the words "Welcome to the world of AIDS". Now, the parish priest of Dungarvan in County Waterford has created a number of controversies by claiming that this particular piece of folklore has become sorry fact.

During a sermon last year, Father Michael Kennedy made the startling assertion that a local woman was deliberately infecting her partners with HIV, by way of revenge on the man who infected her. According to Fr Kennedy, it had first come to his attention after five local men told him that they had become infected with HIV after unprotected sex with the same woman. The woman, who has not been identified, was said to live in London, but had visited Dungarvan in 1994 to see relatives.

GLORIA RAMIREZ: Nerve-gas in the blood?

Fr Kennedy went on to inform his parishioners that he had tracked the woman down to the hospital where she was dying, where she claimed to have slept with "something in the range of 60-80" men since being confirmed HIV-positive. Apart from the original five, a further nine men are supposed to have tested positive, with another 20 awaiting test results.

Of course, it's not that simple. Within a week, claim and counter-claim had begun to fly. A former co-ordinator of Irish AIDS projects, Dr James Walsh, issued a statement that a woman might have to have sex with a man several hundred times in order to pass on the infection through vaginal intercourse. Michael Noonan, the Health Minister, said that there had been no significant increase in HIV rates reported by the sexually transmitted disease clinics in the Waterford, Cork and Dublin areas.

Fr Kennedy subsequently maintained that all the information he gave was correct; the men who approached him for advice had all taken their HIV tests in the UK, to avoid identification. He also chided the media for misunderstanding him: "Often the message that is preached is lost completely and it is the messenger who is attacked. But the truth will out in the end." He maintained that he had told the story as a warning, rather than to cause a mass panic.

The locals have been taking it with characteristic good humour; the *Independent* reports healthy sales of T-shirts reading: "I come from Dungarvan, but I have an alibi". *Independent, 13+14+18 Sept; Independent on Sunday, 17 Sept; Observer 17 Sept 1995.*

Animal Deaths

We've all heard of whales which beach themselves and die, singly or in numbers, but what about other mysterious or amusing animal deaths? What about, for example, the five dead sheep found in a New Zealand tree? Read on...

'DEMON' CROCODILES BURN TO DEATH

A PAIR OF CROCODILES, male and female, captured on the outskirts of Cameroon's capital Yaoundé, were burned to death in public by traditional healers who said the 3ft (90cm) animals were bewitched.

Some 300 residents of Yaoundé's Madagascar and Nkomanka districts watched on 24 September 1995 as the healers adorned the male animal with a beard and trousers, and the female with hair and nail polish on its claws, before setting them ablaze on a wooden funeral pyre.

Locals, who chipped in for the cost of petrol, blamed the male for a spate of road accidents on a bridge under which it lived, and some believed that both of the beasts were behind the disappearance of small children. Sightings of crocodiles are rare in Yaoundé, a city of nearly one million people.

That, at any rate, was how Reuters reported the story. Readers of the *Ethiopian Herald*, which was quoting the official Cameroon News Agency, CAMNEWS, were told that there was only one crocodile, 2.5 metres (8ft) long, captured by the witchdoctors in a pool at Nlongkak, on the outskirts of Yaoundé "at the weekend" (16/17 September).

According to the *Herald*, it was already sporting trousers, with its snout and claws painted red. (We are reminded of the report which appeared in *FT* some time ago that an unknown person was tranquilising gorillas and dressing them as clowns before releasing them.)

The witchdoctors said the crocodile's male companion had escaped, but would be captured soon. They asserted that the reptile was a transformed old woman who had also appeared as a python, and had caused the deaths of many people, especially children, through accidents. After incantations and rituals, the animal was burnt. *Reuters, Ethiopian Herald, 24 Sept 1995.*

AN OTTER RUN OVER by a naturalist in Newark, Nottinghamshire, was the first to have been seen in the county for 40 years. The body of the otter, a male, was given to a museum which prepared it for display. *Mail on Sunday, 27 Aug 1995.*

A MUTILATED cow was discovered near Camlough in County Armagh last September. The carcass had been drained of blood, the flesh stripped from the skull and the vital organs removed. Investigators suggested that the damage was caused by animal predators, but Miles Johnson, an electronics technician and ufologist from Lurgan, maintained that "the organs were sucked out through a clean incision made by some hi-tech laser device".

In keeping with the classic 'mute' scenario in 1970s America, witnesses had told of a large, black, silent helicopter and various UFOs in the area at the time of the mutilation. These included discs and a ball of light with a smaller ball revolving around it. *Newsletter (Belfast), 20 Oct 1995.*

THE FATE OF LES KUPI seems like revenge for the infamous dynamiting of a whale on an Oregon beach. Mr Kupi was among a crowd gathering around a dead whale which had beached on the shore of Northumberland Strait, Nova Scotia. He noticed a trickle of blood from the whale's mouth and bent for a closer look. Without warning, a loud groan issued from deep inside the creature, and Mr Kupi was drenched in a shower of blood and 'other matter'. "It was disgusting," he said. *Toronto Globe-Mail, 13 Dec 1994.*

A DOG IN NEPAL committed suicide three days after his 12-year-old master died in a swimming accident. Sirjan Padrhan died in a pond at Bhairahawa, 190 (300km) southwest of Katmandu. Jackson the dog went to the pool, howled three times and leapt in. *AFP, 1 Dec 1995.*

NOW – THOSE SHEEP. Their bodies were found dangling 100 feet from the ground in one of New Zealand's many forests. Authorities were baffled as to how they got there, until the culprit came forward: an unnamed pilot admitted that they had fallen from his helicopter. *Reuters, 19 Sept 1995.*

IT'S WITCHCRAFT

It may look like something out of a fairy story, but this scene comes straight from modern Russia. Full-time witch Maria Deeva earns more money out of casting one spell than a Moscow doctor typically earns in a year. She left her job as a nursery-school teacher in 1988 for the more profitable field of witchcraft. Her customers request a broad range of magical services, she says. "Many of my clients are wealthy businessmen wanting to find a lost relative or stolen car; or they are caught in a love triangle and want someone destroyed." Maria is one of thousands of Russians who now make a living out of witchcraft.

the paranormal world

MAKE MINE A DOUBLE HELIX

The 1996 crop circle season produced little proof that the circles are made by anything more exotic than groups of hoaxers with a love for conceptual art and country pub ale, but several of the designs set new standards in beauty and sheer complexity. Whether or not the circles are genuinely mysterious, they are often genuinely gorgeous.

1. Stonehenge, Wiltshire. A spiral design of more than 150 separate circles near Britain's most potent ancient site.

2. East Field, Alton Barnes, Wiltshire. Spectacular arrangement of nearly 90 individual circles in barley.

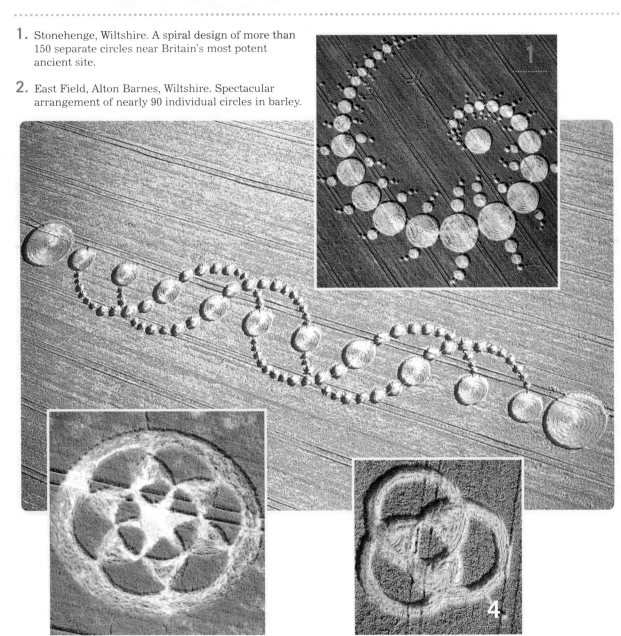

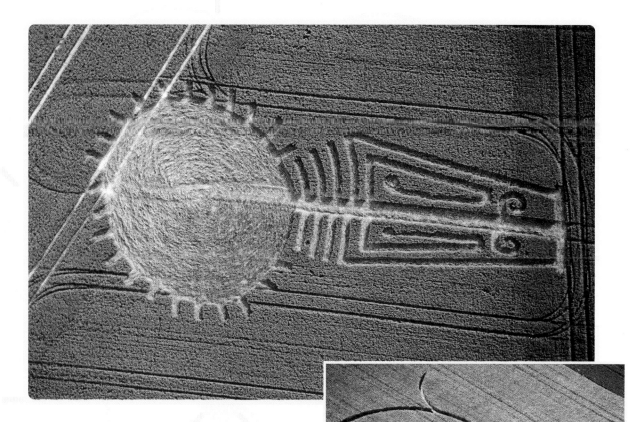

3. Sudbury Hill, Wiltshire. Rosette motif in barley.

4. Clarken Green, Hampshire. Mathematical ven diagram (or possibly a biohazard symbol).

5. East Oakley, Hampshire. Flowerpot design in wheat.

6. Girton, Cambridgeshire. Slightly imperfect tailed circle in barley.

7. Girton, Cambridgeshire. A similar pattern to (6) close by, this time in oil seed rape.

LIFE on MARS?

Just before NASA released the momentous news that meteorites found in the Antarctic ice might contain evidence of primitive Martian life from the distant past, *Fortean Times* published an article by Bob Rickard on that very subject. Although the article predated NASA's statement by some months, its speculations were surprisingly close to the truth, even naming the meteorite which contained the alleged fossils...

SCIENTISTS studying the origins of life generally agree that the fossil evidence of organic carbon dates back some 3.8 billion years, to a time when the Earth was just half a billion years old. In 1991, Thomas Cech of the University of Colorado and Sidney Altman of Yale University shared a Nobel Prize for discovering how RNA, the predecessor of DNA, could assemble itself from a chemical soup. Since then, other scientists have created cell-like structures containing a primitive form of RNA.

David Deamer of the University of California, for example, who studies tidal pools at Monterey Bay, has shown how compounds forming an oily scum can spontaneously curl to make tiny bubbles. Within that membrane organic chemistry can take place away from the chaotic surrounding environment. Dr Deamer calls this "an essential step in the evolution of the first cells." Stuart Kauffman, a biophysicist at the Santa Fe Institute, believes "life is a natural property of complex chemical systems." He theorises that chemical soups have "a certain threshold at which a self-sustaining network of reactions will suddenly appear."

The search for new life is not restricted to tidal pools. One avenue of enquiry – into the ocean depths, where sunlight never penetrates – has proved rewarding. Projecting from the floor of the mid-Atlantic Ridge is a forest of tall, thin volcano-like structures called 'black smokers'. They pour out clouds of chemicals dissolved from fissures in the Earth's crust, propelled upwards by superheated steam. When this caustic smoke hits the ocean waters the minerals freeze out, creating chimneys as tall as three-storey buildings.

The environment surrounding the black smokers is a highly toxic cocktail of hot water, gas, sulphur and heavy metals, yet life has evolved here. Smokers in the Pacific are home to giant worms that live in tube-like structures three metres long. "These volcanoes are like oases in the desert," says Dr Bromley Murton of the Oceanography Centre at Southampton University. "The surrounding area is barren. These animals are only here because of the volcanoes. They are totally interlinked to the geological situation."

Unlike life nearer the Earth's surface, these ecosystems show an adaptation to life in darkness, great pressure, intense heat and poisonous gases. More importantly, their biochemistry is not driven by sunlight, but by bacteria thriving on heat and sulphur-based chemical reactions.

Other bacteria-based ecosystems are coming to light. In October, a previously unknown ecosystem was found in deep aquifers near the Columbia River, Washington State, dependent not on sunlight, geothermal heat or organic matter, but on the chemical interaction between water and basalt rock. Todd Stevens and Jim McKinley of the US govern-

ALH84001,0

ROCK THE WORLD: These tiny structures within meteorite ALH 84001 could be microscopic fossils of primitive, bacteria-like organisms that may have lived on Mars more than 3.6 billion years ago

ment's Pacific Northwest Laboratory in Richmond, Washington, have dubbed these ecosystems SLiMEs (subsurface lithoautotrophic microbial ecosystems).

This implies that terrestrial life has more strings to its bow than the familiar action of photosynthesis. Stevens and McKinley believe that life on Mars, if it exists, is more likely to be a SLiME or similar bacterial ecosystem sheltering deep below the Martian surface. The implication is that we, ourselves, may well be the descendants of Martian SLiME brought to earth on a meteorite.

Earlier this year, astronomers from Manchester University and scientists from the American Museum of Natural History announced they had found the oldest Martian meteorite to date, named 'Allan Hills 84001', in Antarctica. It dates to the time-frame of the 'Lunar Cataclysm', between 3.9 and 4.1 billion years ago, when the moon underwent massive meteoric bombardment. During this time – when Mars had liquid water on its surface – an impact propelled the 'Allan Hills' rock fragment to Earth. If it, or any other meteorite from Mars, carried traces of organic matter, it could have stirred the pre-cellular soup into protolife. The age of the meteorite also falls comfortably within the period during which life is thought to have begun on Earth – 3.5 to 4.1 billion years ago.

The most serious objection to the idea of 'seeds of life' hitching rides on interplanetary meteors is that the intense temperatures of the impact explosion would destroy any organic matter that survived the heating during passage through our atmosphere. Incoming 'seeds' would have a better chance of survival if the object falling from space does not hit full on. Those hitting deep water or slopes, or with a shallow trajectory, may have less damaging explosions. Moreover, there are meteoric objects – for example the Dharamsala meteorite (1860) discussed by Fort – which were found to be cold or even frosted over after their fall and impact. These controversial objects would be perfect vehicles for infecting this earth with proto-lifeforms.

Naturally, heating is related to the speed of fall and size of object; the heat being generated not by friction, but by compression of the relatively thick atmosphere it travels through. Particles of dust and ice crystals, therefore, may well survive the fall to Earth because of their low mass. Indeed, some astronomers believe there is a constant and almost invisible rain of microscopic detritus, any fragment of which may carry germs or organic material. The really interesting implication of this notion is that the genesis events are still happening. In this view, life could be in continual creation and not restricted to a single ancient origin.

It would only take a single bacterium or virus – perhaps only a few lengths of primitive RNA or amino acids – to introduce life to Earth. It needs only to survive the journey and drop into an environment in which it could multiply and adapt. Some epidemiologists have attempted to link the major waves of worldwide illnesses to infections from a meteor shower or passing comet.

Recently, scientists found confirmation that carbon-based material might survive the intense heat of entry from space and shock of impact. It stems from a study of the

...it is now looking more likely that life on earth was kick-started by some external source

huge Sudbury 'impact structure' in central Ontario where the Earth was struck, around two billion years ago, by an enormous comet or meteorite. Around the perimeter of this site – the second largest known on this planet – Jeff Bada and Luann Becker of the Scripps Institution found large deposits of 'buckyballs': a hollow spherical arrangement of carbon-60, called Buckminsterfullerene after Buckminster Fuller, the late philosopher-engineer and Fortean, as they resemble the geodesic domes he invented.

As the Sudbury crater has the world's largest known concentration of buckyballs, Doctors Bada and Becker knew there was some connection with the visitor from space. At the time, they believed the buckyballs had been made in the impact explosion and asked Robert Poreda of the University of Rochester to ascertain what atoms or molecules may be trapped within the spheres.

To their delight, Dr Poreda discovered molecules of helium-3 and heli-

um-4 in a ratio not found within our solar system. This form of helium was almost certainly forged within a red giant star. Around five billion years ago, it was trapped within the forming buckyballs which, in turn, became part of a comet and roamed space for billions of years before colliding with Canada. The temperature of the Sudbury impact is estimated to have been over 5000°C. As carbon molecules begin disintegrating at temperatures above 1000°C, scientists have been searching for scenarios that would allow some buckyballs to survive the heat of the impact: these include fragments flying off during entry and the explosion itself being uneven in temperature.

Whatever the answer, this is a scientifically plausible mechanism for complex carbon-based molecules to arrive here from deep space. "I had believed," said Bada, "as most people did, that these [impacts] were just too energetic for the stuff to survive. Now, all of a sudden, I have a different view."

In answer to the original question, it is now looking more likely that life on Earth was kick-started by some external source than that it began here spontaneously. This external stimulus – dirty meteorites from Mars, rains of cosmic dust or buckyballs from the galactic core – is a constant process and four billion years ago the chemical conditions on this earth happened to be just right, the so-called 'Goldilocks' prescription.

The launch this December of the Mars Pathfinder mission, which includes the Sojourner lander, makes all of this quite topical. The Viking lander of 1976 found no life signs on the surface – this time around, when Sojourner touches down on Mars in July 1997, we know enough to drill deeper into the planetary crust. The first Earthman to set foot on Mars may actually be returning home.

Sources.

SCUM: *South China Morning Post 15 Jan 1995.*
BLACK SMOKERS: *Guardian 11 Jan 1996.*
SLiME: *Science Oct 1995.* CAVE: *NY Times 12 Dec 1995.* OLDEST METEORITE: *[R] 9 Mar 1996.*
BUCKYBALLS: *Science April 1996; Int.Herald Tribune 18 April; New Scientist 20 April 1996.*
PATHFINDER: *NY Times 20 Feb 1996, or point your web browser to http://nssdc.gsfc.nasa.gov/ planetary/mesur.html for latest mission news.*

the natural world

Secret Country

The United Kingdom is dotted with places that have a Fortean or paranormal resonance dating back many centuries. A few are well known, but many are not. Sometimes the site's original purpose has been changed or lost over the years, or it has become the focus of folklore or superstition. It's all grist to the Fortean mill.

fortware

fortware

FORTEAN TIMES PAPERBACK LIBRARY

CHARLES FORT'S BOOK OF THE DAMNED £9.99
The first major revision of the Forteans' founding book. Strange ærial objects, teleportation, rains of blood and fish... the whole damned procession observed with Fort's "gorgeous madman's humour". 320pp.

CHARLES FORT'S NEW LANDS £9.99
This, the second volume of Charles Fort's works, deals mainly with an astonishing selection of strange ærial and astronomical phenomena. 256pp.

FORTEAN STUDIES VOL. 1 £19.99
Fully referenced and all new material — more than 250,000 words by leading researchers. Luminous owls, 1909 airship flap, Devil's hoofprints, giant octopus, etc, plus comprehensive index to 1993 issues of *FT*. 350pp.

FORTEAN STUDIES VOL. 2 £19.99
Another feast of anomalies original and fully referenced. Marine lightwheels, out-of-place coelacanths, mystery cats, Icelandic water monsters, Nazi archæology, etc, plus index to 1994 issues of *FT*. 320pp.

YESTERDAY'S NEWS TOMORROW —
FORTEAN TIMES 1-15 £19.99
Wolf children, moon mysteries, mass hysteria, antigravity, black dogs, sexy spectres, Travis Walton, mystery wounds, leys, etc. Fully illustrated, 400pp.

DIARY OF A MAD PLANET —
FORTEAN TIMES 16-25 £19.50
Levitating nun, coloured rains, Morgawr and the owl-man, fairy encounters, persistent puddles, missile-throwing clouds, skyquakes, etc. Fully illustrated, 416pp.

SEEING OUT THE SEVENTIES —
FORTEAN TIMES 26-30 £14.99
Mystery big cats, spontaneous combustion, parallel lives, bizarre crimes, assorted falls of stuff, Uganda's talking tortoise, etc. Fully illustrated, 320pp.

GATEWAYS TO MYSTERY —
FORTEAN TIMES 31-36 £19.99
Enfield poltergeist, delayed death touch, dinosaur hunting, alien abductions, phantom hitch-hikers, miracle fuels, Kuano river boy, etc. Fully illustrated, 416pp.

HEAVEN'S REPRIMANDS —
FORTEAN TIMES 37-41 £19.99
Entombed toads, rat kings, Australia's lizard monsters, hair-clipping panics, crop circles, stigmatics, sinister clowns, cattle mutilation, encounters with Castor and Pollux, etc. Fully illustrated, 416pp.

IF PIGS COULD FLY —
FORTEAN TIMES 42-46 £19.99
Kenyan stone showers, Exmoor Beast, people with horns, Smurfs on the rampage, killer telephones, possessed dolls, the Holy Foreskin, the Jabberwocks of Quebec, etc. Fully illustrated, 416pp.

FISHY YARNS —
FORTEAN TIMES 47-51 £19.99
Welsh find America, X-ray vision, natural rejuvenation, thylacines, burning hands, the Shrouds of Turin and Liverpool, messages on eyeballs, deaths of Marconi scientists, Men in Black, holygrams, etc. Fully illustrated, 432pp.

BONFIRE OF THE ODDITIES —
FORTEAN TIMES 52-56 £19.99
Multiple Personality Syndrome, cold fusion, humans with tails, sardine rain, record postal delays, teleportations, history of Father Christmas, whale attacks, Muslim wonders, etc. Fully illustrated, 424pp.

STRANGE ATTRACTORS —
FORTEAN TIMES 57-62 £19.99
Phantom social workers, drilling to Hell, incorrupt bodies, Satanic child abuse, trepanation, Mexican wolf boys, near-death experiences, toe-suckers, etc. Fully illustrated, 432pp.

STRANGE DAYS #1: THE YEAR IN WEIRDNESS £9.99
All the weirdness fit to print – the full story of strangeness in 1995. From recreational amputation to SCHWASCAR weirdness awards. US-licensed *FT* book.

THE BOOK OF STRANGE DEATHS £4.99
More than 350 exotic extinctions including: death by doughnut, flying turnip tragedy, chainsaw suicides, cactus revenge. 128pp.

THE BOOK OF WEIRD SEX £4.99
More than 360 phenomenal fornications including: topless robberies, enema bandits, one man and a Barbie, sex after death. 128pp.

NEW! BOOK OF THE MILLENNIUM £9.99
The definitive work – all you need to know about end-of-the-world predictions, doomsday cults and millenarianism. 160pp + 8pp of photos.

NEW! THE PLUMBER FROM LHASA —
FORTEAN TIMES 63-67 £19.99
The face on Mars, blood miracles, Alternative 3, seiche waves, Darwin re-examined, giant penguins, dead sea serpents, and an exposé of Tibetan lama T Lobsang Rampa – really a plumber's son from Plympton. 368 pages.

NEW! THE FORTEAN TIMES BOOK OF INEPT CRIME £4.99
More than 375 farcical felonies, including: don't hide a lobster down your underpants, chilli pepper enema, mugged by muppets, dental floss jailbreak. 128pp.

NEW! THE FORTEAN TIMES BOOK OF LIFE'S LOSERS £4.99
More than 400 tragic tough-luck stories, including: letter bomb returned to sender, harpooned rabbis, the ear that went off, the skydiver who forget his parachute, God gets mugged. 128pp.

Mad Planet

We tend to regard the Earth as a stable, unchanging place, but the truth is very different. Our planet is restless, moving and altering month by month. Whether you regard it as a natural process, the results of mankind's despoiling of the world, signs of the coming millennium or Gaia flexing her shoulders, the fact remains: the only certainty is change.

FISH

THE GULF OF TEXAS suffered from an unusual mass death of spined catfish in early June. Thousands of the fish, which ranged from 4in to 6in in length, were washed up along the Gulf coast. The fish have large barbed spines on their back, coated in a mild poison, which snap off when stepped on. Several people required medical attention to remove the spines from their feet. Motorists also suffered, as the spines are sharp enough to puncture tyres. No cause could be found for the mass death, once the usual one – lack of oxygen in the water – had been ruled out. The catfish began to wash up just as the Gulf coast was recovering from an invasion by Portuguese Men-Of-War and jellyfish.

EARTHQUAKES

MUCH OF SHROPSHIRE was rattled by a comparatively powerful quake (52.8°N, 2.77°W 3.2R Depth: 7.7 km) shortly before midnight on March 7th. Reports of movement were received from Shrewsbury, Telford and Oswestry, varying from "a rumble and a shuddering" to "I felt the settee move sideways". A quake of comparable magnitude took place in nearby Newtown almost exactly a year previously, on March 17th 1994. The tremor lasted eighteen minutes. There were no reported injuries, although the *Daily Telegraph* mentioned that a hamster belonging to 11-year-old Rebecca Morris of Harmer Hill was 'shaken' and 'thrown from its hut', and a parrot was also reported to be 'in shock'.

VOLCANO

HAWAIIAN SCIENTISTS warned that there is a possibility of the island chain's Kilauea volcano erupting for the first time in 14 years. There has been a series of small tremors and a buildup of pressure at the volcano's summit, as well as an 'unprecedented' release of sulphur dioxide gas. The Hawaii Volcanoes National Park was partially closed during recent alerts centred on the volcano. Its last major eruption was in 1982.

After months of rumbling, Mt Ruapehu, on New Zealand's North Island, erupted in mid-June, blasting lava and hot ash into the night sky, followed by a scientific assurance that volcanic activity was subsiding. Local authorites imposed an exclusion zone around the volcano; airports were closed and planes re-routed mid-flight. Maori folklore has it that Mt Ruapehu is the bride of the dormant Mt Taranaki, and is weeping for its husband.

OLD FAITHFUL

THE FAMOUS OLD FAITHFUL geyser in Wyoming's Yellowstone National Park appears not to be quite as faithful as it once was. It gained its nickname on account of its uncannily regular eruptions; at the turn of the century, it was touted as spouting "every hour on the hour". However, the interval between eruptions has been getting longer and more irregular in recent years. In 1950, it was 62 minutes; in 1970, 66 minutes. Now eruptions are 77 minutes apart, give or take ten minutes. Park rangers are blaming earthquakes for disturbing the spout's schedule.

RAIN

SPAIN'S DROUGHT was resolved in the spring, although probably not in the way the Spanish would have preferred. Torrential winter rains not only refilled reservoirs which had been lying half-empty, but caused catastrophic floods in some areas. Seville's schools were closed; dams burst; farms became unworkable; crops were ruined. Some areas which had imposed water rationing now have enough in reserve for the next three years.

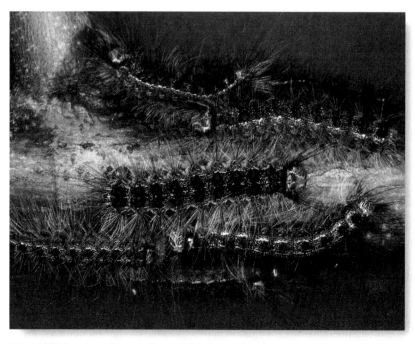

HAIRY ARMY: A good year for caterpillars, as Britain faces an invasion of Asian gypsy moths.

INSECTS

THE SOUTH-WEST POLISH TOWN of Opole found itself playing host to some particularly unwelcome guests: caterpillars. Conservation workers had to be called in to clear hundreds of enormous caterpillar nests from roadside trees. A local pest control official was quoted as saying, "Cocoons 20 inches long, bulging with caterpillars, constitute a traffic hazard when they drop onto the windscreens of speeding cars." An unusually cold winter which had almost wiped out the insects' natural predators was being blamed.

Meanwhile, Britain is reportedly threatened by a plague of moths whose caterpillars could devastate our forests. The Asian gypsy moth has been moving steadily westwards for several years; it reached Germany in 1993, where it stripped entire plantations. Although the moth hasn't become established in Britain yet, there are fears that it might cross the Channel in tourists' cars. A small infestation was reported in South Woodford in Essex last year, but was eradicated. Britain used to have its own gypsy moth species, but it became extinct at the turn of the century.

In Exeter, the university has reported a plague of tropical ants. Since Christmas 1995, the Pharaoh's ants have been slowly taking over the university's Lafrowda accommodation block. The ants are apparently immune to poison, and when threatened simply move their nest to a less hazardous location. Exeter City Council pest control has tried to remove the infestation by spraying the area with growth-reducing hormones, but it will take 200 days before the queen ant dies, destroying the colony.

US SINKHOLE

A THREE-STOREY mock Tudor house in San Francisco collapsed into a sinkhole in December 1995. The hole, in Seacliff, was believed to have been caused by heavy rain, which ruptured a 100-year-old sewer. As well as the house, the hole claimed a tree, a truck, part of a neighbouring house and some power lines. The hole was 200 feet wide and 60 feet deep.

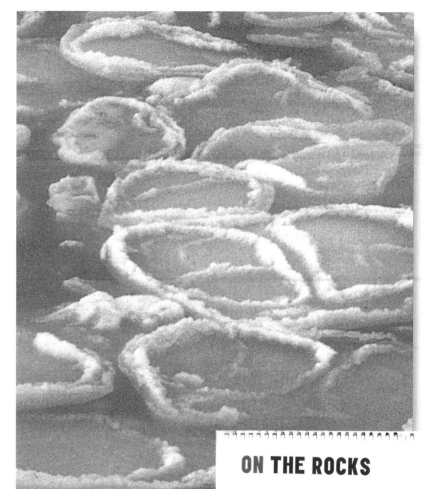

STILL HOTTER

THE WORLD METEOROLOGICAL ORGANISA-TION has issued a statement that the world is officially hotter. Echoing an earlier warning from the Meteorological Office in Britain, they said that worldwide temperatures for 1995 were, on average, 0.72°F higher than any year in the last three decades. Parts of Siberia were 5.4°F hotter. They also noted that 1995 had 19 tropical storms in the Atlantic, of which eleven reached hurricane strength or higher – the second highest total since records began in 1886. The report also said that depletion of the ozone layer started earlier in the year and lasted longer than before. The ozone hole was measured at 8.8 million square miles, just short of its 1993 peak.

COLD

THE USA SUFFERED a 'cold wave' to match its heatwave of the previous year. Over 60 people are believed to

ON **THE ROCKS**

ICE COVERS the area of the Greenland sea where the Odden Feature should appear. The feature is a 'natural pump' which helps control the circulation of the world's oceans. It has formed every year in living memory, but began to falter in 1972. It completely failed in 1994, and has not formed since. The possible effect on the world's oceans is not known.

have died as a result of the record low temperatures, including one unfortunate elderly Chicagoan who managed to survive the city's apocalyptic heat in the summer of 1995, only to freeze to death in her apartment on 1 February. Temperatures as low as -51°F (-46°C) were recorded. After the chill came the thaw, and the inevitable floodwater. The Pacific north-west was particularly badly hit, with much of Oregon being declared a disaster area. The floods were the worst for 30 years, with most of Oregon and Washington's rivers flooding, and thousands being evacuated from their homes.

Fortean Ads

Many people have observed that interest in Forteana seems to have crossed over from the fringes to a sort of mainstream respectability. This was rather nicely illustrated by the sudden spate of 'Fortean' advertising which has hit our screens, papers and billboards this year.

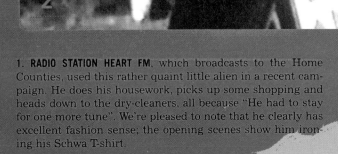

1. **RADIO STATION HEART FM**, which broadcasts to the Home Counties, used this rather quaint little alien in a recent campaign. He does his housework, picks up some shopping and heads down to the dry-cleaners, all because "He had to stay for one more tune". We're pleased to note that he clearly has excellent fashion sense; the opening scenes show him ironing his Schwa T-shirt.

2. **VOLKSWAGEN** presented an amusing twist on the stereotypical alien sighting. A clichéd 'pore white trash' couple are seen describing a mysterious encounter. It came out of nowhere, they tell us, and it had lights on it; they'd never seen anything like it; there seemed to be windows along the side, and so on. All this is accompanied by suitably shaky and grainy footage of the couple running around the forecourt of their service station. The punchline is that "it" bore a symbol on the front, "kinda like a 'V-W'"; their cars are, it appears, so ruthlessly efficient that petrol station attendents might not remember what they look like.

3. **THE PRESENT GOVERNMENT** attracted criticism from the Advertising Standards Authority for a perceived personal attack on Labour leader Tony Blair. They briefly ran a poster which showed Blair with red, demonic eyes in place of his own. This was one in a series of adverts in which voters were apparently warned that a vote for Labour was a vote for the Lord of Darkness; a Conservative party political broadcast even went so far as to show a huge pair of the eyes in the sky over a (presumably Labour-controlled) Houses of Parliament.

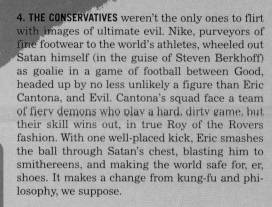

4. THE CONSERVATIVES weren't the only ones to flirt with images of ultimate evil. Nike, purveyors of fine footwear to the world's athletes, wheeled out Satan himself (in the guise of Steven Berkhoff) as goalie in a game of football between Good, headed up by no less unlikely a figure than Eric Cantona, and Evil. Cantona's squad face a team of fiery demons who play a hard, dirty game, but their skill wins out, in true Roy of the Rovers fashion. With one well-placed kick, Eric smashes the ball through Satan's chest, blasting him to smithereens, and making the world safe for, er, shoes. It makes a change from kung-fu and philosophy, we suppose.

5a & b. VODAFONE played on the popularity of *The X Files* by introducing Kyle McLachlan as a Spooky Mulder-like paranormal investigator, tracking down the mysterious Vodafone Network. Coincidentally, McLachlan played alongside Mulder actor David Duchovny in *Twin Peaks*. The Vodafone ads feature all manner of forteana, from time-travel to the yeti. Another interesting piece of trivia is that the 'time-travel' ad featured the late Jon Pertwee in his last role, as a rather familiar-looking figure who emerges from a garage marked 'Doctor On Call'.

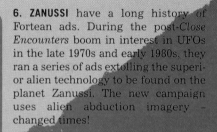

6. ZANUSSI have a long history of Fortean ads. During the post-*Close Encounters* boom in interest in UFOs in the late 1970s and early 1980s, they ran a series of ads extolling the superior alien technology to be found on the planet Zanussi. The new campaign uses alien abduction imagery – changed times!

the human world

FUN pages

All answers on page 128

Step-Words

CAN YOU transform FORT into DATA in five steps, changing one letter each time, so that each step is also a word. Then can you do it a different way?

WEIRD YEARBOOK WEIRD WORDSEARCH

Thirty-one words and acronyms with Fortean connotations are hidden within this cryptic grid of letters. Award yourself bonus points for finding concealed messages from aliens, Knights Templar inscriptions, or the face of Jesus.

```
I  G  A  M  P  U  M  A  A  Z
E  R  P  H  R  U  V  B  N  I
T  O  O  F  G  I  B  C  E  K
S  T  P  N  N  T  A  S  M  O
O  O  T  O  A  E  E  W  I  O
H  O  B  E  S  Y  H  N  N  B
G  O  A  T  S  U  C  K  E  R
T  N  W  R  T  H  S  G  H  A
A  I  A  O  S  R  E  R  P  E
N  I  N  F  O  R  G  E  R  Y
C  T  H  U  L  H  U  Y  P  B
```

If you find all the words, you will be left with seven unused letters, which can be arranged to spell another word that sums up Fortean phenomena.

SPOT THE DIFFERENCE

IVOR CONSPIRACY-THEORY, *our Fortean investigator, has got his pictures jumbled. He knows that one image is the genuine Face on Mars and the other was faked by a rival to discredit his research – but he can't remember which is which! Using your skill and judgement, can you detect the nine differences between the two images – and for a bonus point, tell the real image from the fake?*

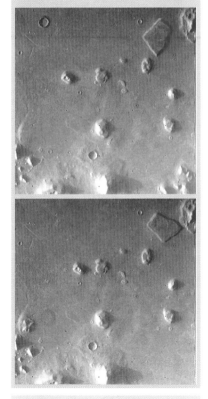

How Fortean are you?

1. It's a warm summer night. You see strange lights moving in the sky. What do you do?

a. *Assume it's a completely natural, explicable phenomenon such as a helicopter display team, firework display or the planet Venus having a jig.*

b. *Assume it's a completely unnatural, alien phenomenon, and start humming the five-note theme from Close Encounters in preparation.*

c. *Assume you've been abducted, and immediately book a course of X-rays and hypnotherapy so you can check for implants and suppressed memories.*

d. *Observe the phenomenon, write down full details of the sighting, then lose the notebook in the pub a week later.*

2. Your favourite newspaper prints a Fortean story. Do you:

a. *Send the editor a letter, calling him a credulous goon for printing such tosh?*

b. *Send the editor a 20,000-word article covering your own investigation of the subject?*

c. *Of course the paper prints Fortean stories – that's why you buy the Weekly World News?*

d. *Cut out the story and send it to Fortean Times, noting the date and paper?*

3. A mysterious stranger promises to send you a document proving that Elvis was Jack the Ripper. A week later, it hasn't arrived. You immediately:

a. *Blame the Post Office, which is probably on strike again.*

b. *Blame mysterious cosmic forces, and write an article about disappearing evidence.*

c. *Blame the Illuminati for suppressing the Truth, and swear vengeance.*

d. *Blame the mysterious stranger for being a flake, and go down the pub.*

4. A fish falls on you. Do you:

a. *Look around for the seagull that dropped it?*

b. *Check to see if its stomach contains that watch you lost five years ago?*

c. *Treasure it as a secret communication from the cosmic masters?*

d. *Wonder how it would go with a white-wine sauce?*

5. The Goatsucker phenomenon is:

a. *Gullible peasants illustrating the depressing power of folklore over rationality.*

b. *Some form of previously unknown animal, using paranormal powers to hunt and travel?*

c. *A vampiric alien life-form placed on this planet by ETs with the collusion of the CIA to gather samples, implant sinister tracking devices and spread genetically engineered diseases?*

d. *You're not sure, but it makes a good T-shirt.*

6. What section of *Fortean Times* do you read first?

a. *'Strange Days', to laugh at humankind's credulity.*

b. *The book reviews, to see if there's a review of your latest pamphlet on the Basingstoke Bat-Beast case of 1733.*

c. *The small ads, to receive the latest communications from the Secret Masters.*

d. *All of it, cover to cover, immediately, over a pint.*

How did you do?

MOSTLY 'a': You're one of life's natural skeptics, you don't believe in anything, and we suspect you bought this book so you could laugh at people who aren't as enlightened and rational as yourself. We recommend you subscribe to *Fortean Times* for more laughs on a monthly basis.

MOSTLY 'b': You're really into Fortean stuff – perhaps a little bit too much. Not that we can criticise, of course, but under 'credulous' in the dictionary there's a picture of you. A subscription to *Fortean Times* could bring a little 20/20 vision to your life.

MOSTLY 'c': You take this stuff way too personally. Get help.

MOSTLY 'd': You are a true Fortean, you have no opinion on anything, you measure circles beginning anywhere, and it's your round.

Coincidence

Coincidence, some magical types maintain, is never just 'coincidence'; any chance coincidence of names, dates, times, or whatever, is an indication from the universe that Great Things Are Afoot. I wonder whether they would feel the same way after reading this little selection?

HE AIN'T HEAVY: Tim Henderson ran into his long-lost brother hithcing a lift to London

Of all the pigeon lofts in all the world...

TWO RACING PIGEONS from Northumberland have settled in Casablanca, independently and four months apart. Both birds belonged to David Dougal, who lives in Humshaugh, near Hexham, Northumberland, last June; and both have settled in a loft owned by Essofi Mohammed. The first bird got diverted during a race from France, and the second flew off from Mr Dougal's allotment. *D. Telegraph, D. Mail, 23 Mar 1996.*

TWIN SISTERS who live 400 miles apart sent their mother in Merthyr Tydfil, Wales, identical Christmas cards with the same message. *D. Mirror, 30 Dec 1995.*

STUDENT TIM HENDERSON, 29, hitched a lift to London with diving engineer Mark Knight, 31, because he couldn't afford the train fare from Newcastle. They were matched by the Freewheelers Lift Share Agency on Tyneside, which has 16,000 names on its register. They started talking about relatives. "There was a complete silence as we stared at each other in disbelief," said Mr Henderson. "Then one of us said, 'You must be my brother.' I always knew I had a half-brother, but never thought we would meet." Tom Henderson, their father, was divorced from Mark's mother; Mark's mother remarried and he took his stepfather's surname. The brothers had met when they were five and three, but had lost touch due to the family rift. *Northern Echo, 23 Feb; Guardian, Sun, 24 Feb 1996.*

A MAN IN HIS SIXTIES suffered a head injury and broken ribs when his Volvo 440 automatic car crashed backwards through a barrier on level four of a multi-storey car park in Canterbury, Kent, and landed upside-down on concrete 70ft below. The roof was completely caved in and the windows shattered. The driver was helped out by firemen and taken to hospital where his condition was said to be stable. The accident mirrors a television advertisement for Volvo in which one of its cars is shown plunging from a building and landing dented but without harm to its test-dummy occupant. *Glasgow Herald, Independent, 13 Jan 1996.*

THE DRIVER'S A DUMMY but it's proof that Volvos live up to claims made in the company's adverts

THE DREDGER *BOWBELLE*, which sank the Thames cruiser *Marchioness* seven years ago with the loss of 51 lives, has sunk off the coast of Madeira. The 260ft sand dredger, working under a new Portuguese name, *Bom Rei*, broke in two on 25 March, drowning one of its crew. The connection with the earlier disaster went unnoticed until 22 May. *Guardian, 23 May 1996.*

Weird 1896

1896 is a fairly momentous year in the study of Forteana, for it saw the beginning of perhaps the most important series of phenomena of the 19th century: the Great American Airship Scare, which prefigured our modern obsession with UFOs. There was still room for some classic Forteana – mysterious aerial objects, *'globsters'* (unknown dead marine animals) and strange aerial bangs.

THE AIRSHIP SCARE which began in 1896 is a Fortean classic. Even today it can provoke a certain amount of debate among ufologists: some maintain that it represents the first recorded wave of true UFOs; others feel it more likely that it was manufactured by the notoriously sensationalist press of the time. Whatever the truth, it's an intriguing case, and one which might well contain a few lessons for modern Forteans.

'Airships' had been reported in the skies over America since about 1880, when a Santa Fe newspaper reported an encounter with a 'balloon' crewed by people speaking an unknown language, apparently holding a party on board. Reports of similar incidents dribbled in from time to time, but it wasn't until 1896 that mystery airships really took off – so to speak.

The first 'airship' report proper appeared in Sacramento, California, on 17 November. Between six and seven o'clock, according to the *Sacramento Evening Bee*, a light resembling an "electric arc lamp propelled by some mysterious force" passed over the city, again accompanied by the sound of a partying crew. Several witnesses also claimed to have seen an object circling the city at a great height, leaving a smoke trail, the previous evening.

This inevitably generated enormous interest and controversy, and soon the press and public were dividing into sceptics and believers. Some denounced the reports as another press hoax, while others pointed to the 'evident sincerity' of the witnesses. Scientists insisted that it must have been a prank.

There was a further sighting on 20 November, when passengers on a streetcar in Oakland saw a balloon-like structure, complete with lights and wings. Within days two more, earlier, reports had come to light – from October and August – and one of them claimed contact with the fliers! William Jordan of San Rafael told the *San Francisco Call* that he had come upon a machine shop in an isolated area of the Tamalpais mountains, and had spoken to mechanics working on an airship. They swore him to secrecy, of course.

Before long, there were sightings and contacts being reported from all over California. Airships were seen on almost a daily basis, while contacts grew ever more baroque. A former attorney general of California, WHH Hart, claimed to be legally representing two airship inventors, and disclosed that they had built their machines to bombard Havana with dynamite. Others put the blame squarely on 'Martians'. A Col. HG Shaw told reporters that on 25 November, three beings answering the description of modern 'grey' aliens tried to snatch him from his coach – the first recorded attempt at a UFO abduction?

By early 1897, 'airship' sightings were coming in from all over the USA. Inevitably, within six months or so of national exposure, interest in the 'airships' waned and reporting petered out. No hard evidence of anything conclusive was ever found. The airships would be back, of course, but that's another story.

FORT REPORTS some classic weirdness from 1896 in his books. A black spot was seen crossing the moon in July, by the director of the Smith Observatory. In Baton Rouge, 'hundreds' of dead birds fell from a clear sky, some with 'strange plumage'. A light was seen in Iowa and Montana, just before the start of the airship wave. Mysterious bangs were heard over Ostend on 18 February. Lights appeared in the sky during an earthquake in Worcester. On 1 December, a strange animal – 21ft long, 7ft long and 4.5ft high – was washed up on the beach near St Augustine, Florida; Fort called it "an appalling thing with the look of a cherub"... A vintage year, all things considered.

Sources: Jerome Clarke, The UFO Encyclopaedia, Volume 2, Charles Fort, Book of the Damned, New Lands, Lo!; John Spencer, The UFO Encyclopædia, The Encyclopaedia of the World's Greatest Unsolved Mysteries (w. Anne Spencer).

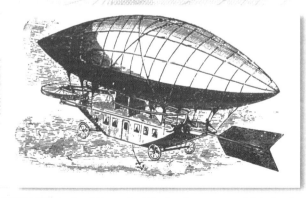

HOT AIR: 19th-century UFOs, or circulation-boosting newspaper fabrications?

FUN PAGE ANSWERS

(The puzzles were created by James Wallis)

Wordsearch

ABCs
Bigfoot
BVM
CIA
Cthulhu
Fang
Forgery
Fortean
Ghost
Goatsucker
Grotto
Grey
Iron
Lost
Magi
Ness
Phenomena
Photo

Popobawa
Puma
Satan
Schwa
SHC
Sheep
Sink
Tor
Twin
UFO
Unit
Yearbook
Yeti

The hidden word is:
BIZARRE

Step-words

Fort
Fore
Fare
Fate
Date
Data
or:
Fort
Fart
Fare
Dare
Date
Data

If you found the one with the word 'Fate' in first, then you can count yourself a real Fortean. If you found the other one... well, try harder.

Spot the difference

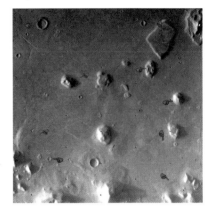

The real face-on-Mars picture is the lower one of the pair.

What's 'Fortean'?

FORTEAN TIMES, from which much of the material in this book is taken, is a monthly magazine of news, reviews and research on strange phenomena and experiences, curiosities, prodigies and portents. It was founded in 1973 to continue the work of Charles Fort. Fort, an American philosopher, was sceptical about scientific explanations, observing how scientists argued according to their own beliefs rather than the rules of evidence and how inconvenient data was ignored, suppressed, discredited or explained away.

Fort spent many years researching scientific literature in the New York Public Library and the British Museum Library. He marshalled his evidence and set forth his philosophy in *The Book of the Damned* (1919), *New Lands* (1923), *Lo!* (1931) and *Wild Talents* (1932).

His dictum "One measures a circle beginning anywhere" expresses his philosophy of Continuity in which everything is in an intermediate state between extremes. He coined the term 'teleportation' and was perhaps the first to speculate that mysterious lights in the sky might be craft from outer space. However, he cut at the very roots of credulity: "I conceive of nothing, in religion, science or philosophy, that is more than the proper thing to wear, for a while."

PICTURE CREDITS AND COPYRIGHTS